Valle-Inclán
Plays: One

Divine Words, Bohemian Lights, Silver Face

One of the most significant anti-naturalistic playwrights and novelists of the early twentieth century, Ramón María del Valle-Inclán (1866–1936) has recently undergone a major reappraisal in Europe. This volume of translations contains *Divine Words*, which draws on the pagan, Celtic traditions of the playwright's native Galicia and the repressive Catholicism of Spain to present a distorted picture of rustic life at its cruellest and most hypocritical; *Bohemian Lights*, the play which first expounded Valle-Inclán's theory of the grotesque (*esperpento*) and *Silver Face*, the first in the trilogy of *Savage Plays*, distinguished by the same sense of anarchy and amorality which runs through *Divine Words*.

These lively but accurate translations by Maria M. Delgado are complemented by her historically illuminating introduction and chronology. Further recommended reading and a list of major productions of the plays in this volume are also included.

Ramón del Valle-Inclán, actor, novelist, poet and playwright, was born on 28 October 1866 in Pontevedra, Spain. His major plays include: *The Italian Farce of the Girl in Love with the King*, *Divine Words*, *Bohemian Lights* and *The Horns of Don Friolera* – all published in Spain in 1920 and 1921; and the trilogy known as *The Savage Plays*: *Silver Face* (published 1922), *Eagle of Honour* and *Ballad of Wolves* (both published in 1907). Valle-Inclán died on 5 January 1936.

Methuen World Classics *and* Methuen Contemporary Dramatists *include*

Aeschylus (two volumes)
Jean Anouilh (two volumes)
John Arden (two volumes)
Arden & D'Arcy
Aristophanes (two volumes)
Aristophanes & Menander
Peter Barnes (three volumes)
Sebastian Barry
Brendan Behan
Aphra Behn
Edward Bond (five volumes)
Bertolt Brecht (six volumes)
Howard Brenton
  (two volumes)
Büchner
Bulgakov
Calderón
Richard Cameron
Jim Cartwright
Anton Chekhov
Caryl Churchill
  (two volumes)
Noël Coward (five volumes)
Sarah Daniels (two volumes)
Eduardo De Filippo
David Edgar (three volumes)
Euripides (six volumes)
Dario Fo (two volumes)
Michael Frayn (two volumes)
Max Frisch
Gorky
Harley Granville Barker
  (two volumes)
Peter Handke
Henrik Ibsen (six volumes)
Terry Johnson
Bernard-Marie Koltès
Lorca (three volumes)
David Mamet (three volumes)

Marivaux
Mustapha Matura
David Mercer (two volumes)
Arthur Miller (five volumes)
Anthony Minghella
  (two volumes)
Molière
Tom Murphy
  (four volumes)
Musset
Peter Nichols (two volumes)
Clifford Odets
Joe Orton
Philip Osment
Louise Page
A. W. Pinero
Luigi Pirandello
Stephen Poliakoff
  (two volumes)
Terence Rattigan
Christina Reid
Philip Ridley
Willy Russell
Ntozake Shange
Sam Shepard (two volumes)
W. Somerset Maugham
  (two volumes)
Sophocles (two volumes)
Wole Soyinka
David Storey (two volumes)
August Strindberg
  (three volumes)
J. M. Synge
Sue Townsend
Ramón del Valle-Inclán
Michel Vinaver (two volumes)
Frank Wedekind
Michael Wilcox
Oscar Wilde

VALLE-INCLÁN

Plays: One

Divine Words
Bohemian Lights
Silver Face

Translated and introduced by Maria M Delgado

Methuen Drama

METHUEN WORLD CLASSICS

First published in Great Britain 1993 by Methuen Drama
Random House, 20 Vauxhall Bridge Road, London SW1V 2SA
and Australia, New Zealand and South Africa
and distributed in the United States of America
by Heinemann, a division of Reed Elsevier Inc.
361 Hanover Street, Portsmouth, New Hampshire NH 03801 3959

Reissued with corrections and a new cover 1997

Copyright © in these translations 1993, 1997 by Maria M Delgado
Introduction and Chronology copyright © 1993, 1997 by
Maria M Delgado
The translator has asserted her moral rights

ISBN 0-413-67090-2

Random House UK Limited Reg. No. 954009

Every effort has been made to trace the copyright owner of the
cover picture, Ramón del Valle-Inclán by Leal da Camara

A CIP catalogue record for this book is available from the British Library

Typeset by Wilmaset Ltd, Birkenhead, Wirral
Printed in Great Britain by Cox & Wyman, Reading, Berkshire

Contents

Acknowledgements

I would like to thank all the directors, designers and actors who have worked on these translations; Stephen Roberts and Nuria Triana Toribio for discussing with me the intricacies of Valle-Inclán's language; Stewart Harcourt and Paul Heritage for reading through early drafts of *Divine Words* and *Bohemian Lights*; Jorge Lavelli, Lluís Pasqual and José Carlos Plaza for sharing with me their experiences of directing Valle-Inclán; Northern Arts for awarding me a travel and training grant which made possible trips to Paris and Madrid in 1991/2 to see *The Savage Plays*; Michael Earley for his editorial guidance and suggestions; Henry Little; and Gwynne Edwards, John London and Rod Wooden for their comments on the texts and introduction and for their encouragement and friendship.

This edition has been translated with the financial assistance of the Spanish Dirección General del Libro y Bibliotecas, Ministerio de Cultura.

Ramón del Valle-Inclán: A Chronology

1866   Born on 28 October in the village of Villanueva de Arosa
        in Pontevedra, the second of the four children of Ramón
        del Valle-Inclán y Bermúdez and Dolores de la Peña
        Montenegro Cardecid y Saco Bolaño. Christened Ramón
        José Simón Ville y Peña the following day.

1868   Liberal military rebellion overthrows Queen Isabel II.

1873   Second Carlist War (resulting from the earlier succession
        to the throne of Fernando VII's daughter Isabel in place
        of Fernando's brother Carlos).

1874   Restoration of the monarchy. Alfonso XII pronounced
        king.

1877   The young Valle attends the Institute of Santiago after
        passing its entrance exams. Spends two years studying
        there.

1881   Attends the Institute of Pontevedra. Graduates after four
        years without distinction, having failed the mathematics,
        Latin and Spanish components of his course.

1887   Enters the University of Santiago de Compostela to study
        Law.

1889   Publishes first poems and short stories 'At Molinares',
        'Babel' and 'At Midnight'.

1890   Death of Valle's father on 14 January. Abandons his
        studies and moves to Madrid in the hope of pursuing a
        career as a journalist. Articles and stories published in the
        liberal newspaper *El Globo*.

1892   Leaves for Mexico in April. Publishes articles, stories and
        poems in a number of Mexican newspapers. First adopts
        the pseudonym of Ramón del Valle-Inclán.

1893   Returns to Spain via Cuba in July. Settles in Pontevedra.

1895   Publication of his first book, *Femeninas. Seis historias
        amorosas* (*Of Women. Six Amorous Stories*).

1896   Returns to Madrid to pursue his literary career.

1897   Publication of his second book, *Epitalamio* (*Wedding
        Song*).

1898   Valle-Inclán's debut as an actor in Jacinto Benavente's *La
        comida de las fieras* (*The Feast of the Wild Beasts*) at

Madrid's Teatro de la Comedia on 7 November. Loss of Spain's colonial empire as Cuba proclaims independence.

1899   In July an argument with Manuel Bueno at a café *tertulia* over an impending duel between the Portuguese caricaturist Leal da Camara and J. López del Castillo results in a cufflink lodging in his wrist. Valle-Inclán refuses to have the injury seen to and gangrene sets in, necessitating the amputation of his left arm. Publication of *Cenizas* (*Ashes*), Valle-Inclán's first play. The play is premièred on 7 December at Madrid's Teatro Lara by the Teatro Artisco Company.

1902   Publication of the novel, *Sonata de otoño* (*Autumn Sonata: Memories of the Marquis of Bradomín*). Gains second prize for a short story *¡Malpocado!* in a literary competition organized under the auspices of the journal *El Liberal*.

1903   Adapts Lope de Vega's play, *Fuenteovejuna*, with Manuel Bueno for Madrid's Teatro Español. Publication of the novel *Sonata de estío* (*Summer Sonata*).

1904   Publication of the novel *Flor de santidad* (*Flower of Sanctity*). Publication of *Sonata de primavera* (*Spring Sonata*), first in the sequence of novels chronicling the memories of the Marquis of Bradomín.

1905   Publication of the novel *Sonata de invierno* (*Winter Sonata*).

1906   Marriage of King Alfonso XIII to Victoria Eugenia of Battenburg. Assassination attempt against the couple by the Catalan anarchist Mateo Morral. Valle-Inclán's first major play, *El Marqués de Bradomín* (*The Marquis of Bradomín*), based on the *Sonata* novels is premièred at Madrid's Teatro de la Princesa on 25 January.

1907   Marries the actor Josefina Blanco. Publication of *Aguila de blason* (*Eagle of Honour*) and *Romance de lobos* (*Ballad of Wolves*), two plays in the trilogy to be known as *Comedias bárbaras* (*The Savage Plays*). Visits the province of Navarre where he meets a number of important Carlists, including General Amador del Villar and Don Joaquín Argamasilla de la Cerda, close friends of the Carlist pretenders to the Spanish throne, Don Jaime and Don Carlos.

1910   Presents himself as a traditionalist candidate for the Government elections in the Monforte de Lemus district of Galicia but is defeated. *La cabeza del dragón* (*The*

Dragon's Head) produced under the auspices of Benavente's Teatro de los Niños Company at Madrid's Teatro de la Comedia on 5 March. *Cuento de abril* (*April Tale*) produced by the Matilde Moreno Company in Madrid's Teatro de la Comedia on 19 March. Appointed Artistic Director of Francisco García Ortega's Theatre Company. Tours Argentina with them. Joins the María Guerrero-Fernando Díaz de Mendoza Theatre Company on a tour of Latin America which encompasses Chile, Paraguay, Uruguay and Bolivia.

1911   *Voces de gesta* (*Epic Voices*) premièred in Barcelona by the Guerrero-Díaz de Mendoza Company. Opens in Madrid's Teatro de la Princesa on 26 May 1912. First real theatrical triumph. Death of his mother.

1912   *La Marquesa Rosalinda* (*The Marchioness Roslinda*) premièred by the Guerrero-Díaz de Mendoza Company in Madrid's Teatro de la Princesa on 5 March. Moves back to Galicia.

1913   Collected works published by Perlado, Páez y Compañía. Establishes a Galician base at a farm near Puebla de Caramiñal. Publication of his play *El embrujado* (*The Bewitched*).

1914   Death of his four-month-old son Joaquín María.

1915   A failed attempt to have himself recognized as the Viscount of Viexín and Señor of Caramiñal.

1916   Publication of his collection of aesthetic essays, *La lámpara maravillosa* (*The Lamp of Marvels*). The Nicaraguan Nobel Prize winning poet, Rubén Darío, a close friend of Valle-Inclán, dies on 6 February in Nicaragua. Valle appointed to the Chair of Aesthetics at the Special School of Painting, Sculpture and Engraving in Madrid. Abandons all formal duties there after 1917. Visits the Western Front as a war correspondent.

1919   Industrial unrest in Barcelona. Martial law imposed in Madrid.

1920   Publication of four major plays: *Farsa italiana de la enamorada del rey* (*The Italian Farce of the Girl in Love with the King*), *Divinas palabras* (*Divine Words*), *Luces de Bohemia* (*Bohemian Lights*) (the first *esperpento*) and *Farsa y licencia de la reina castiza* (*The Licentious Farce of the Chaste Queen*).

1921   Publication of *Los cuernos de don Friolera* (*The Horns of Don Friolera*) (an *esperpento*). Visits Mexico to participate in an official capacity in the country's independence day celebrations. Travels back to Spain via Cuba.

1922   Publication of *Cara de Plata* (*Silver Face*), the opening part of the trilogy, *The Savage Plays*.

1923   General Miguel Angel Primo de Rivera establishes a dictatorship in Spain.

1924   Valle-Inclán returns with his family to Madrid. Publication of *La cabeza del Bautista* (*The Baptist's Head*) (a melodrama for marionettes). The play is premièred at Madrid's Teatro del Centro by Enrique López Alarcón on 17 October, transferring to Barcelona's Teatro Goya on 25 March of the following year. Publication of *Bohemian Lights* with three additional scenes – Two, Six and Eleven. Publication of *La rosa de papel* (*The Paper Rose*), another in the series of melodramas for marionettes.

1926   Forms his own theatre company, El Cántaro Roto (The Broken Jug), which stages *Ligazón* (*Blood Bond*) (a morality play for silhouettes), at Madrid's Teatro Bellas Artes on 19 December. The play is directed by Valle-Inclán. Publication of *Blood Bond*, *Las galas del difunto* (*The Dead Man's Suit*) (an *esperpento*), *Sacrilegio* (*Sacrilege*) (a morality play for silhouettes) and the novel *Tirano Banderas* (*Banderas the Tyrant*).

1927   Publication of *La hija del capitán* (*The Captain's Daughter*) (an *esperpento*). The first edition is confiscated by the authorities because of its attack on the Government. On 27 October Valle-Inclán enters Madrid's Teatro Fontalba and interrupts the performance of Joaquín Montaner's *El hijo del diablo* (*The Devil's Son*) until forcibly removed by the police.

1929   Imprisoned twice for supposed offences relating to the non-payment of fines.

1930   End of Primo de Rivera's dictatorship. *The Dead Man's Suit*, *The Horns of Don Friolera* and *The Captain's Daughter* published together as *Martes de carnaval* (*Carnival Tuesday*).

1931   Alfonso XIII goes into exile on April 14. Inauguration of the Second Republic. Manuel Azaña elected Prime Minister. *The Licentious Farce of the Chaste Queen* premièred by the Irene López Heredia Company at Madrid's Teatro Muñoz Seca on 3 June. Première of *The Bewitched* by the same company at the same theatre directed by Valle-Inclán on 11 November.

1932   Valle-Inclán elected to the presidency of the Ateneo. The Spanish Academy rejects *Banderas the Tyrant* for the Fastenrath Prize. A formal separation from his wife Josefina Blanco after twenty-five years of marriage. The couple are divorced the following year.

1933   Azaña resigns as Prime Minister. A conservative majority is returned in the November elections. The right wing Falange founded under the leadership of José Antonio Primo de Rivera, son of the deposed dictator. Valle-Inclán elected President of the Association of Friends of the Soviet Union. Convenes the first Congress of Revolutionary Writers and Artists at Madrid's Ateneo. Gives a reading of *Divine Words* at Madrid's Teatro Español on 24 March. His nomination to become head of the Spanish Academy of Fine Arts in Rome is approved. Moves to Rome. Première of *Divine Words* by Margarita Xirgu and Enrique Borras's Theatre Company at Madrid's Teatro Español on 16 November.

1934   Illness forces his return to Madrid. The Spanish Academy rejects his candidacy for membership. Guest of Federico García Lorca at the acclaimed première of *Yerma* at Madrid's Teatro Español on 29 December.

1935   Accepts the presidency of the International Association of Writers (Spanish Section). Elected as one of the twelve praesidium members of L'Association Internationale des Ecrivains pour la Défense de la Culture. Unable to attend the first congress due to ill-health.

1936   Dies in the Galician city of Santiago de Compostela on 5 January. Buried the following day in a civil ceremony. Tribute held to him on 14 February in Madrid's Teatro de la Zarzuela featuring speeches by Lorca and the poets Antonio Machado and Rafael Alberti. Posthumous première of *The Horns of Don Friolera*. Military insurrection led by General Francisco Franco on 18 July. The Civil War begins.

Introduction

Ramón María del Valle-Inclán is one of the most significant 'anti-naturalistic' playwrights and novelists of the early twentieth century, though until recently much of his work has remained largely unknown outside his native Spain. In recent years, however, Europe, in particular, has witnessed a major reappraisal. Lluís Pasqual, now Artistic Director of Paris's Théâtre de L'Odéon d'Europe, staged *Bohemian Lights* in 1984 and 1987, claiming it to be the greatest work in Spain's twentieth century dramatic literature. More recently he adapted *Banderas the Tyrant* for a cast of twelve, opening at L'Odéon in May of 1992 before embarking on a tour of Spain, Italy and Latin America. Jean-Marie Broucaret staged *Divine Words* in France in the late-eighties and in 1991 Jorge Lavelli and José Carlos Plaza staged *The Savage Plays* in French and Spanish respectively at The Avignon Festival and Madrid's María Guerrero Theatre. New translations of these plays have been published in France and Germany; only Britain has remained largely ignorant of Valle-Inclán's work, failing to accord him the status he deserves as one of the great innovators of twentieth-century theatre.

II

Ramón del Valle-Inclán was born on 28 October 1866 in the Galician village of Villanueva de Arosa in the North Western province of Pontevedra and christened the following day with the name Ramón José Simón Valle y Peña: Ramón del Valle-Inclán was the pseudonym he adopted from his father's name to reflect what the playwright perceived as his illustrious lineage. He was the second of four children born to Dolores de la Peña Montenegro Cardecid y Saco Bolaño and Ramón

del Valle-Inclán y Bermúdez. Although Valle-Inclán was to
make much of his noble antecedents – the Montenegros were
a well-established Galician clan after which he was to name
one of his most celebrated creations, the nobleman Don Juan
Manuel Montenegro, and the Bermúdez estate owners in Puebla
de Caramiñal – the Valle y Peña family were, at the time of
Ramón's birth, largely impoverished. Ramón del Valle-Inclán
y Bermúdez (1822–1890) sunk his meagre inheritance into a
wealth of minor journalistic ventures which necessitated his
taking on a variety of odd jobs – coastguard, administrative
clerk in local government – to support his family.

Little is known about Valle's early childhood. This is in
part due to his reticence to discuss or write about his early
years, but also to his fondness for embellishing and fabricating
autobiographical details where he felt it appropriate. What
is certain however, is that his father's work as a provincial
journalist – most notably founding the weekly paper *La Opinión
Pública* in Santiago de Compostela and *La Voz de Arosa* in
Villagarcía de Arosa – had a profound influence on the young
Ramón. From an early age he witnessed his father preparing
the weekly editions of *La Voz de Arosa* and the gatherings
of local novelists, poets and historians which took place in
the family home. The family's excellent library contained an
impressive collection of regional writers as well as the foremost
writers of Europe who were to influence Valle-Inclán's own
work. Later, while studying law at the prestigious University
of Santiago de Compostela, he came into contact with a number
of prominent writers of the time, including the playwright
José Zorilla. It was during these years that he published his
first poems and short stories – 'At Molinares', 'Babel' and 'At
Midnight'.

With the death of his father in 1890, Valle-Inclán no longer
felt obliged to continue studying for his law degree and moved
to Madrid to pursue a career in journalism. The family's
precarious financial situation, however, put a halt to his
ambitions to pursue a full-time literary career. His early articles
and short stories met with only a limited success amongst
Madrid's literary intelligentsia and the disappointment resulting
from this lack of instant success and recognition no doubt
played a part in his decision to travel to Mexico in the spring
of 1892, although in contradictory interviews he cited both a

romantic attraction to the land of Montezuma and an intense desire to avoid sitting his final bar examination as reasons for his sudden departure. After a period of travel around Vera Cruz, Valle-Inclán settled in Mexico City, working as a journalist and publishing a prolific number of articles, poems and short stories in various Mexican newspapers. It was in Mexico that he first adopted the pseudonym he was to assume for the rest of his life, Ramón María del Valle-Inclán and here too that his habitual drug-taking, initially dabbled in as a means of reaching the realms of the spiritual, originated.

On his return to Galicia in the summer of 1893, he continued earning a living through journalism and published his first book, *Of Women*, largely ignored by the critics, in 1895. It was during these years too that he cultivated his particular Bohemian look – the long flowing mane, the sweeping beard, small rimmed glasses, loose unkempt clothes and cape – with which he was to be associated for the remainder of his life. When asked once why he refused to cut his hair, he is rumoured to have remarked curtly that no one dared to attempt it, for whenever he entered a barber's each snip would cause his hair to bleed and the barber to abandon the task. To complement his distinct physical appearance, he also developed an inclination towards the hyperbolic, fabricating a dashing biography of his life which was embellished during the period in Madrid after 1896 with claims that he had, at various times, been a lay brother in a Carthusian monastery, a Carlist soldier and a private in the Mexican army. Associations with military personnel, including Sóstenes Rochas, as well as his own support for the reactionary Carlist movement, resulted in the fabrication of numerous anecdotes about his bravery and heroism and the adoption of a further pseudonym, Colonel General of the Armies of Tierra Caliente.

Valle's unusual appearance, lively imagination, lisping, high-pitched voice and forthright opinions made him a distinctive figure at the literary gatherings or café *tertulias* which were the backbone of intellectual life in Spain at the time. The Nobel Prize-winning playwright, Jacinto Benavente, the actor Enrique Gómez Carillo, the novelists Miguel de Unamuno, Alejandro Sawa and Pío Baroja, and the poet Rubén Darío were some of the distinguished figures who met at certain well-known cafés to discuss a range of literary and political matters, accompanied by an emerging generation of young writers keen to associate with and learn from the country's most respected literary figures.

This hectic participation in the *tertulias* led Valle-Inclán to consider a career in acting. Anecdotes tell of his lively, animated performances at the *tertulias*, as well as of his recitals of Romantic plays of the period while walking through Madrid. He contacted the novelist and playwright, Benito Pérez Galdós, in 1898 to request he recommend him as an actor to certain theatre companies. His first opportunity came in Benavente's play *The Feast of the Wild Beasts*. After initial problems with the director Emilio Thuiller, whose work as both actor and director Valle-Inclán had vociferously denounced on various occasions, he began rehearsals in October 1898, taking the part of Teófilo Everit, a character modelled by Benavente on Valle-Inclán himself. The play opened on 7 November of that year, but the fact that his performance was largely ignored by the theatre critics led to his sudden resignation from the company after only three performances. He was to act only once more, in 1899 in an adaptation of Alphonse Daudet's *Kings in Exile* by Alejandro Sawa. A friendship with Benavente developed from the initial acting engagement and Valle-Inclán went on to direct an adaptation of *The Taming of the Shrew* for Benavente's Teatro Artístico, with Benavente then going on to première Valle-Inclán's first play, *Ashes*, at Madrid's Teatro Lara in December 1899. Such occasional ventures – Valle-Inclán continued to work as a director sporadically – failed to provide him with any degree of financial security and he was obliged to take on a number of minor literary projects, including the co-translation of a piece by Alexandre Dumas, the adaption into a novel of Carlos Arniches' play *The Face of God* and translations of the Portuguese writer José María Eça de Queiroz.

It was however, the amputation of his left arm in 1899 which convinced him that his future in theatre lay in writing rather than acting. A heated argument with his friend, the writer Manuel Bueno, in the Café de la Montaña became violent when Bueno drove one of Valle-Inclán's cufflinks into his wrist with a swift blow of his cane. Valle-Inclán refused to have the injury examined until gangrene set in. While in hospital, on reading that the bullfighter Angel Pastor had died of a similar condition, he is said to have insisted that the whole arm be amputated. He later bragged that the operation had been performed without chloroform.

He drew on this experience in his own writing. His alter ego, the aristocratic Marquis of Bradomín, a forerunner of the despotic womanizing protagonist of *The Savage Plays*, Don Juan Manuel Montenegro and the protagonist of Valle-Inclán's first major novel, *Autumn Sonata*, has his left arm amputated in the later *Winter Sonata*. A subsequent accident with a pistol that went off accidentally while Valle was out riding in La Mancha left him lame. 'One-armed like Cervantes and lame like Byron', he was fond of repeating to friends with regard to his own disabilities; blindness the only other requisite to greatness eluding him. A fascination with blindness is, in fact, to be seen in his later works. *Divine Words* and *Silver Face* both feature the sly Blind Man of Gondar and *Bohemian Lights* has a blind protagonist, Max Estrella.

The publication of the Sonata novels gained Valle-Inclán further prestige and notoriety. After 1903, when the evening *tertulias* convened at the Nuevo Café de Levante beside La Puerta del Sol, Valle-Inclán dominated the proceedings with his flamboyant, outspoken style. Here the visiting Henri Matisse and Diego Rivera are known to have joined Antonio Machado, Picasso and Valle-Inclán in dissecting the latest literary publications and discussing the burning political questions of the day. It is at one of the *tertulias* at the Café Candelas that Valle-Inclán is thought to have met the Catalan anarchist Mateo Morral, responsible for the assassination attempt against King Alfonso XIII and his bride Victoria Eugenia of Battenburg on their wedding day in 1906, and supposedly the figure on which Valle-Inclán based the character of the Catalan prisoner in *Bohemian Lights*. It is thought that Valle-Inclán was responsible for identifying Morral's body at the City morgue.

Political and social concerns were often discussed at the *tertulias*. The definitive loss of empire and Spain's decline as a world power, brought sharply into focus by the loss of Cuba in 1898, became a serious concern for the intellectuals gathering at the various café *tertulias*, who felt their work needed to reflect and comment on their declining nation. Although Valle-Inclán is often regarded as part of the 'Generation of '98' as they came to be known, 1895–1916 should really be seen as his *modernista* phase, characterized by an overt concern with the

aesthetic over ideas and content. Later his increasing interest
in the political and social fate of his country would lead to
his rejection of *Modernismo*, clearly visible in the satirical
portraits of the *modernistas* in *Bohemian Lights*. But in general
Valle-Inclán's prolific and varied body of work resists simplistic
categorization, reflecting his reluctance to adhere to any one
stylistic trait. If any generalization can be made with regard to
his dramaturgical and novelistic output, it must involve his clear
rejection of photographic imitation and a substitution of realistic
detail with cinematic, sweeping statements: atmosphere and
mood prioritized in an attempt to capture and express the more
elusive reality behind deceptive appearances.

Valle-Inclán's increasing involvement with theatre during
these years, both as spectator and director, in many ways
focused his aspirations as a playwright. At a time when the
rest of Europe was witnessing a bold rejection of pictorial
realism, Spain remained largely untouched by such innovations.
The neo-romantic plays of José de Echegaray, as well as
the sentimental drama of the Quintero brothers, Eduardo
Marquina and Manuel Linares Rivas, all conspicuously
avoiding potentially controversial or delicate subjects, reinforced
the conservative middle-class values which Valle-Inclán so
much despised. His refusal to accept the vulgar mediocrity
of bourgeois society was in part responsible for his attraction
towards the occult and the esoteric, aesthetic elements of
Schopenhauer, Baudelaire and Wagner. Symbolism provided
him with a means of transcending the mundane reality of
contemporary Spain, providing him with the possibility of
creating alternative worlds of the exotic and the exquisite
invisible to the naked eye. Rather than plot, mood, atmosphere,
ritual, myth, non-linearity and musicality of language were
to prove the crucial hinges on which his plays revolved. An
increasing frustration with the theatrical fare on offer in Madrid
led to a vociferous defence of playwrights he admired, like
Benavente, against a hostile public, and a vicious attack on
minor playwrights, like the Andalusian José López Pinillos.
Unable to limit his outbursts to journalistic comment, he
organized an outspoken formal protest at the national tribute
prepared for the comic dramatist José de Echegaray when
he was awarded the Nobel Prize for Literature in 1904. His
criticism of Echegaray and the complacent theatre he so

embodied was to continue over the next two decades, resulting in such episodes as addressing a letter to a friend living in Echegaray Street with Street of the Old Idiot – the letter, in fact, reached its destination. Another incident involved locking his wife, the actor Josefina Blanco, in her hotel room when she was due to appear in Echegaray's *The Stain that Cleans*.

It was while he was working as Artistic Director of Ricardo Calva's Theatre Company that he had met the young Josefina Blanco, marrying her in 1907. She was to bear him six children – Joaquín María, Carlos Luis, María Beatriz, Margarita Carlota, Jaime Clemente and María Ana Antonia – all given Carlist names and sharing the added name of Balthasar, after one of the Magi. Although Valle-Inclán failed to develop his career as a dramatist/director in the manner of Brecht, it is known that he was a demanding and meticulous director whom actors tended to fear. He was to gain the support of the prestigious María Guerrero–Fernando Díaz de Mendoza Theatre Company, undertaking a tour of Latin America with them, but his uncompromising stance with regard to his own writing led to a definitive break with them in 1912 when they dropped *Epic Voices* from their repertoire. This, in effect, put an end to the company's plans for staging *The Bewitched* in their 1912–13 season. The play was also rejected by Pérez Galdós, then director of the Teatro Español. A proposed reading at Madrid's Ateneo on 26 February 1913, preceded by an angry outburst by Valle-Inclán on the Teatro Español's failure to present the play, resulted in the forcible removal of the dramatist by the police. The actual reading had to be postponed until later that week.

It was such eccentricities, such outrageous gestures of defiance which marked his reputation and which were, in part, responsible for his ostracism from the Spanish theatrical establishment. A catalogue of disappointments – only six of the nine plays published by that time had received any kind of production, and *Eagle of Honour* and *Ballad of Wolves*, the two major plays of his *modernista*/symbolist period, had been completely ignored – led to Valle's temporary withdrawal from theatrical activity, as well as to the temporary removal of his family to Galicia. It was a stance he would maintain until the publication of *The Licentious Farce of the Chaste Queen* in 1920.

Valle-Inclán had entertained notions of settling in Galicia as Viscount of Viexín and Señor of Caramiñal on a comfortable

estate in the manner of the feudal nobleman Don Juan
Manuel Montenegro, immortalized in *The Savage Plays*.
Financial problems however – even in his most illustrious days
Valle-Inclán was not a wealthy man – necessitated a move back
to Madrid. Plagued with ill-health for much of his later life,
Valle-Inclán became accustomed to spending long periods in
bed as a means of conserving his strength. Extreme poverty
and the burden of supporting a large family often reduced
him to the ignominy of regular periods of fasting, although he
continued to channel great energy and vitality into his writing.
Forced to sell personal copies of his work in times of need, he
proudly refused to compromise his artistic integrity by agreeing
to cuts in his work for publication or re-publication. Such rash
gestures were to mark his reputation and ensure he remain
largely ignored by the cultural establishment, as in the case of
his exclusion from the select membership of The Spanish Royal
Academy while other lesser writers were honoured. Anger at
the Academy was often reflected in his work – most noticeably
in Scene Four of *Bohemian Lights* in Max's comments to those
assembled outside the café.

Abroad, however, his work was beginning to generate
interest. *Ballad of Wolves*, translated by his friend, the former
Consul General of France in Spain, Jacques Chaumié, was
due to be premièred in Paris in 1914, but fell victim to the
sudden outbreak of World War One. The War was to have a
profound influence on Valle-Inclán. He was appointed Special
War Correspondent of the newspapers *El Imparcial* and *La
Nación* and visited the War front in 1916–1917. Although
anecdotes tend to concentrate on images of Valle-Inclán
parading through the battlefields in his Carlist uniform, there
is no doubt that the suffering witnessed in France severely
traumatized him, and this is reflected in the sharp satirical edge
to his post-1917 work. The death in the previous year of his
close friend, the Nicaraguan *modernista* poet, Rubén Darío, to
whom Valle-Inclán had dedicated the 1906 edition of *Summer
Sonata* and to whom he was to make reference in *Bohemian
Lights*, *Banderas the Tyrant* and *The Pipe of Kif*, marked the
end of *Modernismo* in his work. Although *Modernismo* had, in
effect, been a response against Zola's assertion that Naturalism
provided an accurate reflection of reality, and was a movement
which could appeal to the senses as much as to the intellect,

Valle-Inclán's realization of its inappropriateness to what was happening around him, did not involve by any means a wholehearted adoption of Naturalism. On the contrary, he came to realize that the naturalistic mode of discourse was no longer adequate as a means of reflecting the complexities of life in a society irrevocably changed by the First World War. Although the War had initially brought prosperity to Spain – she was able to supply the allies with much needed raw materials – the boom had been short lived and had led to inflation, political instability and industrial problems. In effect these events politicized him, creating an awareness of the need to express his disenchantment with the political regime and its brutal handling of the proletarian disputes witnessed in Madrid and Barcelona in 1919. Domestic unrest was also aggravated by the impact of the Russian revolution, felt in Spain more deeply than in any other European country: the impact of Socialism evident not only in the labour disputes which rocked Spain's two major cities but also in the increasing hostility to the monarchy which was eventually to lead to the exile of the King and the establishment of the Second Republic in 1931. Valle-Inclán's enthusiasm for Communism lay in his perception of it as a twentieth-century answer to Carlism: an anti-democratic movement which had sought to question the vulgar capitalist ethics and mediocrity of bourgeois society.

The numerous ideologies embraced by Valle during the course of his life – Carlism, Communism, Anarchism – no doubt added to his unpopularity. The Carlists had sought to revive the notion of the classic, feudal king, supporting the right of succession of Don Carlos, brother to Fernando VII. On his death in 1833, Fernando had been succeeded by his young daughter Isabel under the regency of her mother María Christina. The First Carlist War (1834–39) had failed to restore Don Carlos to the throne, but Valle-Inclán saw in the Carlist movement the spirit of the *conquistadores* who had made Spain such a great colonial power during the reign of Phillip II. The ethical ideals and sense of sacrifice of the Carlist movement (which in 1931 awarded Valle-Inclán its highest decoration) provided him with material for his historical novels published under the general title of *The Carlist War*. His taking up of the Carlist cause in this series of novels, the Carlist sympathies of the Marquis of Bradomín in *Winter Sonata*, in *Epic Voices* the

veiled allegory of the relentless efforts of a community led by
La noble shepherdess Ginebra to restore the rightful sovereign
to the throne, and Silver Face's departure in *Eagle of Honour*
to the Carlist War, led to a certain disapproval of his work
in the Spanish press. His post-1917 espousal of Communism
and his rash, satirical treatment of the reign of Alfonso XIII's
grandmother, Isabel II, in *The Licentious Farce of the Chaste
Queen*, was to prove equally unpopular to the post-1923
dictatorship of Miguel Angel Primo de Rivera. The insecurity
of the political situation, which made for constant changes of
government, and the annihilation of a large part of the Spanish
Army in Morocco during the rebellion led by Abd-el-Krim was
to lead to Primo de Rivera's suspension of the constitution and
eventual dictatorship. Miguel de Unamuno's forced exile after
a vociferous campaign against the regime produced widespread
dissent from other writers outraged by the Government's action
against such a major writer. The King's compliance in Primo
de Rivera's seizure of power also provoked anti-monarchist
comments on Valle-Inclán's part. Government representatives
were required in consequence to attend all theatrical events and
public ventures in which Valle-Inclán was involved and the first
edition of his last play, *The Captain's Daughter*, was confiscated
because of its blatant satirical attack on the Government.
His honorary presidency of the Association of Friends of
the USSR in 1929 was no doubt in part responsible for the
Government's refusal to grant him a passport to visit France.
The following year his signing of the San Sebastian Pact, part
of a mounting anti-monarchist campaign, complemented his
writing in registering his opposition to what he perceived as an
incompetent and unjust government.

These tumultuous political years (1917–1930) produced much
of Valle-Inclán's most respected work, characterized by an
increasing recourse to the grotesque, malicious wit and irony –
in the tradition of Quevedo's black, pessimistic views of human
existence – and a sharp cynicism not evident in his earlier
modernista writings. For Valle-Inclán an unquestioning reflection
of reality could not provide any kind of criticism of that reality.
The recording of reality in a concave mirror, advocated in his
theory of the *esperpento*, exposes the inadequacy of mimetic art
as a means of commenting on and recreating history. As with
Modernismo, Valle-Inclán perceived the grotesque as a reaction

against the constraints of capitalist society at its ugliest and
most mediocre, lamenting the change of values and priorities
which governed such an unsettling world. It is no coincidence
that his most savage portraits in *Bohemian Lights* are those
of the Home Secretary and Zarathustra – marionette-like
representatives of the Government and the entrepreneurial
middle class respectively.

The fall of Primo de Rivera's dictatorship in 1930, the
abdication of the monarch and the elections which followed
in 1931, returned a left of centre Government which set to
work on a new liberal constitution. A wave of social reforms
followed, including a widespread campaign to eradicate
illiteracy. Federico García Lorca's travelling theatre company,
La Barraca, was at the forefront of this process. To prevent
Valle-Inclán having to lecture in America in order to make ends
meet, the new Prime Minister, Manuel Azaña, created a new
post for him – Curator General of the Artistic Patrimony and
Head of the Palace Museum at Aranjuez. Despite persistent
ill-health, including a painful bladder infection, he undertook
his duties with a diligence not witnessed in any of his previous
official posts. But as in the case of his brief appointment
in 1916 to the Chair of Aesthetics at the Special School of
Painting, Sculpture and Engraving in Madrid, where he had
insisted on calling impromptu lectures and had convened
classes in such venues as the Prado and the Café Levante on
the grounds that they had more influence on contemporary
culture than any university, problems of communication with
his superiors brought about his resignation. This, of course,
put paid to any possibility of a regular income at a time where
penury was also proving an excessive strain on his marriage. He
continued to earn meagre amounts from occasional articles but
influential friends had to rally round to help support him and
his children – he was awarded custody of all but the youngest,
María Ana Antonia, when he and Josefina finally separated
in 1932. Although *Banderas the Tyrant* was shortlisted for the
Fastenrath Prize that year, the Spanish Academy's prejudiced
jury again refused to recognize Valle-Inclán's worth, rejecting
what has come to be regarded as one of the most innovative
Spanish novels of the twentieth century. In France however,
he was perceived as one of Spain's leading writers. He was
the only Spaniard invited to join an international committee

convened to compile an agenda for the Grand Congrès Mondial Contre la Guerre. Ill-health again prevented his attendance at its meeting in Amsterdam, but in 1933 he was well enough to travel once more when the proposal that he head the Spanish Academy of Fine Arts in Rome was finally approved, despite opposition from the Prado Museum and the Academy of Fine Arts in San Fernando who put forward less controversial candidates. Although recurring bladder infections forced him into hospital again in early March, he was able to give a reading of *Divine Words* at Madrid's Teatro Español on 23 March, leaving for Rome with five of his children soon after. He returned to Spain briefly in November of the same year for the controversial première of *Divine Words* at Madrid's Teatro Español. It was the last of his plays to be staged in Spain during his lifetime. Returning to Rome, he remained there until recurring haematuria forced his return to Spain in November of the following year. In Italy he embarked on a brief romantic affair and cultivated links with writers, artists and directors including Anton Giulio Bragaglia, founder of Teatro Sperimentale degli Indipendenti and Teatro delle Arti who, despite the efforts of the Fascist censor, premièred *The Horns of Don Friolera* in 1934 at the Teatro delle Arti.

A new Prime Minister – Alejandro Lerroux – replaced Azaña in August 1933, and the conservative majority returned in the November elections ensured that a more precarious political climate greeted Valle-Inclán on his return. Despite recurring bladder problems, he continued his lecturing, his preparation of texts for publication, his attendance at theatre performances and his political activities. Later that year he was elected Honorary President of the National Campaign Against the Death Penalty. Although elected too as one of the twelve praesidium members of the Association Internationale des Ecrivains pour la Défense de la Culture – alongside Henri Barbusse, Romain Rolland, André Gide, Heinrich Mann, Thomas Mann, Maxim Gorki, E.M. Forster, Aldous Huxley, G.B. Shaw, Sinclair Lewis and Selma Lagerlöf – ill-health again prevented Valle's attendance at the first Congress convened in Paris in June 1935. He returned to Galicia in the late summer, relying on the support of friends and admirers who, though unable to raise the money needed to purchase an estate, rallied around him to make his final months as comfortable as possible. He died in the holy city of Santiago

de Compostela at 2 pm on 5 January 1936, leaving instructions
for a simple, non-religious funeral. Buried the following day
– appropriately the feast of the Magi – which was proclaimed
an official day of mourning in Santiago, he was to prove as
controversial in death as in life, for the sculptor Modesto Pasín
threw himself onto the coffin as it was being lowered into the
grave in order to remove the cross which had been placed there
in spite of Valle-Inclán's stipulations. Proceedings were brought
to a temporary halt as the mourners attempted to retrieve the
lid which had broken, revealing the body beneath.

The tributes which followed that year were marked by similar
controversy. In February, the homage held at Madrid's Teatro
de la Zarzuela, culminating in a performance of *The Horns
of Don Friolera*, was boycotted by Valle's children who felt
that their father did not want his plays produced, that they
were written to be read, and that no director in Spain had
sufficient insight to stage them. He was writing for the theatre
of the future. His time, as Lavelli, Plaza and Pasqual have
demonstrated in 1992, has come; it is only appropriate that a
man perhaps best known for his personal extravagances and
eccentricities should now receive the acclaim his work deserves.

III

The difficulty of staging theatre works which are realized
so vividly on the page has meant that Valle-Inclán's plays
have remained largely unperformed in his own lifetime and
beyond. Few directors have felt able to meet the challenge
of rescuing his theatre from the bookshelves on which much
of it has languished since his death. Lacking a director in
his own times of the stature and imagination of Meyerhold
or Piscator to realize the spectacular world of his texts, Valle
was never in a position to direct his own work on a regular
basis. The detailed, allusive nature of his stage-directions –
a poetic guide to the surrounding dialogue and an intrinsic
component of the dramatic text – has often led to a perception
of the plays as failed cinema scripts rather than works for the
stage. The intertextual resonances present in the texts – the
incorporation and deployment of techniques from melodrama,

cinema, *commedia dell' arte*, the drama of the Golden Age and the theatre of Shakespeare – gives his plays the appearance of a mosaic, a literary anarchy of sorts which renders them awkward to classify. By drawing on a wide body of texts, Valle-Inclán made constant reference to the intellectual tradition he was part of, utilizing and revising the vocabulary of his cultural predecessors – most noticably Quevedo, Calderón, Cervantes, Velázquez and Goya – thus reflecting the fundamental post-structuralist notion that all plays are only ever about other cultural artefacts, literary or otherwise. Each text is, in effect, a pretext, offering Valle-Inclán the possibility for reworking and modification. Characters are rewritten from text to text – the Blind Man of Gondar appears both in *Divine Words* and *Silver Face*, Don Juan Manuel Montenegro in each of *The Savage Plays*. Each play operates in a state of aesthetic and structural evolution towards what Valle-Inclán came to recognize as an unattainable ideal – perfection; an acknowledgement that the autonomous text is ever anything but complete. The text is constantly reinvented in Valle-Inclán's work. Fictional characters, for example, Max Estrella in *Bohemian Lights*, jostle with historical characters, like Rubén Darío. Just as he invented and rewrote his own life so, in *Divine Words* and *The Horns of Don Friolera*, he rewrote the tragedies of Calderón for his own time, as a parody of the Golden Age husband obsessed with honour and self-respect.

In the sense that they are anti-Aristotelian, Valle's plays have been labelled Shakespearean and Brechtian. Although he lacks the didacticism regarding the need to change society so visible in Brecht's work, in many ways he anticipates Brecht's concepts of alienation and epic theatre. The open-ended nature of his theatre questions the fundamental notion of the 'well made' play with its single, closed ending by offering a possibility of openings to the reader: a multiplicity of voices jostling with each other to produce a decisive rupture with the dominant dramaturgical structures, an effect analogous to that created by Arnold Schönberg in his operas. As in Shakespeare, the action proceeds through short, self-contained episodic scenes which often contrast in mood and language with those preceding or following them. The strange, unnerving fusion of myth and reality, the epic and the insular, the physical and the spiritual and the sacred and the profane, so reminiscent of Shakespeare, remain, with the exception of Genet, unequalled in twentieth-century theatre.

Valle's plays reflect the aesthetic and structural influence of Shakespeare, their dialogue too contains many Shakespearean echoes. In Scene Fourteen of *Bohemian Lights*, the two gravediggers recall those at Ophelia's grave in *Hamlet*, a coincidence noted by the Marquis of Bradomín who reflects Valle-Inclán's admiration of Shakespeare and denigration of his contemporaries through the populist Quintero brothers:

> THE MARQUIS. During my period of literary flirtation I chose him as my mentor. He is exquisite! With a shy philosopher and an unbelievably silly girl he miraculously created the most beautiful of tragedies. In our Spanish theatre, my dear Rubén, Hamlet and Ophelia would become two comic characters. A shy boy and a silly girl! Just imagine what the glorious Quintero brothers would have done with them!

The parodic aspects of his work – the sarcasm, irony and macabre humour (often misunderstood by his contemporaries) and his overt anticlericalism (the irreverent, burlesque and grotesque treatment of religion) – were certainly unpopular with the more reactionary members of the establishment. His reinvention of dramatic language which was to prove such an influence on a generation of new dramatists – including Lorca whose *The Shoemaker's Wonderful Wife* was directly inspired by Valle-Inclán's *commedia*-influenced pieces such as *The Marchioness Rosalinda* – and his constant exploration of the relationship between stage, actor and audience proved frustrating to a theatrical establishment keen to promote domestic comedies where refined dialogue was of paramount importance. Just as he was able to expound two distinct political viewpoints in the same conversation, so his plays reflect the contradictions present in his character. The fact that ideological discrepancies are espoused and highlighted rather than negated – the dichotomy between liberalism and tradition, the pagan and the Catholic, the radical and the reactionary visible in the struggle of the worlds of Séptimo Miau and Pedro Gailo in *Divine Words* – provides an unnerving experience for the reader/audience accustomed to the closed text of naturalistic theatre. This may, in part, explain the influence he has exerted over dramatists like Lorca and Arrabal as well as the film-makers Luis Buñuel and Carlos Saura, similarly concerned with non-naturalistic modes of discourse. Only now, over fifty years after his death, is Valle recognized as the true initiator of a revitalization of Spanish theatre not witnessed since the Golden Age.

IV

Drawing on the pagan, Celtic traditions of his native Galicia and the repressive Catholicism of Spain, *Divine Words* – arguably Valle-Inclán's most resonant play – presents a grotesque, distorted picture of rustic life at its cruellest and most hypocritical. There is no longer any of the pastoral idealism found in Valle-Inclán's earlier work. Instead, through colour, odour, taste and a concentration on the odd and the distinctive, we are presented with an intense vision of an ugly, dehumanized society which simultaneously attracts and repels. Sentimentality for the old Galician feudal order has disappeared, replaced by a colder, more clinical view which is developed further in the equally unheroic *Silver Face*. This is a superstitious society with few positive values, a primitive region governed by amorality, adultery, avarice, lechery, cruelty, incest, cowardice and homophobia. Valle-Inclán succeeds in creating a distance between himself and his subject while simultaneously capturing the particular local character of the places and people described, thereby creating a tableau which had a direct relevance to turn of the century Spanish society. There are no irrevocably 'good' characters to compensate for the inhumanity and intolerance displayed by the community. Miau, although an outsider, is equally cynical and cruel, using Mari-Gaila for his own sexual gratification and then abandoning her to the wrath of the village when they are caught fornicating in the canefields. His ability to see into the future further reinforces the demonic associations suggested by one of his pseudonyms – Lucero. He is, however, more honest and direct than the other characters, less concerned with pleasantries and rituals of decorum. Hence his direct comments to Simoniña in Act Three, Scene Three regarding the now non-existent possibilities for exploiting the hydrocephalic dwarf. The villagers are more covert in their plans to exploit Laureano. Marica del Reino and Mari-Gaila both resort to meaningless rituals of mourning as a necessary prelude to the fight for the cart. The desperate wailing does not fool the village women who recognize the hypocrisy of Mari-Gaila lamenting a sister-in-law who despised her. They merely recognize the need for ritual in a society where appearances are all important.

Laureano, or the idiot or cart as he is dismissively referred to by the other characters, is the central pivot on which the action hinges. It is Juana la Reina's death which sets the narrative in motion, for it provides a lucrative legacy over which her family can argue. Laureano is never regarded as a human being, merely as an exploitable source of profit. Behind Marica and Mari-Gaila's lofty claims that they are motivated by a sense of benevolence and charity, lies a practical realization – expounded by the chorus-like figure of Rosa la Tatula – that the dwarf offers the possibility of a substantial income. The façade of mourning is only maintained until a settlement is reached. Bastián de Candás's suggestion that they divide the cart – recalling Solomon's decree and one of the numerous Biblical parodies present within the text – is egoistically accepted by both parties involved as a practical, workable solution. Laureano provides Mari-Gaila with access into an unfamiliar, picaresque world of beggars, pilgrims and tinkers – carnivalesque characters who live by their wits, exploiting the weakness of those more innocent than themselves. In this world he suffers horrendous abuse which eventually brings about his death, a death as violent and undignified as that of his mother. No one mourns his passing, only the loss of income which accompanies it. His continued presence in Act Three, as a stench-ridden bloated corpse left to rot outside the church, serves as a constant reminder of the ugly nature of the characters' lives.

In Mari-Gaila, Valle-Inclán presents a spirited anti-heroine, a descendent of Venus and Ceres, the goddesses with whom Miau associates her. Voluptuous, confident, opportunistic and egocentric, she is for Valle-Inclán a figure of pagan antiquity for whom the hedonistic and the sensual are paramount. Like the egocentric Miau, she is a constant reminder of the pagan, Celtic roots of Galicia. Dionysiac animalistic lust, in which love

really plays no part, governs her behaviour. This is emphasized
by her association with the Goat Goblin – the lascivious devil
of Galician folklore – who appears to her after the physical
consummation of her relationship with Miau. Her nocturnal
encounter with him functions both as a re-echoing of her own
sordid sexual encounter with Miau and as a manifestation of her
erotic subconscious.

Attracted by Miau's notoriety, Mari-Gaila embarks on a
relationship with him which flaunts the rules of the society to
which she belongs. She refuses to play the part of the dutiful
wife and has no real affection for her husband and daughter,
treating both with impatient disdain. Her treatment of
Laureano is equally dismissive; the few gestures of generosity
motivated solely by financial incentives. She audaciously
displays his genitalia to the assembled crowds for extra profit
and shows no respect for the arrangement reached with Marica
over the cart. In addition, she is thrilled by the thought that
Miau may be the infamous Polish Count and titillated by the
possibility that he may be a murderer. She is not, however,
wholly negative. Her physical beauty singles her out from the
community and she demonstrates an endearing naive piety when
faced with the pilgrim's pleas for food, for no other character
is moved by his stories of fasting and humility. It is this
'otherness' which sets her apart from her neighbours, whose
malicious jealousy and unrelieved sexual frustration rather than
any sense of moral indignation motivate their brutish behaviour
on discovering Mari-Gaila with Miau in the cornfields. Their
primitive instincts and animalistic lust mirror her own. The
bacchae-like procession through the fields into the village with
its frenzied Dionysiac associations brings the action to a climax:
Pedro Gailo's traditional Roman Catholic morality brought face
to face with the community's aroused pagan instincts. He is
able to tame the wolves through the Latin of the divine words
he utters – Christ's words to the baying crowd as they are about
to stone the adulteress. These primitive instincts are moved
only by words the community cannot understand, words whose
magical, semantic properties override any literal significance
they may have.

Valle-Inclán's perceived assault on the hypocrisy of the
Church – through his portrait of the drunken, weak-willed
sexton, Pedro Gailo and his direct handling of taboo subjects

– incest, adulterous sex and nudity – was no doubt responsible for the play's delayed theatrical première, over twelve years after it was first published. Even then it met with mixed responses, shocking the more conservative audiences who felt that such moral filth should never have been staged by the company of such an illustrious actor as Margarita Xirgu.

V

Bohemian Lights, the play which first expounded Valle-Inclán's theory of the grotesque, the *esperpento*, was, like *Silver Face* never staged during the author's lifetime. Although the play was first published in 1920, it lacked Scenes Two, Six and Eleven which were added at a later date (1924). As in the case of Brecht's epic theatre, the form of the play is itself a dramatic statement, its episodic scenes providing, like Joyce's *Ulysses*, a modern day Odyssey, charting the journey of an anti-hero through a capital city – here an absurd, brilliant and hungry Madrid – as much a product of the author's imagination as of historical reality. The play's episodic structure functions both as a reflection of and as a comment on the fragmentary, divisive nature of Spanish society in general. It is an uneasy reflection of urban life in the turbulent post-1918 years as Valle-Inclán perceived it, reflecting his anger at the country's religion (which is compared by Max in Scene Two to that of an African tribe), her political instability and corruption (the Home Secretary can provide Max with a pension, appropriated from other funds, only while he remains in power) and the police brutality (seen in the skirmishes between the police and the workers we hear of, the glass-strewn streets, the disturbance outside Tight Arse's tavern, Max's arrest, the death of the innocent child and the notorious *ley de fugas* whereby prisoners were shot by the authorities on the way to or from a police station and subsequently reported shot trying to escape). The darkness of much of the play – Scenes One to Twelve chart a twelve hour period from dusk to dawn, Scene Thirteen takes place in the darkened attic room where Max's funeral-wake is taking place, Scene Fourteen in the cemetery's fading light and the final scene in Tight Arse's dingy tavern – reflects not only

Max's despair but the dark nature of Spanish reality at the time. The lighting is often described as dim and subdued with Max and Don Latino forced to grope their way unsteadily from place to place. Many characters are themselves like shadows, disappearing into and out of the night which Max illuminates with his bitter perceptive comments.

This was the first play this century to be set in a contemporary Spain, clearly identifiable as post-World War One Madrid with specific allusions to streets, cafés and monuments, as well as to historical figures – politicians, writers and artists. In addition, a number of the characters are modelled on people Valle-Inclán knew, a fact which accentuates the ambivalent relationship between fictional situations and historical reality within the text. Enriqueta is thought to be based on a seller of lottery tickets known as Ojo de Plata – literally Eye of Silver. Dorio de Gadex, though the pseudonym of the *modernista* writer Eduardo de Ory, was also thought to be based on another writer, Ciro Bayo, and Basilio Soulinake on the Russian anarchist writer, Ernesto Bark. It is in Max Estrella however, that Valle-Inclán creates the most direct portrait of a contemporary – the Sevillian poet, novelist and translator, Alejandro Sawa (1862–1909). Described by Valle-Inclán in a letter written to Rubén Darío as 'blind and mad', terms used in association with Max, circumstances conspired to deprive Sawa of the respect his work deserved. He too had resided in Paris for many years and had developed close friendships with Paul Verlaine and a number of the symbolist poets. His wife, Jeanne Poirier, was French and they had a single child, a daughter by the name of Elena. Neither, however committed suicide after Sawa's death. Author of a number of Zolaesque naturalistic novels and a known contributor to newspapers of the time, he found it increasingly difficult to earn a living from his writing and died in abject poverty. Like Max he suffered at the hands of an establishment unwilling to appreciate his talent.

In *Bohemian Lights* there is a close identification between Valle-Inclán and his protagonist which is not the case in the later *esperpentos*. The fate of Spain, of peripheral concern to Valle in his *modernista* period, is here of prime importance. The country's mediocrity is evident not only in what we see and how the characters comment on it but also in the sly, self-satisfied figure of Don Latino of Hispalis. Like Don Latino, the pretentious, pompous *modernistas* who so irritate and annoy Max remain unmoved by the social unrest around them. Max, however, as witness to the turmoil around him, recognizes the responsibility of the artist in the face of a chaotic society. He differs from those around him – a point noted by the prisoner when he talks of Max speaking as if he were from another era – evoking the blind poet/seer of classical mythology – there are echoes of both Homer and Oedipus in the vivid descriptions of him provided by Valle-Inclán. In such a contemptible, uncaring society, however, Max cannot assume the tragic role which would have been his in a previous era. Although presented to us as a classical hero in the opening scene, he is made progressively aware of his own insignificance as the play progresses, forced to act out the role of a starving Bohemian, only really recognized by a prostitute and, even then, not as a poet of repute but as a compiler of cheap verses. His death is as irrelevant as his life to a society that has failed to value him. It comes, ironically, as dawn approaches, but is not the climax of the play, as would be expected in a tragedy. His neighbours are more preoccupied with their daily chores than with mourning his death. In such conditions there is an incongruity in the tragic role that Max has been allocated. Heroic values cannot exist independently of the social and cultural context which endorses them. Like a puppet, Max acts out a tragic role created by others which has no place in such a dehumanized society. The tragic means of discourse is incompatible with the social context in which Valle-Inclán attempts to use it. The true image of Spanish reality can only be captured in a grotesque literary form. Existing literary forms, as Valle-Inclán's recourse to tragedy reveals, do not suffice.

The theory of the *esperpento* (meaning 'scarecrow') is expounded by Valle-Inclán in Scene Twelve through the dying Max Estrella and is part of a tradition of deformation evident previously in the paintings of Velázquez and Goya which perturbs and disturbs the reader/spectator but is at the same time beautiful in the mathematical precision of its distortion. For Valle-Inclán, the tragic sense of Spanish life could only be rendered through an aesthetic that was systematically deformed. Distortion through a convex or concave mirror distances the viewer from the subject, highlighting the unnaturalness of events or figures otherwise taken for granted. By shattering the world as we recognize it, the *esperpento* reorientates the reader/spectator, calling into question the possibility of a clear distinction between the tragic and the comic, the bizarre and the conventional, the real and the unreal, fiction and history. Thus we laugh at what, in different circumstances, would produce awe and pain. Max's funeral-wake is therefore not the solemn occasion one would expect but a catalogue of chaotic misunderstandings which proves both embarrassing and ridiculous and an unnecessary prolonging of the suffering of his widow and daughter. The play is full of such incongruous situations – the tragic and the comic existing uncomfortably side by side in a world where characters do not behave in the manner expected of them. If, as Ionesco claims, the absurd is that devoid of purpose, then Max's life is absurd. Like a frustrated puppet he plays the part of the blind poet before an insensitive, uncaring audience – a companion who steals mercilessly from him, a prostitute who refuses his tenderness, a corrupt Home Secretary who ignores his pleas for justice and buys his compliance and a gnarled bookseller who cheats him of a few much needed pesetas. By the time of his death, Max can view his surroundings from a different perspective. He thus responds with sarcasm to Don Latino's heartless comments, laughing and joking in the midst of his own tragedy. The catharsis to be found in tragedy is here denied to us. Valle-Inclán himself described the *esperpento* as a means of recontextualizing the world. He believed there were three primary modes of viewing the world: from one's knees where the characters appear superior to their creator, heroic or godlike as in Homer: face to face as if they are our equals sharing our strengths and our weaknesses, as in Shakespeare: and from above, which allows the writer to see his characters from a superior plane, to look down on them with a sense of distance as inferior beings, as Goya and Quevedo had done. From this perspective the characters' gestures appear alien and unfamiliar. For this reason Valle-Inclán's characters often appear distinctly unhuman, as if they were puppets – stunted, awkward, mechanized figures with distinctive traits singled out for the reader's attention. Thus Zarathustra – a reference to Nietzsche's hero, emulating his namesake in his ability to cheat the weak – is described as 'a hunched figure with a face reminiscent of rancid bacon and with a green, serpent-like scarf wrapped around his neck . . . at once sharply distant and painfully immediate'. The animal dehumanization is taken further in the later *esperpentos* such as *The Horns of Don Friolera* where the marionette show is seen to be a more perceptive means than tragedy of dramatizing the meaninglessness and banality of human existence.

In the idea of the reader as mathematician/scientist, Valle-Inclán preempts the philosophies of Roland Barthes. The fact that the *esperpento* was not promoted in Spain when first published in its complete form may, in part, be responsible for the fact that Valle-Inclán failed to generate interest abroad in the 1920s. Had his *esperpentos* been staged in Spain at the time they were written, it is distinctly possible that Valle-Inclán may have been perceived today as one of the foremost innovators of theatrical language this century. But his plays were staged too late – post-Brecht, Beckett, Ionesco and Genet – to be perceived as pioneering.

VI

Although Valle-Inclán did not call it an *esperpento*, *Silver Face* is characterized by the same deflating techniques and systematic distortion as are evident in *Bohemian Lights*. The first play in the trilogy, *The Savage Plays*, displays none of the nostalgia for the feudal system so pivotal to the earlier *Eagle of Honour* and *Ballad of Wolves*. Certainly there remains the same fascination with Galicia's history, landscape, myths and traditions, but the treatment is far more detached and distanced.

The character of Montenegro, an uncle of the fictitious Marquis of Bradomín, first appeared in print in 1902 in *Autumn Sonata*. Although Montenegro was one of Valle's mother's surnames the character itself was supposedly based on Don Juan Manuel Pereira, a family friend who had died in 1902 and whom Valle-Inclán had referred to as 'my uncle' in a lecture at the Ateneo where he had set out to describe the way of life of a certain aristocratic class near extinction, a feudal ascendancy replaced by an emergent middle class represented in the text by the herdsmen and tenant farmers who challenge

Montenegro's right over access to the bridge. This nostalgia for the disappearing order, lamented by Montenegro in *Eagle of Honour* when he deplores the fact that there are no longer men prepared to die for an idea, is not as clear in *Silver Face*. Although the play marks in a sense a return to the heroic subject matter of his pre-*esperpento* works, its treatment is distinctly unromantic. The Carlist issue, so prominent in *Eagle of Honour*, is here conspicuously absent – Silver Face betrays no intention of joining the Carlist cause – and is perhaps an indication of the playwright's disillusionment with Carlism as a solution to Spain's problems. In addition, the timescale of the action, which Valle-Inclán saw as analogous to El Greco's deployment of space, is more reminiscent of that at work in *Bohemian Lights* – there it is dusk to dawn, here an eighteen-hour period from dawn to midnight – than the other two sprawling *Savage Plays*.

The character of Montenegro is, as his name suggests, a Galician Don Juan; a confident, compulsive and energetic womanizer, an autocratic feudal lord first introduced strolling casually through his estate. Although the play takes its title from Montenegro's favourite son's nickname it is the father who is, as in *Eagle of Honour* and *Ballad of Wolves*, the main focus of attention, the central pivot on which the various conflicts hang – father versus son, aristocracy versus clergy, male versus female. The rupture between father and son which takes place in the play's final scene – bringing together the three main characters for the first and only time – destroys any possibility of Silver Face succeeding him as the next lord of the manor. Although Silver Face shares many of his father's qualities and vices, he lacks his decisiveness. His other brothers, all similarly described, seem to have inherited only their father's less redeeming characteristics. Montenegro carries out what Silver Face can only threaten to do, abducting Sabelita and making her his whore. Sabelita is to Montenegro what Pichona is to Silver Face – a sexual object on which to vent anger and frustration. Sabelita is an ambiguous figure, both angel and whore. She appears first in Act One, Scene Two, singing amongst the lemon trees in the early morning light, an endearing angelic figure flirting innocently with Silver Face. As night falls – half-way through the play – she is carried away into the night by the demonic Montenegro.

Nightfall marks the loss of her innocence, a transition marked by the new importance attached to Fuso Negro, a peripheral figure in the action in the daylight scenes. He is in many ways the catalyst for much of the action which occurs in the second half. His assault on Sabelita attracts Montenegro who comes to the latter's defence. His theft of the bag of gold from the pathway where the Abbot has thrown it provides him with the means to solicit sexual favours from Ginera and Pichona, thus placing him in a central position to comment on and bring together the various threads of the action which is occurring around him. He functions as a means of deflating the ridiculous plan devised by the Abbot to avenge himself on Montenegro, appearing at climactic moments as the Abbot is conjuring Satan in Act Two, Scene Two and as Blas is preparing to die in the following scene. He is an altogether more carnal, dangerous and frustrated figure than in *Ballad of Wolves* where he exists primarily as a fool-like foil to Montenegro's raging Lear.

It is in the vain, arrogant Abbot of Lantañon, his avaricious sister and his lascivious sexton, however, that Valle-Inclán provides his most brilliant *esperpento* creations. Each described in terms of a few specific details – as with Zarathustra, the Home Secretary and the *modernistas* in *Bohemian Lights* – they present a damning indictment of a rural clergy and its sponging dependents, more preoccupied with power and material wealth than matters of the spirit. When defied by Silver Face, the Abbot can only respond with violence and aggression. Sacrilege is never really an issue. The Abbot's wrath and indignation spring from the insult he believes he has suffered at the young man's hands. He allows the incident to escalate out of all proportion, refusing to accept Silver Face's offer of peace. Silver Face becomes for him the Devil incarnate, a worthy opponent for the agent of God. This battle between the supposed forces of light and darkness is reflected in the interplay between day and night and light and darkness in the text itself. The early morning light of the first three scenes is darkened only by the Abbot's black figure, which anticipates the menace of the night in terms of the darkness which he casts over the action – the dark doorways of his house, his black cassock an ominous shadow over Silver Face's light colouring and the bright colours of the scenes at the fair. Revenge alone motivates his decision to remove Sabelita from her home, a decision which sets in motion a pattern of escalating violence and terror which ends with the antagonistic final confrontation of the play's three main characters.

The play is distinguished by the same sense of moral grotesqueness which runs through *Divine Words*. The clergy, aristocracy, peasants, herdsmen, peddlers and pilgrims – with the exception of Pichona and Silver Face – are as callous as their counterparts in the earlier rural tragicomedy. Friendship, as indicated in the unholy alliance between the Abbot and the herdsmen, is merely pragmatic. All exploit each other mercilessly: materialism, as the Abbot's avaricious sister and the penitent indicate, is all pervasive. There is a sense of inevitability to the action – the penitent indirectly prophesying what Silver Face is to attempt in the play's final scene: the murder of his father – a pattern of confrontation (sons versus father, tenant versus landlord) repeated both in *Eagle of Honour* and *Ballad of Wolves*, which finally renders the play as much a *Savage Play* as an *esperpento*.

VII

The problems of translating Valle-Inclán's plays are multiple. This is partly because his language defies any simplistic categorization – it does not adhere to any specific set of speech patterns or any tangible idiom. Filled with contemporary references to people and places, and references back to a nation's literature, the effect is rather that of linguistic displacement – nothing proceeds quite as expected, and our expectations as readers and spectators are constantly frustrated. The comic and the erotic are unexpectedly juxtaposed; characters speak 'out of character', in a mode counter to what we expect – prostitutes and low-life figures declaim in elevated Spanish, anyone and everyone quotes from some literary source or other when least expected. Valle-Inclán's language is extraordinarily dense, filled with parodies of Biblical and literary language, neologisms, slang and colloquialisms, and Galician, Portuguese and Latin American expressions. His work is, in effect, a montage of languages which clash and collide

– drawing constant attention to their own artificiality and self-reflexivity. It is part of what critics are fond of referring to as the 'spirit' of Valle-Inclán. How, though, does one remain faithful to the 'spirit' of Valle-Inclán while rendering a text which, while capturing the ambiguities and idiosyncrasies of his writing, does not read awkwardly in translation?

This question has preoccupied translators for many years. Translations like Anthony Zahareas' *Bohemian Lights* (1968) seek to produce a text which is, above all, literal, providing a mass of explanatory footnotes which aim to clarify textual references both to contemporary people and events and to a nation's literary heritage. This is beneficial to the reader who has the opportunity to consult the notes but is quite irrelevant to questions of staging. Translating entails decision-making, prioritizing and interpreting, and for this reason I would refer to my translations of these plays as 'versions'. I have attempted to write, or rather re-write Valle-Inclán; to provide a theatrical text in English which captures the quirkiness and originality of the original without rendering the language unidiomatic. Spanish is an excessively rhetorical language, Valle-Inclán a rhetorical dramatist. A literal translation into English can read awkwardly and appear a mistranslation. When translating *The Savage Plays* into French, Armando Llamas had noted a similar experience and employed a more 'neutral' French in order to retain the elusive 'spirit' of Valle-Inclán's original. Commenting on a Polish translation of *Bohemian Lights*, Urszula Aszyk has spoken of translation as not revolving merely around a comprehensive knowledge of the language one is translating from, providing something that may prove linguistically correct, but rather as the breaking away from an accurate linguistic translation in order to capture the theatrical concepts at the heart of the piece. It is impossible, as the critic Miguel Pérez Ferrero argued on seeing a French translation of *Divine Words* at L'Odéon in 1963, to re-create, the particular characteristics of Valle-Inclán's writing. One can however, attempt a reflection of the original.

As regards my own attempts to achieve some sort of 'reflection' regarding *Divine Words*, *Bohemian Lights* and *Silver Face*, the cast list of either of the three plays appears a sensible place to begin. Valle-Inclán's use of names is especially pertinent as Don Latino indirectly explains in Scene Seven of

Bohemian Lights, when informing the *modernistas* of the history of his own pseudonym, Don Latino of Hispalis:

> I am named Latino after the Baptismal waters of our own beloved Church and for being a pain on the streets of Paris and Hispalis after the Andalusian lands of Spain where I was born. In the language of the occult, Latino becomes transformed into a mysterious magical word, onital.

An attempt to capture a sense of the meaning behind the name, so to speak, has led previous translators to find literal translations for the proper names. The resonances of Max's surname, Estrella, meaning 'star', ironically comment on his own physical blindness as well as being a reference to Calderón's *Life is a Dream*, where a number of the characters have names related in some way to astronomy and the cosmos. If the name is anglicized into Max Star or Stella, it mitigates somewhat the particular cultural context of the piece. In *Silver Face*, Don Miguel's nickname, Cara de Plata (literally Face of Silver), had to be anglicized to obtain the significance and the spirit of the original. With regard to other nicknames, however, I felt I needed to capture more of a sense of the original which a literal translation could not always offer. For example, Enriqueta is known as Marquesa del Tango, literally Marchioness of the Tango, a term in Spanish for a woman of loose or easy virtue, but in English the phrase does not have the same connotations. I felt therefore that modifying the English into Her Ladyship the Tango Tart captured more of the playful spirit of the original. She is also known as Enriqueta la Pisa Bien in Spanish but Enriqueta Tread Well sounds dull and plodding in English, and so I chose to adapt it into the chirpier and more rhythmic Enriqueta the Street Walker. A similar reasoning governed my decision to transfer Serafín el Bonito, literally Serafín the Dandy or Serafín the Pretty into Slick-Back Serafín.

The abundant literary quotations or homages and the allusions to historical and literary figures in *Bohemian Lights* present similar problems. My decision to keep the references to literary and historical figures intact stemmed largely from the realization that since a number of them were second rate figures in their own time, they would mean little even to a native Spanish audience today. Literary figure-spotting is not what the play hinges on. Experiments with finding English alternatives in an early draft were soon dismissed after workshops with actors quick to pick up and comment on literary and cultural discrepancies. What I have come to regard as a workable solution has depended on the context of each reference. Sometimes this has involved a half-way house between a literal translation and an English alternative, as in Scene Seven when Dorio de Gadex ridicules the Prime Minister, García Prieto, by shouting aloud his parliamentary rallying cry, 'Santiago y abre España a la libertad y al progreso', literally, 'St. James and open Spain to liberty and progress'. Playing on the fact, noted by the critic Anthony Zahareas, that this echoes the war cries of medieval Spaniards in battles against the Moors as well as parodying Prieto's own cliché-filled speeches, I used *Henry V*'s Act Three, Scene One rallying cry, 'Cry God for Harry, England and Saint George', to re-frame the phrase, 'Cry God for Freedom, Progress, Spain and Saint James'.

Although I originally attempted something similar for Max's entry to Zarathustra's cave in Scene Two, where he quotes from Rosaura's opening speech in Calderón's *Life is a Dream*, '¡Mal Polonia recibe a un extranjero!' (literally 'Badly does Poland receive a stranger!') the possibility of pillaging a Shakespearean alternative did not capture the irony of the Parrot's 'Long live Spain!', which precedes the quote or the specific reference to what Max believes is a hostile welcome in what should be friendly territory. I therefore kept the original in a fairly literal but literary translation, 'Is this, Poland, the way to greet a stranger?' In the case of Dorio de Gadex's greeting of Max in Scene Four, which is an appropriation of the opening line of Rubén Darío's 'Responso a Verlaine', in order to make the literary reference and Dorio's plagiarism clear, I reframed it within a line spoken by the first witch in *Macbeth*: 'Hail to thee, Thane of Glamis'. It thus becomes 'All hail Maestro, Hail to thee Father and Masterful Magician', which, while pronouncing its self-reflexivity, just as the Spanish does, also retains something of the content of Darío's verse.

Divine Words has similar intertextual resonances – most noticeably in the Calderónian language employed by Marica del Reino in Act Two, Scene Four, when she chastises her brother for failing to discipline his wayward, adulterous wife. There is none of the rustic, plainer dialogue employed by the character elsewhere in the play, but instead a measured attempt through heightened declamation to provide a sharp parody of the rigorous and ultimately destructive concept of honour evident in such plays as Calderón's *The Surgeon of Honour* and *The Painter of his Dishonour*. Such an apparent anachronism in the language may result in an awkward reading in naturalistic terms, but the translator must respect Valle-Inclán's stylistic idiosyncrasies. Here the language seeks to work towards the resonant critique of the inflexible codes of behaviour which govern the characters' conduct. Behaviour perceived as heroic in seventeenth century Spain is here reflected in a concave mirror which distorts and deflects it. Pedro Gailo cannot emulate the principled behaviour of his illustrious fictional predecessors. His grotesque attempts to do so merely lead him further into sin and vice, culminating in a desperate attempt to rape his own daughter.

I do not believe that any of the above examples are necessarily 'right' or 'wrong' ways of reinterpreting Valle-Inclán. All a translator can do is ask him or herself questions about how a text functions in a certain language and how it can be made to function in a different language. Contextually he or she then makes decisions about how to translate or transpose, say neologisms or words with no equivalent in the language one is translating into, in the case of *Bohemian Lights*, for example, *tertulia* and *esperpento* – signifying respectively a literary café gathering and Valle-Inclán's aesthetic of the grotesque. My own collaboration regarding these translations with actors and directors and consultation with writers and translators, makes a slight mockery of the notion of reworking Valle-Inclán into a different language as a pursuit for which I am solely responsible. Translation is the art of the imperfect and of misreadings. All one can ever hope to achieve is a faithful betrayal.

Maria M Delgado, 1992

Divine Words

A Village Tragicomedy

This translation of *Divine Words* received a rehearsed reading at The Soho Poly Theatre, London on 9 January 1990, with the following cast:

MARICA DEL REINO	Kate Binchy
SIMONIÑA	Claire Cathcart
ROSA LA TATULA	Maureen Glackin
BASTIÁN DE CANDÁS	Stephen Hodson
PEDRO GAILO	Patrick Keeley
SÉPTIMO MIAU	John Lynch
MARI-GAILA	Veronica Quilligan
MIGUELÍN EL PADRONÉS	Patrick Toomey

All other parts read by the company.

Directed by   Mark Ravenhill

Characters

LUCERO otherwise known as SÉPTIMO MIAU or
COMRADE MIAU
POCA PENA, his woman
JUANA LA REINA
LAUREANO, her idiot son
PEDRO GAILO, sexton of San Clemente
MARI-GAILA, his wife
SIMONIÑA, their daughter
ROSA LA TATULA, an old beggar woman
MIGUELÍN EL PADRONÉS, a pot mender
A HERDSMAN
PEASANT WOMEN WHO FILL THEIR PITCHERS AT
THE FOUNTAIN
MARICA DEL REINO with OTHER PEASANT
WOMEN
BASTIÁN DE CANDÁS, a local mayor
A GIRL
THE BLIND MAN OF GONDAR
THE LEMONADE SELLER
A PILGRIM
TWO CIVIL GUARDS
A PEASANT COUPLE and THEIR SICK DAUGHTER
AN INNKEEPER
SERENÍN DE BRETAL
AN OLD WOMAN AT A WINDOW
A PREGNANT WOMAN
ANOTHER NEIGHBOUR
A SOLDIER WITH HIS DISCHARGE DOCUMENTS
LUDOVINA, another innkeeper
A CHORUS OF NOISY CHILDREN
PIOUS WOMEN OF ALL AGES
BENITA THE SEAMSTRESS
QUINTÍN PINTADO
MILÓN DE LA ARNOYA
COIMBRA, a wise dog
COLORÍN, a fortune-telling bird
A GOBLIN WHO MANIFESTS HIMSELF IN THE FORM
OF A GOAT

AN ANONYMOUS TOAD WHO SINGS AT NIGHT
A FINAL SCREAMING CHORUS

The translator recommends that the play be performed by
Irish actors.

Act One

Scene One

San Clemente, near Viana del Prior. A village church beside the crossroads; its churchyard filled with tombstones and cypress trees. Under the Romanesque portico PEDRO GAILO, the sexton, is snuffing out the burning candles. He appears a funereal old man, dressed in a cassock and surplice, with a roughly shaven sallow face and yellowing hands. He shakes his fingers, attempting to blow off the gathered soot on his fingertips, and then finally wipes them on the pillars of the portico. His gestures are awkward, his speech is at times incoherent, and he can be frequently seen talking to himself.

PEDRO GAILO. . . . They come and just throw themselves on the road, staring at the altar, wandering from one place to another, lazy blighters! I wouldn't wipe the floor with them! A bunch of good for nothings! Causing havoc wherever they go! Look where they've planted themselves! Scum of the earth! People who don't work and spend their lives on the road! . . .

PEDRO GAILO wipes his forehead and the four remaining hairs on his head stand on end. His squinting eyes look out towards the road where two travellers are resting; a man and a woman with a small child, the fruit of their lust. She is sad and slim, dressed in a short skirt and a blue shawl, her curly hair arranged with combs. The man wears a peaked cap, carries a guitar still in its case and holds Coimbra, the wise dog, by a filthy red lead. They are sitting in a ditch facing the portico of the church. Only the man can be heard; the woman listens, rocking the crying child. The woman is known by different names, depending on where the couple find themselves – Julia, Rosina, Matilde, Pepa la Morena. Although her partner's true identity is another enigma, she calls him LUCERO. In turn, he gives her the name POCA PENA.

LUCERO. As for that brat, we'd be best off dumping him at the next place we kip for the night.

POCA PENA. You're his father for Christ's sake!

LUCERO. What if I'm not?

POCA PENA. Calling yourself a cuckold?

LUCERO. Well then, assuming my responsibilities as the kid's father, I only think it fair to add that I wouldn't really like to see him pick up my filthy habits.

POCA PENA. What's going through that disgusting mind of yours? I'm not asking for anything for myself, I'd just like you to show some paternal instinct every now and then!

LUCERO. That's what I'm doing!

POCA PENA. If my son disappears or dies through any of your doing, I'll stick this knife between your ribs. Don't take my child, Lucero!

LUCERO. We'll have another.

POCA PENA. Show some pity, Lucero!

LUCERO. Drop it!

POCA PENA. Jailbird!

LUCERO *swipes her forcefully across the mouth. Whimpering, she wipes her mouth with a corner of her shawl. Seeing the blood on the garment, she begins to cry. The man coughs contemptuously, rhythmically striking sparks from his tinderbox. PEDRO GAILO, the sexton, standing between the pillars of the portico, raises his arms to heaven.*

PEDRO GAILO. Go on, off with you! Have you no shame displaying such disgusting behaviour outside the Lord's house.

LUCERO. God's not watching us. He's turning a blind eye!

PEDRO GAILO. Heathen!

LUCERO. Too true! It's been twenty years since I last set foot in a church!

PEDRO GAILO. Are you a friend of the Devil?

LUCERO. We're soul mates.

PEDRO GAILO. You may well laugh now but the hour of weeping and gnashing of teeth will soon be upon you.

LUCERO. I've nothing to fear.

POCA PENA. Even the strongest fear the day of reckoning.

PEDRO GAILO. Each will reap what they have sown, thus teaches our Holy Mother Church.

LUCERO. Change the tune, my friend. It's getting a bit repetitive.

PEDRO GAILO. My silence won't hold back the wrath of the Lord.

LUCERO. Good!

An old woman wearing a mantilla of rough brown cloth emerges from the portico, followed by two others, all three walking in single file. In their cupped hands they carry holy water, which they sprinkle on the graves. The last of the three pulls a four-wheeled cart converted into a shoddy makeshift bed. On it lies a sleeping hydrocephalic dwarf. She is JUANA LA REINA, an old dark barefoot shadow-like figure known to beg at fairs and local pilgrimages with her abnormal offspring. She stops to question the sexton, her brother.

JUANA LA REINA. Why didn't you give communion at mass?

PEDRO GAILO. There were no wafers left in the chalice.

JUANA LA REINA. I had hoped to receive the Lord. The earth is calling me.

PEDRO GAILO. You certainly do look pale.

JUANA LA REINA. This mother of a womb's gnawing away at my insides.

PEDRO GAILO. The Earth's your mother! The mother and protector of all sinners! And how is my nephew, sister? Is he not awake yet? It looks to me as if he's showing some signs of improvement.

JUANA LA REINA. Improvement! In this Godforsaken creature! You must be joking!

PEDRO GAILO *squints at the dwarf who shakes his head in a totally uncoordinated manner. His mother shoos away the flies that gather around his dribbling swollen mouth. Dragging the cart along behind her, she then crosses the churchyard and disappears into the roadside shadows. Lucero's dog, sitting up on her hind legs, begins a slow dance of death in front of the dark earthy figure. Slowly the dog doubles up, her tail between her legs, and howls in an unmistakable premonition of death.* LUCERO *then whistles and the dog, back on her hind legs, moves towards her master who laughs and winks mischievously.*

LUCERO. I'm sure this dog has a pact with our mutual friend the Devil.

PEDRO GAILO. Till the day he stumbles on an exorcist and that'll be the end of him.

LUCERO. That'll be the end of us both.

PEDRO GAILO. You shouldn't doubt the word of God.

LUCERO. My weakness.

POCA PENA. It's all a lot of nonsense if you ask me!

LUCERO. Coimbra! Over here! Listen to what I'm going to ask you and then answer carefully. Right paw up for yes, left for no. Use your tail if you're not sure. And no lying. It's about our friend over here, has his wife ever done the dirty on him?

COIMBRA, *still on her hind legs, remains pensive, gently nodding her spotted black and ginger head. Gradually, as the prophetic spirit takes hold of her, she stiffens, staring at her master. Then, after a slight moment of hesitation when only the bells decorating her ears can be heard tinkling, she begins to shake her left paw furiously.*

LUCERO. Well, my friend, Coimbra says no. Now she's going to tell us something else. Coimbra, do you have the prophetic insight to tell us whether our friend here will one day be called to the Guild of Cuckolds? Right paw up for yes, left for no. Use your tail for anything else you may want to tell us.

COIMBRA *wags her tail, barks, and again jumps up onto her hind legs. She begins shaking each paw alternately while staring intently at Lucero. The bells attached to her ears give a gentle but prolonged tinkle.* LUCERO *smiles, winking mischievously. The dog then suddenly raises her right paw.*

LUCERO. Are you sure Coimbra? Well then, give a bow and apologize to the gentleman for slandering his good name.

PEDRO GAILO. Hypocrites! Your insults can't touch me!

LUCERO. My friend, one has to take these things with a pinch of salt. Let's go, Poca Pena!

PEDRO GAILO. I'd like to see how loud you'll be laughing in Hell!

POCA PENA *adjusts her shawl, slipping the child between its folds, while* LUCERO *lifts the cage of the wise bird onto his back. They begin to walk away.*

POCA PENA. Please Lucero, an occasional display of paternal feelings wouldn't come amiss!

LUCERO. Shut up!

POCA PENA. I'm getting out of this slave-like existence. I'll break free, you'll see.

LUCERO. If you think I'm going to go running after you, think again.

POCA PENA. You've run before, run and killed for me.

LUCERO. Pure fluke!

POCA PENA. Well if you aimed at me, how did you miss?

LUCERO. Drop the subject! Has the bird got any seed?

POCA PENA. It's not eating.

LUCERO. Coimbra, where will we find another bird like him? Do you think we should ask our friend Satan?

POCA PENA. You talk such shit.

*The restless child tosses and turns in its mother's arms. The bird's
cage sways gently across LUCERO's back, catching the sun's rays.
It is an image of the most pure illusory hope.*

Scene Two

*A clump of trees at the side of the road. There, half-hidden
amongst the shadows, with her flowered hankerchief open, JUANA
LA REINA can be seen begging. Her idiot son LAUREANO,
smothered in the cart's straw mattress and patched blankets, groans
and grimaces in his accustomed manner.*

JUANA LA REINA. Show a little charity for this wretched
creature bereft of the light of reason! Find pity in your hearts
for him, exposed to all evils!

*Throughout this speech JUANA LA REINA groans, clutching
her side. ROSA LA TATULA, also known for begging at
harvest fairs and pilgrimages, stops to give JUANA LA REINA
some sound advice.*

ROSA LA TATULA. You should be in the hospital at
Santiago. It's a wicked pain you're in!

JUANA LA REINA. I've been like this for years!

ROSA LA TATULA. You're lucky that son of yours keeps the
cash rolling in!

JUANA LA REINA. I'd allow him to attack me with a dagger
just to see him rise up from that cart!

ROSA LA TATULA. The Lord our God gave you this cross to
bear. Bearing it graciously you fulfil his will on earth.

JUANA LA REINA. Have you ever known me question it?

*Sighing and limping with pain, a pewter dish in her hands,
JUANA LA REINA goes off in search of rich fairgoers. A
HERDSMAN driving young bulls down from the mountains rises
up in his stirrups, beckoning all those around to clear the way.*

A HERDSMAN. Go on! . . . Off with you! Keep away from
the cattle!

JUANA LA REINA, *clutching her side, returns to the shade
of the oak trees. She has a glazed look about her and her mouth
appears the colour of earth. The herd of bulls rushes past in a
cloud of dust.* THE HERDSMAN, *ruddy-faced and well-built,
trots along behind. He possesses a striking Roman profile.*

JUANA LA REINA. I'm dying! I'm dying!

ROSA LA TATULA. Is the pain that bad?

JUANA LA REINA. A viper's eating away at my very soul!

ROSA LA TATULA. A bad case of cramp if you ask me!

JUANA LA REINA. A drop of anis wouldn't come amiss!

ROSA LA TATULA. Someone's bound to come by with
a bottle.

JUANA LA REINA. May the Lord open the gates of Heaven to
receive me!

ROSA LA TATULA. Blessed be those who struggle here on
earth for theirs is the kingdom of God.

JUANA LA REINA. This day will see the end of me!

JUANA LA REINA *doubles up in pain and then falls face
down, her hair hanging over her face and her hands clutching
the grass. Her bare waxen legs and feet protrude from beneath a
frayed underskirt.* ROSA LA TATULA *looks visibly shocked.*

ROSA LA TATULA. Juana, try getting up. Don't relinquish
your soul in this Godforsaken place! You have to confess and
make your peace with God!

JUANA LA REINA. What a feast! There's no fasting
around here!

ROSA LA TATULA. You're losing grip of yourself.

JUANA LA REINA. I can't fit any more coins on that
handkerchief, pick it up! . . . Ssh Laureano! . . . That's
better! . . .

ROSA LA TATULA. Jesus Christ! Has she lost her marbles?

JUANA LA REINA. Marelo, give me a glass of lemonade! Yes

Marelo, I've got enough money to pay for it! . . . I've got enough!

ROSA LA TATULA. Juana Reina, don't end your days here, people will talk! Try to hold on until we get to the village!

JUANA LA REINA. Look at that star in the sky!

ROSA LA TATULA *tries to lift up the decaying woman, but the limp and shrivelling carcass simply slips down, its arms spread out like sails.*

ROSA LA TATULA. What a way to go!

In the distance, beneath some low-lying vines supported on stone pillars, a young man can be seen. Behind him, the profile of another shadowy figure can just be made out. Picking up his stick, the young man throws his tool bag onto his back. He is MIGUELÍN EL PADRONÉS, *another wandering traveller, often teased and hounded at fairs and pilgrimages for his effeminate nature. He wears an earring in one ear.*

ROSA LA TATULA. Over here Christian soul!

MIGUELÍN. If it's help you want I'm near enough already.

ROSA LA TATULA. Come quickly for the love of God!

MIGUELÍN. Which god are you referring to?

ROSA LA TATULA. I've no time for silly stories now. Juana la Reina's just had an epileptic fit!

MIGUELÍN. Give her the once over with a pile of nettles.

ROSA LA TATULA. Get over here, you disrespectful heathen!

MIGUELÍN. Here comes Comrade Miau!

COMRADE MIAU, *who was lying in the shade of the grapevines, is now on his feet and moving into the sunlight. It is the same traveller seen earlier with the long suffering woman who called him* LUCERO.

MIGUELÍN. Should we go over Comrade Miau?

COMRADE MIAU. There's nothing to see but the face of death.

MIGUELÍN. How the devil did you know that?

COMRADE MIAU. Coimbra got the message some time ago.

ROSA LA TATULA. What are you two afraid of?

COMRADE MIAU. We might as well head over.

The two friends walk down towards the road. MIGUELÍN uses his tongue to moisten a curly hair growing from a mole at the corner of his mouth. MIAU strikes a match from his tinderbox. In the shade of the oak trees JUANA LA REINA lies silent and still. Her bare legs still protrude from the flannel underskirts like a pair of wax candles.

ROSA LA TATULA. Juana Reina! Juana Reina!

COMRADE MIAU. Don't expect a reply. The best thing you can do is notify the family. But don't tell them the whole truth, just tell them that she's having a fit. This woman's dead and gone.

ROSA LA TATULA. Jesus Christ! That'll mean the police! Well, that's the price I have to pay for having a heart of gold.

COMRADE MIAU. Let's take it for granted that you don't mention my name in connection with all of this . . .

ROSA LA TATULA. But who noticed she was dead?

COMRADE MIAU. Don't mention me.

ROSA LA TATULA. And if I'm made to swear on oath?

COMRADE MIAU. Don't mention me.

ROSA LA TATULA. What are you afraid of?

COMRADE MIAU. Your safety.

COMRADE MIAU sits down in the shade of the trees and uses his jackknife to spear two cigar butts together. ROSA LA TATULA, worried but wise enough to judge the situation, puts on her clogs at the side of the road. She then picks up her bag of grain and, leaning on her staff, marches off to deliver the bad news. THE IDIOT can be seen amongst the leaves of the oak-tree. He is covered in flies and making his usual faces. MIGUELÍN EL PADRONÉS, *the tip of his tongue resting on his mole, crawls across to him and slips his hands under the mattress. He brings out a patched handbag filled with heavy coins.*

COMRADE MIAU. It sounds like silver!

MIGUELÍN. So do a lot of things.

COMRADE MIAU. Well let's see for ourselves.

MIGUELÍN. This is my business.

COMRADE MIAU. My! My! I never thought you so greedy! If you don't want this business shared we'll have to seek independent arbitration.

MIGUELÍN. In which court?

COMRADE MIAU. My friend, shall I ask Coimbra to judge the case?

MIGUELÍN. I don't want my case resting on the Devil's whims.

COMRADE MIAU *gets up and rolls a cigar, using his jacknife. He takes a few steps and sits down on* MIGUELÍN's *tool bag.* MIGUELÍN *tries hard to smile but looks unmistakably worried as he tucks the handbag into his belt. He squints in order to catch a lone curl which has fallen over his forehead and then sticks out his tongue in his customary manner.*

COMRADE MIAU. Poofter, if the bag doesn't get handed over pretty quick you're going to find this knife lodged between your ribs!

MIGUELÍN. I was wondering – what happened to that woman you used to hang around with?

COMRADE MIAU. She's on her way home.

MIGUELÍN. Is she going far?

COMRADE MIAU. Very far!

MIGUELÍN. It wouldn't be to the ends of the earth, would it?

COMRADE MIAU. Just Ceuta.

MIGUELÍN. To the prison there?

COMRADE MIAU. To Ceuta, pride and joy of Spanish cities.

MIGUELÍN. You know it well?

COMRADE MIAU. Listen poofter, that's where I've just come from. What of it?

MIGUELÍN. You wouldn't want the bother of this cash if you were on the run!

COMRADE MIAU. Drop the subject! Or would you rather I drew your attention to a recent hit and run job on the church in Viana.

MIGUELÍN. I was held overnight on suspicion, then released the next morning for lack of evidence.

COMRADE MIAU. Do you remember just after that when we were having a few drinks at the bar in Camino Nuevo?

MIGUELÍN. Well?

COMRADE MIAU. Well, Coimbra implied that you'd done the job.

MIGUELÍN. Rumours!

COMRADE MIAU. They may be rumours but while Coimbra was sniffing around the window from where the thieves made their getaway she just happened to stumble across this earring. You might as well take it since it matches the one you're wearing. And while I'm here we'll divide the cash. Of course, if you don't want it back I'd be only too pleased to hand the earring over to the Civil Guard.

MIGUELÍN. Money! Who needs it! I can't believe we nearly argued over it. A lover's tiff!

Scene Three
A path winding through a village. Around the edges of the rooftops pumpkins are ripening. On the ground dogs' chains rattle. The

*path leads to a fountain enclosed in the cool shade of poplar trees.
Blackbirds sing while the village women, eagerly exchanging gossip,
allow their buckets to overflow.* ROSA LA TATULA *arrives
breathless, the bearer of bad news.*

ROSA LA TATULA. Blessed be God who works in mysterious
  ways! Juana la Reina's back there unconscious. I tried talking
  to her but she didn't reply. She looks like death itself. I
  was in such a rush to get here that I didn't bother calling
  into her sister's house at Cruz de Leson. Do any of you live
  around there?

FIRST PEASANT WOMAN. I live next door.

ROSA LA TATULA. Could you give her the bad news?

FIRST PEASANT WOMAN. Are you sure she's dead?

ROSA LA TATULA. All I said is she looks like death itself.

A SECOND PEASANT WOMAN. She'd been in pain for
  ages. And the cross she had to bear! Day after day, come rain
  or shine, dragging that cart from village to village. What'll
  happen to the little runt now? Where will he end up?

ROSA LA TATULA. That child's more of a blessing than a
  hindrance, it all depends on which way you look at it. Juana
  la Reina guzzled more alcohol in one night than most of us
  manage in a year. Now we all know brandy doesn't grow on
  trees, so she must've got the money from somewhere. I tell
  you that halfwit kept her in drink. You can't imagine what a
  cart like that brings in! There's nothing like it for pulling the
  heart strings. Juana la Reina made at least seven reales a day.
  I don't even make half that!

*Two women, a mother and daughter with empty pitchers on
their heads, come down along the path leading to the fountain.
The mother is fair-skinned and blonde with smiling eyes and
an exquisite body. Her voice is melodious and engaging. The
daughter on the other hand is large and stupid with a round
moon-like face and clumsy gestures.*

FIRST PEASANT WOMAN. There's the Gailas. They're
  Juana la Reina's family.

ROSA LA TATULA. Mari-Gaila's the wife of the deceased's brother, Pedro Gailo, the sexton.

A SECOND PEASANT WOMAN. They don't look as if they've heard the news.

ROSA LA TATULA. Mari-Gaila, hurry. Your sister-in-law's had an epileptic fit, she's lying unconscious at the side of the road.

MARI-GAILA. Which of the two?

ROSA LA TATULA. Juana la Reina.

MARI-GAILA. Tatula, don't be afraid to tell me the worst, I can bear it!

THE GROUP OF WOMEN. We know no more than you do.

MARI-GAILA *lets her pitcher fall and unties the scarf around her head. She then turns to face her daughter, raising her arms in a tragic, over-emphatic manner. Her daughter merely sighs subserviently. Murmuring softly, almost religiously, the row of women turn to the mourning woman who radiates a classical, histrionic beauty beneath the shadows of the fountain at the top of the path. She begins an almost classical mourning elegy, her sensuous voice exquisitely complementing the graceful movements of her arms.*

MARI-GAILA. Cast down your pitcher, Simoniña! Cast it down and mourn, mourn the cruelty of fate! Juana la Reina suffered the fate of a despot's daughter! Snatched by the earth, the downtrodden earth of the roadside, far from the bosom of the family she rejected! Cast down your pitcher, Simoniña!

FIRST PEASANT WOMAN. You've got to hand it to her! No one can match her when it comes to mourning!

A SECOND PEASANT WOMAN. It's a talent you're born with.

A THIRD PEASANT WOMAN. She handles language like a professional.

MARI-GAILA. Beloved sister-in-law, condemned in this world

to roaming the streets, day after day, come rain or shine! Sister-in-law, you were driven from your family by malicious gossip! You had it in for me sister-in-law! Poisoned against your own by vicious tongues!

ROSA LA TATULA. You can hardly call it a family when they barely speak to one another.

FIRST PEASANT WOMAN. Blood's thicker than water.

ROSA LA TATULA. Not always.

MARI-GAILA. It is for me, Tatula!

ROSA LA TATULA. So it seems.

MARI-GAILA. And even if I have to starve myself, I'll make sure the idiot doesn't go without.

ROSA LA TATULA. Keep the cart on the road and you'll be rolling in it.

MARI-GAILA. It hardly makes up for the suffering involved in abandoning my house and home.

ROSA LA TATULA. You could always hire him out. Give it some thought and then get back to me.

MARI-GAILA. I'll do that. I do think that it's best that the cart comes to me. The deceased was my husband's sister. She had no closer family than us.

ROSA LA TATULA. The case will be between yourselves and your sister-in-law Marica del Reino.

MARI-GAILA. Case? What case? I'm doing this out of charity, it's an act of kindness. Who is going to contest the fact that the cart should go to the man in the family? If the case goes to court, they'll decide in favour of the male or there's no justice in the world!

ROSA LA TATULA. Well if you're given the cart, remember what we agreed.

MARI-GAILA. Hold on, I've not agreed to anything.

ROSA LA TATULA. Not technically, but when you think about it . . .

MARI-GAILA. I'll think about it.

ROSA LA TATULA. I'll drop by sometime.

MARI-GAILA. Whenever you want.

FIRST PEASANT WOMAN. That idiot's worth a small fortune.

A SECOND PEASANT WOMAN. At least!

MARI-GAILA. Yours was a tragic fate, sister-in-law! An example to fallen women everywhere! What it is to die alone, without confession, at the side of the road!

Pale, stupid, plump-faced SIMOÑINA closes her eyes and imitates her mother's mourning, stretching her arms out towards the broken pitcher.

Scene Four
A group of oak trees by the side of the high road: JUANA LA REINA is lying on her back. A cross of green branches has been placed on her breast. Her bare waxen legs still protrude from beneath her skirt like candles. BASTIÁN DE CANDÁS, the local mayor, is guarding the corpse. He issues orders with one arm raised, as if in benediction.

BASTIÁN DE CANDÁS. You men keep watch over here, don't lose sight of the body. And whatever happens, don't allow it to be moved until the authorities arrive to inspect it.

Peasant women can be seen drawing near, their lanterns burning brightly amidst the black shawls. Amongst them is a stooping woman, groaning with her head in her hands. Every so often she allows herself to fall to the ground and begins to recite ritual mourning prayers. This woman praying with outstretched arms is MARICA DEL REINO, the sister of the deceased.

MARICA DEL REINO. Juana! Where are you? Condemned to eternal silence! Our heavenly Father has called you into his kingdom, forgetting those of us who remain here on earth! Where are you, Juana? Where is it you lie, beloved sister?

A GIRL. Be brave, Marica!

MARICA, *supported by the women and covered in a blanket continues her slow stooping march. When she reaches the corpse, she falls to embrace it.*

MARICA DEL REINO. Oh Juana, beloved sister, now pale and cold! Your eyes no longer see me! Your mouth no longer greets me! Never again will you knock at my door for a bowl of bread and stew! How you'd lick your lips at the thought of it! Remember all those afternoons at fairgrounds when we'd both sit and share a bowl! You'd have killed for that special fried bread and stew!

Having finished this lament, she remains on her knees, moaning continually. The women sit around her, gossiping about road accidents, sudden deaths, and souls in distress. Whenever the noise drops MARICA DEL REINO renews her emphatic wailing. The GAILOS are seen approaching through the oak trees. MARI-GAILA has a shawl draped over her shoulders. Her husband wears a long cloak and carries an ornate walking stick with a gold-plated handle. As MARICA DEL REINO watches them approach, she gets up and raises both arms dramatically.

MARICA DEL REINO. Have you only just heard the news? I've been here most of the day, frozen with cold.

PEDRO GAILO. Marica, a working man can't just drop everything at the slightest occurrence. Now tell me, how did this unfortunate incident occur?

MARICA DEL REINO. Brother, it was the will of God!

PEDRO GAILO. That goes without saying! But what actually happened?

MARICA DEL REINO. How should I know? You'd better ask the deceased, she's the only one who'll have an answer!

PEDRO GAILO. Beloved sister, now deceased, a lifetime spent on the roads and on those roads you met your death!

MARICA DEL REINO. My very thoughts! May God protect us from such a fate!

THE SEXTON *wipes his eyes. His squint now appears more pronounced. He approaches* THE IDIOT's *cart.*

PEDRO GAILO. You're an orphan now Laureano and you can't understand it! Your mother, my sister, is no more and you can't quite believe it! I will adopt you as my own!

MARICA DEL REINO. I'll take it upon myself to care for this innocent creature.

MARI-GAILA. We couldn't possibly relinquish responsibility, sister-in-law.

MARI-GAILA *looks relaxed but confident. Her dazzling eyes shine provocatively.* MARICA DEL REINO *tosses her head indifferently.*

MARICA DEL REINO. I was talking to my brother!

MARI-GAILA. Yes, but I replied!

BASTIÁN DE CANDÁS. That's enough.

PEDRO GAILO. What are we waiting for, Bastián?

BASTIÁN DE CANDÁS. The arrival of the authorities.

PEDRO GAILO. I can't see what they'll have to say about it. As far as I can tell, the deceased drank from some contaminated stream and it proved fatal. It's well known that sulphate from the vines can poison water. Drink that, and you've had it.

BASTIÁN DE CANDÁS. Do you remember that spotted cow I had?

MARI-GAILA. A beautiful cow if I recall!

BASTIÁN DE CANDÁS. Well, she was at death's door, you know. I saved her with one of those herbal potions which cost an arm and a leg at the chemist's.

AN OLD WOMAN. Water can be deadly.

PEDRO GAILO. No doubt about it. And if you're already ill, well, you don't stand a chance. It rots your insides.

MARI-GAILA. The well-to-do should talk less about the evils of brandy and more about the dangers of water.

BASTIÁN DE CANDÁS. They wouldn't be so quick to talk about the evils of drink if that was the only pleasure they could afford.

MARI-GAILA. An iced anis on the rocks!

A JUDGE *can be seen approaching along the high road, mounted on a grey horse with tassled blinkers and striped saddlebags. A* CLERK *strides along beside him like a groom.* THE PEASANT WOMEN *rise, blow their hands, and turn up the flames of their lanterns. A solemn prayer begins.*

MARICA DEL REINO. Juana, beloved sister, if you should come across my dead husband in the kingdom of Heaven, tell him that I was always true to his memory! Tell him that I never considered marrying again, despite many good offers! Now I'm old and past my prime, but he left me when I was still young and attractive. Tell him that a tall, wealthy, virile Cuban was after me, but I didn't even look at him!

MARI-GAILA. Sister-in-law, rose of the roads! You are now at the side of the Lord our Father! Blessed were you who suffered, for now you are rewarded, forever at God's table, beside the angels, with food in abundance! If only I too could be there with you, listening to the tales of Saint Peter!

Scene Five
San Clemente. The portico with the church in the background. The moon shines through the branches of the trees. A number of lanterns placed on the ground project rays of light around the body of the deceased, which lies outlined beneath a white sheet. Masked in cloaks and mantillas, the villagers drink brandy while keeping vigil in the shelter of the church. The murmuring voices, the endless pacing, and the long shadows all combine to create an intense, almost unreal effect.

PEDRO GAILO. I've sworn all along that she met her end through drinking at some poisoned fountain. There's been some strange things happening to humans and animals recently.

MARI-GAILA. The idiot must have had a sip or two of that

same water. I'm not sure if I should mention it, but you should have seen the filthy state his straw was in! He had to be washed like a baby. And to look at him down there, you'd never believe he was a dwarf!

MARICA DEL REINO. Enough of such talk, sister-in-law! Don't worry, you won't need to do many more of such chores when I take over the care of the cart.

MARI-GAILA. Your brother is over here! Sort it out with him, Marica.

MARICA DEL REINO. Well brother, what have you got to say about this?

PEDRO GAILO. A man's arms are better equipped to carry such a heavy burden.

MARICA DEL REINO. It was my dead sister's last wish that I take care of the cart. She told me herself!

MARI-GAILA. Can you produce any witnesses?

MARICA DEL REINO. I was talking to my brother.

MARI-GAILA. I couldn't help overhearing.

MARICA DEL REINO. If only the deceased could declare her wishes!

PEDRO GAILO. Speak, deceased sister! Was it your intention to defy the laws of the family?

ROSA LA TATULA. I wouldn't expect an answer if I were you! Death doesn't usually say much.

BASTIÁN DE CANDÁS. No words without breath, no flame without air.

PEDRO GAILO. Miracles do happen.

BASTIÁN DE CANDÁS. Not any more they don't. I've never seen anyone cheat death.

MARICA DEL REINO. All this bickering over who should support our own flesh and blood!

MARI-GAILA. There'd be no bickering if you'd respect the rights of the male.

MARICA DEL REINO. We'll consult a lawyer.

BASTIÁN DE CANDÁS. There'll be even more bickering if you bring a lawyer into it! You've enough wise men in the village, there's no need to go looking for a lawyer.

PEDRO GAILO. What's your opinion, Bastián de Candás?

BASTIÁN DE CANDÁS. If it were up to me, neither of you would receive it. The law favours neither party!

MARI-GAILA. What about the rights of the male?

BASTIÁN DE CANDÁS. One cannot simplify the intricacies of the law. The law works in mysterious ways!

MARI-GAILA. But here we have a Latin scholar who could clarify all this!

BASTIÁN DE CANDÁS. Clerical Latin is not quite the same as legal Latin.

PEDRO GAILO. Bastián de Candás, what's your honest opinion?

BASTIÁN DE CANDÁS. Why ask, if you have no intention of following it?

MARICA DEL REINO. If we require your advice, you should give it willingly.

BASTIÁN DE CANDÁS. Had the deceased left two cows, instead of the idiot, you would have each had one apiece. That much I know. And had she left two carts again there would have been one each.

ROSA LA TATULA. And there'd be no problems.

BASTIÁN DE CANDÁS. Well, as she left only one, you should apply the same principle and share the responsibility.

ROSA LA TATULA. I think you mean profit, not responsibility.

BASTIÁN DE CANDÁS. In legal terms it is referred to as an undivided inheritance.

MARI-GAILA. It's all very well for you to suggest that we share the cart, Bastián, but how do you propose to arrange it? I'd like to see you try to fit two feet in one shoe!

BASTIÁN DE CANDÁS. In my time I've seen a good many mills grind for different masters.

A GIRL. My father grinds twelve hours a week at András's mill.

MARICA DEL REINO. In other words, you're suggesting that we share the cart between us, and work out who has it which days.

BASTIÁN DE CANDÁS. Let's suppose for a moment that you both own a mill. One of you takes charge from Monday to Wednesday and the other from Thursday to Saturday. On Sunday you alternate.

ROSA LA TATULA. That would put an end to the problem.

MARICA DEL REINO. Well brother, what do you think?

PEDRO GAILO. Our honourable neighbour has given us some worthy advice. The decision rests with us whether to take it or leave it. I've made my opinion clear, it's now up to you.

MARICA DEL REINO. I'll go along with your decision, brother.

MARI-GAILA. A crafty response if ever I heard one.

MARICA DEL REINO. I don't see anything crafty about it.

BASTIÁN DE CANDÁS. I'm not sure if I catch your drift, Marica del Reino. Are you saying that you'll go along with whatever your brother decides?

MARICA DEL REINO. Yes!

BASTIÁN DE CANDÁS. What do you say, Pedro?

MARI-GAILA. He'll agree to anything!

BASTIÁN DE CANDÁS. Well then, we'll leave it at that.

MARICA DEL REINO. So for three days then I'll take care of the cart, the next three days it goes to my sister-in-law.

BASTIÁN DE CANDÁS. Sundays will remain undivided.

ROSA LA TATULA. All arranged without legal hassles.

MARI-GAILA. This calls for a celebration drink. Husband, go and find the brandy.

PEDRO GAILO. There's a bottle right there, beside the deceased.

MARI-GAILA. And we mustn't forget to give a sip to our crippled friend.

BASTIÁN DE CANDÁS. I wonder if he's tasted it before?

MARI-GAILA. Tasted it! He can't get enough. It's in his blood.

ROSA LA TATULA. All that trekking, day after day, in all weathers . . . He would have died without it.

MARI-GAILA. Do you want a swig, Laureano?

ROSA LA TATULA. Just show him the bottle, he'll soon understand what you mean.

MARI-GAILA, *captivating and elegant, glides over to the deceased. She fills a glass to the brim and relishes the aroma of the brandy.*

MARI-GAILA. Bastián, you take the first swig. After all, you settled the problem.

BASTIÁN DE CANDÁS. Well, cheers everyone.

MARI-GAILA. And after you comes the idiot. Come on, take a sip, Laureano.

ROSA LA TATULA. Don't give it to him until he lets out one of his thunderclaps. He can do it really well if he tries!

MARI-GAILA. Quickly, over here! Just look at the way he's poking his tongue out!

THE IDIOT. Ugh! Ugh! Here, give, here.

MARI-GAILA. Who's giving what?

THE IDIOT. Na! Na! Na!

MARI-GAILA. What is it, Laureano?

THE IDIOT. Here! Here!

MARI-GAILA. Now, what do you say?

THE IDIOT. Shit! Here! Here!

MARICA DEL REINO. Just give him a drink and stop all this disgusting business.

MARI-GAILA. No fart, no drink!

THE IDIOT. Miau! Fu! Miau!

MARI-GAILA. No stupid, that's a cat!

ROSA LA TATULA. Laureano, give us one of your very own rocket blasts and we'll give you a drink!

MARICA DEL REINO. How can you encourage him like that?

THE IDIOT *farts*.

BASTIÁN DE CANDÁS. He's earned his swig!

MARI-GAILA. We'll not be short of laughs with him around!

PEDRO GAILO. It's disgusting!

MARICA DEL REINO. Our deceased sister certainly had him well trained! Sister or not, she was one hell of a businesswoman! Oh Juana, what a way to meet your end!

MARI-GAILA. Sister-in-law, you've plenty of days of mourning ahead. I'm tired of holding out the bottle, so for now just drink up!

MARICA DEL REINO *sighs, wiping her lips with the corner of her mantilla before drinking the brandy. She takes a sip and her face contorts, as if unaccustomed to the alcohol. She then drains the glass in one swig. MARI-GAILA drinks the remainder of the bottle and then joins the others sitting in a circle. An OLD*

WOMAN *begins a story and* THE IDIOT, *his enormous head lying on the straw pillow, screams in the damp cemetery.*

THE IDIOT. Here! Here!

A TOAD. Croak! Croak!

End of Act One

Act Two

Scene One

*Lugar de Condes, an old village with canopies of grapevines
enclosing the doorways. Garden plots, granaries and balconies. From
over the walls, the sound of barking dogs. The day is dawning,
the stars are disappearing, and the voices of those rising with the
new day can be heard. Cows and calves are mooing. Indiscernable
shadow-like figures, carrying lanterns and bundles of grass, come
and go from the dark stables. The smell of baking bread and
wild flowers pervades the atmosphere. MARICA DEL REINO,
crouched in the doorway of her house, is indulging in a breakfast of
boiled cabbage.*

A NEIGHBOUR. Are you waiting for the cart, Marica?

MARICA DEL REINO. I've been waiting since yesterday.

A NEIGHBOUR. Your sister-in-law's taking her time.

MARICA DEL REINO. Sister-in-law! It makes me sick to hear
   her mentioned! Out on the roads after dark like nobody's
   business, wandering recklessly from inn to inn, throwing her
   reputation out of the window.

A NEIGHBOUR. She can be hilarious when she's had a drink
   or two. Holy Jesus! We had such a laugh not so long ago at
   Ludovina's inn! The blind man of Gondar was there trying to
   get his end away and she shut him up every time . . .

MARICA DEL REINO. He's usually pretty sharp with his
   tongue.

A NEIGHBOUR. Nothing compared to her. You should have
   seen them both singing it all in verse, him on the barrel
   organ and her on the tambourine.

MARICA DEL REINO. Well that says a lot about the wine
   and precious little about her behaviour.

A NEIGHBOUR. Most of the time she doesn't even have to
   buy her own drinks! Many pay up because of her cheek,
   others just to hear the verses she comes out with.

MARICA DEL REINO. One of her many talents, which I've

been lucky enough not to witness! If only there were some
way of taking the idiot away from her greedy clutches! She
doesn't care a thing about him. She doesn't change his straw
or wash his goolies. He's got more sores than poor Lazarus
had. She's an evil bitch!

A NEIGHBOUR. And that halfwit earns his keep twice over. I
know many who'd be glad to have him!

MARICA DEL REINO. She'll not want for anything with that
dwarf, not the way she's going, dragging him from fair to
fair whatever the weather. It's different for me. He's my flesh
and blood and I care about what happens to him, there's no
profit in it for me. I drag that cart around from sunrise to
sunset and I'm no better off than when I started!

A NEIGHBOUR. You'd never believe how quickly your
sister-in-law drinks her profit away.

MARICA DEL REINO. And me, a decent, God-fearing
woman.

A NEIGHBOUR. Mind you, whenever she drinks she always
gives the idiot a swig.

MARICA DEL REINO. There's no charity in that! He
earns it.

A NEIGHBOUR. If you ask me, I can't see that anis can be
doing the idiot much good.

MARICA DEL REINO. Well it depends on how much he's
being given. If you've got worms, a glass of that stuff will do
you the world of good.

A NEIGHBOUR. If only it was just one glass . . .

MARICA DEL REINO. Don't tell me!

A NEIGHBOUR. And don't convince yourself for one minute
that your sister-in-law, Mari-Gaila, is going to set foot 'round
here today!

MARICA DEL REINO. I don't want to hear anymore! Sister-
in-law! Sister-in-law! Sister-in-law! That bitch is no relation
of mine! And my brother, deceived by it all!

A NEIGHBOUR. While Pedro sings at funerals, his wife sings in the roadside inns.

MARICA DEL REINO. How true it is that we women are born of the serpent! If only my brother was aware of what's going on around him!

A NEIGHBOUR. He's aware of the money she brings in.

MARICA DEL REINO. He hasn't a clue!

A NEIGHBOUR. I bet Mari-Gaila's dragging that cart as far as Viana today. You can trust her not to miss a single fair.

MARICA DEL REINO. But I should have the cart today! Well this'll be the last time she gets away with it! I'll get that cart back and she'll never set eyes on it again. Between you and me, my sister's ghost came knocking at my door. She sees how her son suffers and she no longer wants to see him in strange hands. She begged me to take sole control of the cart and forewarned me that my shameless sister-in-law would end up under lock and key, if not in this world then in the next! May I be condemned to eternal damnation if it isn't the truth, the whole truth and nothing but the truth!

A NEIGHBOUR. It sounds like a dream to me.

MARICA DEL REINO. I was wide awake.

A NEIGHBOUR. You actually talked to Juana's soul?

MARICA DEL REINO. Yes! But not a word to anyone.

A NEIGHBOUR. My lips are sealed.

THE NEIGHBOUR *enters her house to see to the fire. A broody hen and two chickens are hovering around the entrance, whilst in a nearby fig-tree three dirty, semi-naked children are eating their breakfast.*

Scene Two
A chestnut grove, the meeting place for beggars, pot-menders and tinkers who attend the annual August fair at Viana del Prior.

MARI-GAILA, *relishing this new adventure, appears breathless and smiling, dragging the cart along the sundrenched road.*

MIGUELÍN. You've a goldmine there, Mari-Gaila.

MARI-GAILA. You must be joking.

THE BLIND MAN OF GONDAR. You've been rolling in it ever since you decided to flash his goolies!

MARI-GAILA. These are hard times, money doesn't grow on trees, you know.

THE LEMONADE SELLER. Those who make most are always complaining.

THE BLIND MAN OF GONDAR. Well, we're always complaining!

MIGUELÍN. There's no money around here. And if any appears, Comrade Miau gets his hands on it and that's the end of that!

MARI-GAILA. Séptimo Miau this, Séptimo Miau that! All I seem to hear nowadays are the latest adventures of Séptimo Miau and his dog Coimbra! He must be quite a character!

MIGUELÍN. A jailbird!

MARI-GAILA *drags the cart to the shade of the chestnut trees and sits on it, her eyes and mouth lighting up mischievously.*

MARI-GAILA. There's something nasty making its way up my thigh and I'm going to try to stop it. Don't look, Padronés!

MIGUELÍN. What are you afraid of? Are you trying to hide some ghastly physical defect? It's a known fact that you've got bandy legs.

MARI-GAILA. Bandy and spindly!

THE BLIND MAN OF GONDAR. You've got it made! If we got together and tackled every fair and pilgrimage, we'd make a fortune. I can't honestly see you giving up this new life of yours.

MARI-GAILA. I'm chained to it by my disfigured inheritance.

MIGUELÍN. And there's me thinking that you willingly left the Royal Palace to join us!

MARI-GAILA. I left my home, where I was queen.

THE LEMONADE SELLER. Times may be hard but you're looking better than ever.

ROSA LA TATULA. There's colour in your cheeks!

MARI-GAILA. I've always looked a bit flushed and, of course, it's always been blamed on drink. My good health stems from my virtuous way of life!

The dirty, lazy BEGGARS laugh whilst resting in the shade of the trees. A GIRL dressed in a long robe approaches along the road, leading a pregnant lamb. She laughs merrily, walking between her parents, two old peasants. GIRLS wearing their Sunday best go by singing, accompanied by HERDSMEN and PALLID PILGRIMS carrying offerings.

THE LEMONADE SELLER. The fair at Viana looks as if it's going to be the event of the year.

MIGUELÍN. As far as I'm concerned there's nothing like the one at Bezán.

MARI-GAILA. It's alright for you lot to sing the praises of all these fairs in the back of beyond, you're all free. There's no way I can drag this cart seven leagues.

THE BLIND MAN OF GONDAR. Get yourself some help and take the journey slowly. If you really want to make the most of the idiot, you should head up to the fairs in the mountains. They're a Godsend!

MARI-GAILA. I'm definitely not missing San Campio de la Arnoya this year!

THE BLIND MAN OF GONDAR. There could be a lot more in it for you if we came to some sort of agreement.

MARI-GAILA. We've got an agreement. Just respect it and stop trying to sleep with me because you don't stand a chance.

ROSA LA TATULA. It's thanks to God that you haven't been at it already!

MARI-GAILA. Do you honestly think I'd let this rough animal get his mucky paws on my baby soft skin? Get your hands off me!

THE BLIND MAN OF GONDAR. Don't go, Mari-Gaila!

MARI-GAILA. Catch me if you can.

THE BLIND MAN OF GONDAR. Do you want to be a wealthy woman?

MARI-GAILA. You read my thoughts!

THE BLIND MAN OF GONDAR. The delicious smell of sardines! Care to sit and share my sardines, Mari-Gaila?

MARI-GAILA. I can provide a couple of herrings I was given this morning while begging, but we'll need something to wash them down with.

THE BLIND MAN OF GONDAR. Check in my bag, there might be something in there.

MARI-GAILA. You live like a lord, you crafty bastard!

Rolling her sleeves and tucking her hair under a floral scarf, MARI-GAILA *sets to work, lighting a makeshift fire from a few branches. The smoke gives off a fragrant aroma of laurel and sardines, which mingles with the bitter wine and badly baked bread remaining in the bag. A decrepit old man who appeared asleep slowly gets up. His chest is a mass of rosaries and he wears the cloak of a* PILGRIM.

THE PILGRIM. It is with great lament, good Christian souls, that I regret having nothing to share with you.

MARI-GAILA. Your bag looks full enough.

THE PILGRIM. It's filled with my penitence.

THE BLIND MAN OF GONDAR. A couple of joints of meat!

THE PILGRIM. Only the stone on which I rest my head at night.

He opens his bag and brings out a large round polished river stone, visible proof of endless penitential dreams. MARI-GAILA *is visibly moved by* THE PILGRIM's *gesture.*

MARI-GAILA. It's your lucky day! Come over here and share our meal.

THE PILGRIM. Praise be to God!

MARI-GAILA. Forever and ever, amen.

MARI-GAILA *removes the sardines from the fire and places them on a pewter dish. She then brings out the bread and wine from* THE BLIND MAN's *bag and clears a place for* THE PILGRIM *around the patched cloak, which serves as a makeshift tablecloth. They begin to eat,* THE BLIND MAN *smelling his sardines spread out on a chunk of bread. He perks up his ears.*

THE BLIND MAN OF GONDAR. Stone pillow or not, he sounds as if he's grinding rocks. I thought penitence involved fasting as well as sleeplessness . . . some saint!

THE PILGRIM. I've been without food for the past three days.

THE BLIND MAN OF GONDAR. Indigestion?

THE PILGRIM. Penitence!

THE BLIND MAN OF GONDAR. I know every trick in the trade, my friend.

THE PILGRIM *humbly resigns himself to these words, while* THE BLIND MAN, *refreshing himself with a swig of wine, bursts out laughing.* MIGUELÍN EL PADRONÉS *is whistling loudly and winking mischievously while mending an umbrella in the shade. A pair of* CIVIL GUARDS, *easily recognized by their dusty black three-cornered hats, make their way through the shadows where the unsavoury gang are having their siesta. Silence descends among the group as the snooping* CIVIL GUARDS *approach.*

FIRST CIVIL GUARD. Have any of you seen a man travelling around these fairs with a whore? He's known as the Polish Count.

THE BLIND MAN OF GONDAR. There's no royalty around here.

SECOND CIVIL GUARD. That's the name he's wanted under.

THE BLIND MAN OF GONDAR. A name's easily changed.

MIGUELÍN. This 'Count' you're looking for, what's he done?

FIRST CIVIL GUARD. It doesn't bear thinking about. I'm surprised you haven't heard of him.

THE BLIND MAN OF GONDAR. Some of us look for trouble in this world and some of us don't.

MARI-GAILA. I'm sure that these Civil Guards have the sense to realize this.

SECOND CIVIL GUARD. Well, since we have the sense to realize this, we'd probably be best off taking you all down to the prison. So watch out, because we've got our eyes on you!

MARI-GAILA. Gentlemen, please, we're as honest as they come!

FIRST CIVIL GUARD. Just watch it!

The two CIVIL GUARDS *march off, looking sullen and morose. Looks of fear and ridicule accompany them. Their belts, guns and distinctive hats glimmer in the bright sunlight.*

THE BLIND MAN OF GONDAR. How wondrous is the gift of sight! They're blinder than we who live in darkness.

MIGUELÍN. Maybe.

THE BLIND MAN OF GONDAR. Are we referring to the same person?

MIGUELÍN. My lips are sealed.

MARI-GAILA. Playing cautious, are we?

THE BLIND MAN OF GONDAR. I think we all understand each other.

MIGUELÍN. Miau!

MIGUELÍN *slyly stretches himself out on a tree trunk. He opens his umbrella to judge how well he's mended it and begins whistling again.* MARI-GAILA *listens attentively, trying to catch the tune.*

MARI-GAILA. What a lovely tune. It sounds like a habanera.

THE LEMONADE SELLER. Comrade Miau brought it with him from the ends of the earth.

MARI-GAILA. It'll be ridiculous when we finally catch up with each other! I've never even met him and yet I've been dreaming about him and that dog of his for the past three nights.

MIGUELÍN. Let's hope the man of your dreams has Séptimo Miau's face!

MARI-GAILA. If he has Padronés', then he's the Devil himself!

Scene Three

MARI-GAILA *is entertaining the crowds with her witty comments as she drags the cart along. She uses her tambourine to help attract their attention. Bursts of sunshine accompanied by sudden showers throughout the afternoon. The fair at Viana del Prior. In a corner, beneath the church's portico, stalls and stands; a collage of reds and greens with pack-saddles, harnesses and other such items. A hill leading up to the church. Cattle are grazing beneath the shade of the oak trees. Outside the inn, groups of* HERDSMEN, MEN *of all ages and* BEGGARS *are drinking and discussing a diverse range of subjects.* MIGUELÍN EL PADRONÉS *is repairing a blue flowered bowl under the watchful eye of the innkeeper.* COIMBRA, *dressed in bright colours, rushes in through the crowds.* COMRADE MIAU *is just behind her, carrying the fortune-telling bird's cage on his shoulder. His left eye is covered by a green taffeta eye patch. He stops at the door of the inn and begins playing the flute.* COIMBRA *dances to the tune, while the fortune-telling bird flies in and out of the cage.* MARI-GAILA *adjusts the flowered scarf around her shoulders. In the hope of catching* COMRADE MIAU's *attention, she begins to accompany him, keeping to the rhythm of the habanera.*

MARI-GAILA.
>My dream's to live in Havana
>Who cares about the heat!
>I'll leave the house when the sun goes down
>For a nice cool ride in the street!

MIGUELÍN. Do you recognize the man of your dreams?

MARI-GAILA. Apart from the eye he keeps covered.

MIGUELÍN. Comrade Miau, could we obtain from your goldfinch some indication of this lady's fortune. I'll pay.

COMRADE MIAU. It's on the house. She deserves better than your charity. Colorín, tell us this good lady's fortune. Consult the stars, Colorín.

MARI-GAILA. My fortune's misfortune.

COLORÍN, *wearing a little pointed hat and yellow breeches, appears at the door of the cage with the magical message in its beak.* MARI-GAILA *picks up the tiny, folded piece of paper and hands it to* COMRADE MIAU *who reads it, surrounded by the awestruck faces of the crowd.*

COMRADE MIAU. Venus and Ceres, here, reveal your destiny. Ceres offers you her fruits, Venus unadulterated pleasure. Your destiny is that of all beautiful women. Your throne that of spring.

MARI-GAILA. That's not what I see! All I see ahead of me is misery and misfortune.

Under the vines running above the doors of the inn, the figures are silhouetted by a green aquatic light. Having mended the bowl, MIGUELÍN EL PADRONÉS *now swaggers over to join the group. His tongue locates the mole, allowing him to fold his arms smugly and give a sly smile.*

MIGUELÍN. Why are you wearing that eye patch, Comrade Miau?

COMRADE MIAU. One eye's more than enough to see what you're up to, poofter.

MARI-GAILA. Try again, Padronés.

COMRADE MIAU. Tell me, good woman, don't you think it suits me?

MARI-GAILA. Take it off, my friend, and I'll let you know.

COMRADE MIAU. I'll take it off later, when we're on our own.

MARI-GAILA. Well what?

COMRADE MIAU. Do we meet up or not?

MARI-GAILA. If that's what you want.

THE BLIND MAN OF GONDAR *emerges from the inn. His hat is at an angle and he has a large glass of wine in his hand. His laughter appears prompted by good food and good wine.*

THE BLIND MAN OF GONDAR. Mari-Gaila, come and have a drink.

MARI-GAILA. My pleasure.

THE BLIND MAN OF GONDAR. It'll clear your throat. I heard you singing from inside.

MARI-GAILA *wipes her mouth with a corner of her headscarf and takes the overflowing red glass from the hands of the sharp old man. She drinks, gurgling the wine in her throat.*

MARI-GAILA. Nectar!

THE BLIND MAN OF GONDAR. Wine from Condado is the best money can buy!

MARI-GAILA. Just the thing for this heat.

THE BLIND MAN OF GONDAR. Care to try a drop of white wine now? It's from Amandi and tastes like strawberries!

MARI-GAILA. You certainly know how to live!

THE BLIND MAN OF GONDAR. Well, if you want some, come in with me.

MARI-GAILA. What if I get a little drunk?

THE BLIND MAN OF GONDAR. We'll climb into some loft and sleep it off!

MARI-GAILA. You're at it again! Why haven't you got some young girl with you?

THE BLIND MAN OF GONDAR. Young girls are useless. A blind man needs a woman he can enjoy.

COMRADE MIAU. Surely the opposite is true! A blind man can't appreciate beauty. He'd be better off with some firm flesh that won't slip between his fingers.

THE BLIND MAN OF GONDAR. How firm is your flesh, Mari-Gaila?

THE INNKEEPER. Flesh sags once you've given birth.

MARI-GAILA. It all depends on the woman. I was in better shape after giving birth than I'd ever been before.

THE BLIND MAN OF GONDAR. Well, let's take a look at you now.

MARI-GAILA. If you want me to go inside with you, you'd better keep your hands to yourself.

COMRADE MIAU. If you leave, you'll not be able to make the comparison!

MARI-GAILA. I trust you're referring to the eye patch.

COMRADE MIAU. What else could it be?

MARI-GAILA. I'll see you later.

COMRADE MIAU. Will you wait at the inn?

MARI-GAILA. I'll wait with our mutual friend, but not for too long.

MARI-GAILA *slaps the old man on the back and goes into the inn, dragging the cart behind her. As she is entering the door, she turns and winks to those remaining outside.*

COMRADE MIAU. What a wit! That woman's wasted around here.

THE LEMONADE SELLER. Well, there's no shortage of sharp pretty women in these parts! You must have heard of one, she's well known throughout the world. Carolina Otero, the daughter of a navvy from San Juan de Valga. You may not believe this but she sleeps with the King of France!

COMRADE MIAU. There's no king in France.

THE LEMONADE SELLER. Then it must be the man who's in charge there.

COMRADE MIAU. France is a Republic, like Spain ought to be. In a Republic power lies with the people, people like you and I, comrade.

THE LEMONADE SELLER. Well who did the navvy's daughter from San Juan de Valga sleep with? She must have slept with someone, because it's a true story! Now, there's a girl who doesn't forget her mother! She took her off the roads where she was begging and set her up in an inn!

ROSA LA TATULA. And to think Mari-Gaila could have had luck like that!

MIGUELÍN. Don't believe a word Miau says.

THE LEMONADE SELLER. Your friend ought to know, after all he has travelled around.

COMRADE MIAU. With the right guidance, there'd be no stopping her.

THE LEMONADE SELLER. Now that's saying something!

COMRADE MIAU. I'm not the first to say it. Colorín predicted it and he holds the secrets of the future in that beak of his. Roll up ladies and gentlemen, roll up! This fortune-telling goldfinch has the power to disclose every mystery the future holds! So, roll up ladies and gentlemen for the fortune-telling bird!

Scene Four
The churchyard at San Clemente. Early evening, the hour of the angelus. Birds and purple shadows fill the churchyard. PEDRO

GAILO, *the sexton, is strolling under the portico, jangling his keys. His grey stubble and sallow, sunken cheeks remind one of the yellow flames of candles. The last of the peasant women are leaving the church. Only* MARICA DEL REINO *remains behind, praying over a fresh grave.*

PEDRO GAILO. Goodnight Marica! Don't forget to close the gate as you go out.

MARICA DEL REINO. Don't go, I need to speak to you. Let me just finish this prayer.

PEDRO GAILO *sits on the wall of the portico and jangles his keys.* MARICA DEL REINO *crosses herself. Her brother watches her approach without moving an inch.*

MARICA DEL REINO. Do you remember what we agreed?

PEDRO GAILO. What are you talking about, Marica?

MARICA DEL REINO. Don't you understand? Well it's pretty clear to me!

PEDRO GAILO. You'll need to explain . . .

MARICA DEL REINO. What did we agree regarding the cart?

PEDRO GAILO. You know what we agreed.

MARICA DEL REINO. Is that why you let your wife roam the country!

PEDRO GAILO. She knows what she's doing.

MARICA DEL REINO. Brother, I remember you as proud and virile, now you let that woman walk all over you! What has she done to make you lose all self-respect?

PEDRO GAILO. You've a serpent's tongue, Marica!

MARICA DEL REINO. Why? Because I speak the truth?

PEDRO GAILO. You shouldn't believe every rumour you hear, Marica!

MARICA DEL REINO. Rumours! I wish they were rumours!

That fallen woman's behaviour has brought shame on our family!

PEDRO GAILO. All gossip; malicious, fabricated gossip! Well, I'm getting sick of all this gossip so you'd better watch your step!

MARICA DEL REINO. That's right! Now you stop torturing yourself and lash out at your sister with the rage of your wounded pride!

PEDRO GAILO. I wasn't referring to you although I could have been. Everyone gossips!

MARICA DEL REINO. You'll wake up to what's going on soon enough, brother!

PEDRO GAILO. What the hell do you want me to do? You want to see your own brother ruined!

MARICA DEL REINO. I want to see you stand firm!

PEDRO GAILO. You want to see me ruined!

MARICA DEL REINO. You'd still have your honour and self-respect!

PEDRO GAILO. The self respect of a life in prison!

MARICA DEL REINO. I'm not asking you to kill her, just show her who's boss.

PEDRO GAILO. She'll turn on me.

MARICA DEL REINO. Not if you thrash her hard enough.

PEDRO GAILO. Don't forget, I've got a weak heart!

MARICA DEL REINO. How could I forget?

PEDRO GAILO. If there's going to be any lasting change I'll have to kill her. No kind of thrashing is going to stop her from getting her own back! Forget it!

MARICA DEL REINO. Then split up.

PEDRO GAILO. That won't solve anything.

MARICA DEL REINO. That evil bitch has got you tied around her little finger.

PEDRO GAILO. If I kill her, that'll be the end of me.

MARICA DEL REINO. Why don't you wake up?

PEDRO GAILO. You want to see me off the rails! You won't be happy until I'm climbing the steps to the gallows! Evil tongues are calling the hangman and tying the noose! There's no way out! Your brother will be hung, Marica! I'll sharpen the knife tonight! I can do without your remorse on my conscience!

MARICA DEL REINO. Always blaming me! If you've lost all your self respect and you want it back, then it's your problem.

PEDRO GAILO. My problem's been created by wicked tongues. I'd like to see them fry in Hell! Because of them, a good man who's never harmed a soul is damned! Woe is me! Marica, my own sister, how can you just stand there and watch me suffer?

MARICA DEL REINO. I've hardened my heart.

PEDRO GAILO. How can you abandon me to such a dark prison?

MARICA DEL REINO. Dismal was the hour you were born! If you carry out your evil desires, these mourning clothes will remain with me forever! Oh brother, it's better to see you surrounded by four candles than sharpening your knife! Backbiting jealousy never gives good advice! Brother, don't sentence yourself without a hope! If you want to defend your honour and self-respect, beware of those who will bind you forever in chains! Hide your knife, brother! Don't sharpen it! Don't endanger yourself! Whenever I think of it my soul cries out against that evil bitch! That great harlot's disappeared with the cart! Oh brother! Pride and self-respect are cruel. How can they expect you to search for this woman in the depths of the earth?

Amongst the violet shadows, the carefree flight of the birds and the delicate scent of the evening dew, the old woman's declamatory words create an atmosphere of sinister foreboding. PEDRO GAILO *hurries off along the road to the village.*

The black cassock and pointed cap give his shadow a devilish dimension. He turns and looks around, lost in the dark murmuring cornfields. He then raises his long, thin, dark arms to heaven and pleads:

PEDRO GAILO. Why have you forsaken me? Why have you forsaken me?

Scene Five

A starry night. A rickety sentry box on the beach. Silvery waves break on the rocks. Shadowy masts and beacons burn in the distance. In the harbour inn, the sound of jovial singing and card-playing. MARI-GAILA arrives, dragging the cart. She stops to listen, crouching in the shadows of the sentry box. The soft sound of tinkling bells as COIMBRA runs along the beach, sniffing around. The dark figure of SÉPTIMO MIAU appears, silhouetted against the brightly lit doorway of the inn. MARI-GAILA softly calls out to him and he then joins her in the shadows of the sentry box.

MARI-GAILA. Let's go.

SÉPTIMO MIAU. There's no need to be afraid.

MARI-GAILA. I've my reputation to think of. If anyone catches us together, that'll be the end of me.

SÉPTIMO MIAU. We can hide in the sentry box.

MARI-GAILA. I don't want you this close, my friend. Do me the favour of moving your hand away.

SÉPTIMO MIAU. Threatening me already.

MARI-GAILA. That's the way I am. Why haven't you got some pretty young thing travelling with you?

SÉPTIMO MIAU. I haven't found the right one yet.

MARI-GAILA. You must go for the wrong kind of woman.

SÉPTIMO MIAU. Women are a menace.

MARI-GAILA. But you want them.

SÉPTIMO MIAU. I only want one and that's you.

MARI-GAILA. Well, we are feeling passionate tonight! . . .
You were travelling with another woman not so long ago.

SÉPTIMO MIAU. You know her.

MARI-GAILA. People talk. What happened to her?

SÉPTIMO MIAU. Suicide.

MARI-GAILA. What did you say?

SÉPTIMO MIAU. She killed herself.

MARI-GAILA. Because you abandoned her?

SÉPTIMO MIAU. She was a bit soft in the head.

MARI-GAILA. Maybe she loved you too much.

SÉPTIMO MIAU. Has no man killed himself over you?

MARI-GAILA. You must be joking!

SÉPTIMO MIAU. Well, I'll be the first then.

MARI-GAILA. I'm not worth it.

SÉPTIMO MIAU. Let me be the judge of that.

MARI-GAILA. What a charmer!

SÉPTIMO MIAU. Do you want to see me dead?

MARI-GAILA. No, but then I don't particularly want to see
anyone else dead either. Hey! Get away! What are you doing
with that hand?

SÉPTIMO MIAU. Ticklish, are we?

MARI-GAILA. Yes. Keep still! Someone's coming!

SÉPTIMO MIAU. No one's coming.

MARI-GAILA. You can't be sure of that. You've got the cheek
of the Devil!

SÉPTIMO MIAU. Let's get into the sentry box.

MARI-GAILA. Don't you ever give up!

SÉPTIMO MIAU *gently pushes the woman towards the sentry box. She reacts in a mischievously amorous manner; teasing him playfully while leaning her head against his chest. The colourful fireworks explode above the water. Evening church bells begin tolling. The magnificent light of the fireworks illuminates the church tower. MARI-GAILA kneels at the door of the sentry box to pick up a card which is lying on the sand.*

MARI-GAILA. The seven of spades! What does that mean?

SÉPTIMO MIAU. As compensation for seven misfortunes you will sleep with Séptimo tonight!

MARI-GAILA. And if I sleep with Séptimo Miau all week?

SÉPTIMO MIAU. How about forever.

MARI-GAILA. Who do you think you are? God?

SÉPTIMO MIAU. I don't think I've ever met him.

MARI-GAILA *stops resisting and enters the sentry box. Merry with wine she closes her eyes; her gentle, breathy laughter offering* SÉPTIMO MIAU *the encouragement to take her in his arms. She murmurs contentedly.*

MARI-GAILA. Are you the Polish Count?

SÉPTIMO MIAU. It doesn't concern you.

MARI-GAILA. Well, are you?

SÉPTIMO MIAU. No, but that's not to say I don't know him.

MARI-GAILA. Well, if he's a friend, you'd better warn him that the police are after him.

SÉPTIMO MIAU. Why? Don't you think he knows? He's one step ahead of them!

MARI-GAILA. Are you sure it isn't you?

SÉPTIMO MIAU. Just drop it.

MARI-GAILA. All right.

SÉPTIMO MIAU. Let's go in.

MARI-GAILA. What do I do with the cart?

SÉPTIMO MIAU. Leave it out here. Why? Are you proposing we take it in with us?

MARI-GAILA. Very funny!

SÉPTIMO MIAU. Let's go!

MARI-GAILA. Séptimo, I'll have to teach you not to take me for granted!

SÉPTIMO MIAU *bites* MARI-GAILA's *lip. She relaxes in his arms, sighing in ecstasy. They are lit by the moonlight which pours in through the door.*

SÉPTIMO MIAU. I've tasted your blood!

MARI-GAILA. I'm yours.

SÉPTIMO MIAU. Do you know who I am?

MARI-GAILA. The Devil!

Scene Six
The GAILOS' *house. A dirty rustic kitchen lit by a greasy, smouldering oil lamp. Hens scurry across the floor, seeking warmth beside the stone fireplace.* SIMONIÑA *is undressing for bed behind a cane screen, only her head is occasionally visible.* THE SEXTON *is climbing down from the loft. He is dressed in an old cassock and is barefoot. He has a black butcher's knife in one hand and a tankard in the other. As he slumps down beside the fireplace we become aware of the fact that he is talking to his shadow.*

PEDRO GAILO. I've got to win back my honour and self-respect! It's my duty! Women are a curse on mankind! Blessed Mary, if only it wasn't so! But we have proof in the scriptures! The serpent was born of woman and woman alone! The seven-headed serpent!

SIMONIÑA. Father, what's all this ranting and raving? Go on to bed!

PEDRO GAILO. Children should be seen and not heard.

SIMONIÑA. I'm too tired to listen to all this nonsense now. Go to bed, you're drunk!

PEDRO GAILO. I've got to sharpen this knife.

SIMONIÑA. Drunkard!

PEDRO GAILO. It'll be an all night job! . . . It's my self respect at stake, my pride, my reputation, I've got no choice! Look, it's getting sharper! I'm destined to lose my way! Simoniña, you'll find yourself without a father or mother! Think about it! Look how sharp the blade is! Watch the light catch it! Like lightning! You're so young, how will you manage in this vale of tears? Oh Simoniña, the demands of honour and self-respect will leave you fatherless!

SIMONIÑA. It's the bloody brandy talking!

PEDRO GAILO. You'll be fatherless! I'm going to use this knife to cut that whore's head off. And then, holding it by the hair, I'll take it to the mayor. I'll ask him to arrest me there and then. This is the head of my lawful wedded wife. In defence of my self-respect I was forced to slice it off. I trust that you will use your infinite wisdom to ensure that I receive a just punishment.

SIMONIÑA. Father! Please, be quiet! You make my blood run cold! It's all wicked gossip, don't believe a word of it! It's the work of evil souls!

PEDRO GAILO. What kind of example does a woman set walking out on her husband? What does she deserve? A knife! A knife! A knife!

SIMONIÑA. Stop it, father! Cast aside these wicked thoughts!

PEDRO GAILO. It is written in the Scriptures! She will pay for her whorish ways with her head on a plate! . . . You'll be an orphan, and you deserve it because you're a troublemaker. And I don't care that you're about to become an orphan. I've got to get back to my business. Just look how that knife glimmers!

SIMONIÑA. Bastard! You're not my father, you're the Devil

in disguise. You make me sick! What's my mother done?
Come on, tell me what she's done that's so terrible.

PEDRO GAILO. Can you not see her guilt? You look but see
nothing! Can you not see the tiles being ripped off the roof
under your very eyes? Your mother is condemned to die!

SIMONIÑA. Father, let God be the judge of that! Don't stain
your own hands with blood because it'll never wash off! And
besides, who says mother won't come back?

PEDRO GAILO. She's a lost sheep who'll screech loud enough
when she's is butchered! Stay out of this Simoniña, don't get
involved! Let me grab that whore by the hair! I'll drag her
through this kitchen! Go|on! Scream, you bitch! I'm going to
stick this stone between your teeth as if you were a pig!

SIMONIÑA. Father, please, calm down. Have another drink
and go to bed.

PEDRO GAILO. Shut up, you shit-stirring cow! Why did you
open the door and let her out of the house? We could bury
her here under the fireplace, no one would ever suspect . . .

SIMONIÑA. It's going to have to be a very deep hole, you'd
better have another drink to keep you going.

SIMONIÑA, *dressed in a nightshirt which leaves her shoulders
bare, takes the tankard and lifts it to her drunken father's lips.
He pushes it aside and closes his eyes.*

PEDRO GAILO. You drink first, Simoniña.

SIMONIÑA. It's anis!

PEDRO GAILO. Go on! Drink it! Just leave me enough for a
final swig. Shame on the woman who abandons her home!

SIMONIÑA. Finish it off and wash away those evil thoughts.

PEDRO GAILO. A wife belongs to her husband, a husband to
his wife. They surrender their bodies to each other according
to the requirements of the Holy Sacrament of matrimony.

SIMONIÑA. Well, if it's a woman you want, I'm sure you'll
find one. You're not bad looking and there's a few years of

life inside you yet. Just don't bring any lady friends here. I don't want anyone else giving orders in this house.

PEDRO GAILO. What if I'm seized by temptation in the middle of the night? The Devil strikes when least expected, Simoniña!

SIMONIÑA. Use your Latin to scare him off.

PEDRO GAILO. What if he tempts me to sin with you?

SIMONIÑA. Demon away!

PEDRO GAILO. Cover your shoulders, Simoniña! Temptation's getting the better of me.

SIMONIÑA. Drink up and go to bed.

PEDRO GAILO. You've got great, stocky legs Simoniña!

SIMONIÑA. You can't expect a fat person like me to have skinny legs.

PEDRO GAILO. And your skin's so white!

SIMONIÑA. You shouldn't be looking!

PEDRO GAILO. Put some more clothes on and we'll dig her grave together.

SIMONIÑA. What? Not more delirious ranting!

PEDRO GAILO. My head's exploding!

SIMONIÑA. Go to bed.

PEDRO GAILO. Bed, my sweet? I'm not going to bed unless you come with me.

SIMONIÑA. Put down the knife. What kind of joke is that? You and me going to bed together!

PEDRO GAILO. Let's get one up on her.

SIMONIÑA. Are you no longer planning to slice off a certain person's head?

PEDRO GAILO. Shut up!

SIMONIÑA. Stand up and leave my legs alone!

PEDRO GAILO. You smell good enough to eat!

SIMONIÑA *leads her drunken father to the bed behind the screen and pushes him down onto it. She looks exhausted. Her nightshirt has fallen around her shoulders and her hair is no longer in neat plaits. She picks up the lamp and climbs up to her bed in the loft.* THE SEXTON *can be heard mumbling from his straw mattress behind the screen.*

PEDRO GAILO. Simoniña, come over here! Come on, sweetie! She's playing around, why can't we do the same? Where are you? I want to touch you. You're my woman now but if you kick me around, you won't be my woman anymore. We'll give her a dose of her own medicine! The Devil's laughing at me! He's here inside me! Get rid of him, Simoniña! . . . Please! Get rid of him!

SIMONIÑA *remains on the stairs, crouching with the lamp in her hands, listening to her father's words. As the drunken sexton begins to snore his words become increasingly unintelligible.*

Scene Seven
Viana Del Prior. Tolling bells. A starry night. An inn. Beggars and pedlars of all descriptions; grimy harvesters, peasant couples, women who live by the river selling lace, lively travellers and sallow faced invalids, who, with blankets over their shoulders and sticks in their hands, beg for money to get to the Holy Hospital. Chance has brought them all to the porch of this inn, a porch lit only by the flames of the open fire and the dull flicker of an oil lamp hanging by the entrance to the stable. ROSA LA TATULA *appears, dragging the idiot's cart. She goes over to the counter and begins looking through her purse, her face lit by a broad toothless smile.*

ROSA LA TATULA. Ludovina, does this peseta look all right to you?

LUDOVINA, *a short, plump, ruddy redhead, drops the coin on the counter and rubs it between her fingers. She then examines it by the light of the oil lamp and throws it back onto the counter.*

LUDOVINA. It looks genuine to me. What do you think,
   Padronés?

MIGUELÍN. There's nothing wrong with that.

ROSA LA TATULA. Here Ludovina, take it and give me
   some change if you can. I thought it might be a fake as I
   don't really trust the person who gave it to me. You know
   who I'm talking about, that Castillian who goes around with
   the little bird.

MIGUELÍN. Comrade Miau.

ROSA LA TATULA. That's him! A lazy good-for-nothing
   who's run off with Mari-Gaila. They're watching the
   fireworks in the square like a couple of lovestruck teenagers.
   Since there's such a crowd of people there, they asked me to
   take care of the cart. Let the youth enjoy themselves.

LUDOVINA. Youth! I don't think either of them are
   that young.

MIGUELÍN. That's as may be but they're two of a kind.

*A tall young man with a slight beard appears in the darkness of
the porch. He wears an army cloak over his shoulder and his
discharge papers displayed on his chest. One of his arms has been
amputated. Begging for money, he uses the remaining hand to
play the accordion.*

THE SOLDIER. Mari-Gaila's not the right woman for a
   man like that. His last partner had much more style, and a
   lovely lisp!

MIGUELÍN. She also had a baby round her neck. This one's
   got a first-class source of income in that cart. Comrade Miau
   intends to drag that swollen-headed monster all across Spain,
   he'll make an absolute fortune!

THE SOLDIER. There's nothing special about this dwarf.
   Once you've seen one freak you've seen them all.

ROSA LA TATULA. I doubt if you've ever come across one as
   badly behaved as this one!

MIGUELÍN. Look what Miau made of that mangy flea-ridden dog he stumbled across. Coimbra's a walking goldmine.

ROSA LA TATULA. Mari-Gaila owns that idiot. Well, partly owns him, and she's not done a thing with him.

THE SOLDIER. There's nothing special about him.

MIGUELÍN. Well, I think he's good enough to go on show in Madrid. Ludovina, give him a drink, I'll pay. And bring some paper because I want to make him a hat.

THE SOLDIER. For a head that size you're going to need a lot of paper.

THE IDIOT. Hou! Hou!

THE SOLDIER. You'd make a fortune if you had a beard, a hump and a red hat.

THE IDIOT. Hou! Hou!

MIGUELÍN. That's what will be in store for you if you finish up with Comrade Miau.

ROSA LA TATULA. Buy him another drink and watch. With two drinks there's no stopping him. Laureano, croak like a frog.

THE IDIOT. Cua! Cua!

MIGUELÍN. Do you want another drink, Laureano?

LAUREANO. Hou! Hou!

MIGUELÍN. Give him another, Ludovina.

LUDOVINA. That's three you owe for.

MIGUELÍN. The army will pay.

LUDOVINA. Long live the army!

MIGUELÍN *smiles sarcastically. He licks the mole at the corner of his mouth and forces the idiot to drink. Sitting up in the straw,* LAUREANO *licks his lips and rolls his eyes. His epileptic cries echo around the chimney cover.*

THE IDIOT. Hou! Hou!

MIGUELÍN. Drink up, Napoleon Bonaparte.

THE SOLDIER. Give him a moustache like the Kaiser.

MIGUELÍN. I'll shave him a crown.

ROSA LA TATULA. What sinful ideas.

Beside the fireplace, an OLD PEASANT COUPLE *and a pale* LITTLE GIRL *in a purple robe are eating an evening meal of fresh buns, wine and cherries wrapped in a handkerchief. The dream-like child looks like a wax doll sitting between the old couple who give the impression of having stepped out of an altar engraving; their wrinkled honey and ochre coloured faces resemble those of shepherds in a nativity scene. The idiot's cry brings a smile to the little girl's sad face.*

THE LITTLE GIRL. Would you like some bread, little Laureano? Or would you prefer a bun?

THE IDIOT. Shit!

ROSA LA TATULA. Just look at the way he's looking at the girl. What a devil!

THE IDIOT *stares blankly ahead and madly waves his hands in an epileptic frenzy.* THE LITTLE GIRL *leaves some buns and cherries in the cart and then happily rejoins her parents. Her purple robe and wax-like hands give her the appearance of a martyred virgin between the two altar-piece figures.*

THE MOTHER. Ludovina, don't let them give him that much to drink. It could kill him!

ROSA LA TATULA. Well I never!

THE IDIOT *is breathing with increasing difficulty. His eyes are rolled back and his tongue hangs out from between his blue lips. The enormous head – glutinous, sallow and dishevelled – rolls around the cart as if decapitated.* MIGUELÍN EL PADRONÉS *stretches his tongue out towards his mole and wets it with saliva. Other shadows lean over the cart.*

LUDOVINA. Don't crowd him.

MIGUELÍN. If you stick his head in the well, he'll come 'round soon enough.

LUDOVINA. Tatula, take him outside. I don't want any trouble around here.

LAUREANO's *mouth remains contorted as he begins to rip the bedding in the cart, his hands shaking frantically.* THE LITTLE GIRL *and her* PARENTS *maintain a Christian sense of decorum, remaining in their positions beside the fireplace.*

THE FATHER. This would never have happened if his mother had been alive. She knew how to handle him. There was none of this brandy business with her around . . .

LUDOVINA. Get that cart out of here, Tatula.

MIGUELÍN. Throw him in the well for a second or two, it's nothing serious.

THE SOLDIER. Nothing more serious than death!

LUDOVINA. Get out! I don't want that cart under my roof any longer!

ROSA LA TATULA. He may not be dying!

LUDOVINA. I've got my reputation to think of and you're putting it in jeopardy, poofter!

MIGUELÍN. I see. I pay for the drinks so I get all the blame.

THE IDIOT *stops shaking. His tiny, dark, waxen hands are locked together above the patched blanket, and his bluish head, with glazed eyes and tongue hanging out, appears decapitated. The flies swarming around the cattle have already gathered around the corpse.* LUDOVINA *moves away from the counter.*

LUDOVINA. I don't want any trouble in my establishment! So clear out, go on, the lot of you!

ROSA LA TATULA. I'm going, but everyone had better keep their mouths shut about how this happened.

LUDOVINA. No one saw anything.

ROSA LA TATULA *begins dragging the cart away just as*

MARI-GAILA *appears in the moonlit doorway, her graceful figure silhouetted in the silvery night.*

MARI-GAILA. Good evening to you all!

LUDOVINA. You've arrived just in time.

MARI-GAILA. What is it?

ROSA LA TATULA. Death brings no warning.

MARI-GAILA. The idiot?

LUDOVINA. Dead.

MARI-GAILA. I knew there was more bad luck in store for me. I've got to let Séptimo know what's happened. I need his advice!

MIGUELÍN. Where did you leave him?

MARI-GAILA. He had to go to the Gentlemen's Casino.

LUDOVINA. My advice is to bury him as soon as possible.

MARI-GAILA. In consecrated ground?

LUDOVINA. Where else were you planning to bury him? At the foot of a lemon tree?

THE FATHER. Do what's right and bury him beside his mother.

MARI-GAILA. I'll have to trudge all night with that corpse in the cart. Damn the Devil! You'd better pour me a drink, Ludovina, it'll help me drown my sorrows. Pour me another while you're at it to round off the bill. If Séptimo comes around asking for me . . .

LUDOVINA. I'll know what to tell him. Now get going, Mari-Gaila! I don't want the smell of death around here any longer!

MARI-GAILA. Merciful God in Heaven, you've taken away my livelihood and left me destitute! He who kept me nourished has left this world! Oh Blessed Jesus of Nazareth, you force me to leave this wandering life with nothing else to turn to!

Perform a miracle for me, Jesus of Nazareth! Fill my cup till it overfloweth!

Scene Eight

A starry night filled with the sound of rustling cornfields. MARI-GAILA *is dragging the cart along a moonlit road. A cuckoo's call is heard. It is immediately followed by the laugh of* THE GOAT GOBLIN, *who sits on a craggy rock with his long grey beard blowing in the night wind.* MARI-GAILA *attempts to exorcise him.*

MARI-GAILA.
At one the light of the moon!
At two the light of the sun!
At three the tablets of Moses

THE GOAT GOBLIN. Jujurujú!

MARI-GAILA. Damn you! Go!

THE GOAT GOBLIN. You've really twisted my horns tonight!

MARI-GAILA. At four the cock crowing!

THE GOAT GOBLIN. Jujurujú! Kiss my tail!

The scene changes. MARI-GAILA *is now following a path which crosses a shimmering estuary.* THE GOAT GOBLIN, *sitting on his hooves in the middle of the path, is laughing louder. The laughter appears amplified by his knotted beard.*

MARI-GAILA.
At five the word which lies written!
At six the star of kings!
At seven the flame of death!

THE GOAT GOBLIN. When you finish, we'll dance.

MARI-GAILA.
At eight the fire of purgatory!
At nine three eyes and three iron rods!
At ten the sword of Saint Michael Archangel!
At eleven the bronze doors open!
At twelve the might of the Lord destroys Satan's entrails!

MARI-GAILA *awaits thunder but hears only* THE GOAT GOBLIN's *laughter. The scene changes again. We now see a church by a crossroads. Witches are dancing around the church. A brilliant red light emerges from the church door and the smoky wind brings with it the aroma of grilled sardines.* THE GOAT GOBLIN *cries out from the weathervane on the church tower.*

THE GOAT GOBLIN. Jujurujú!

MARI-GAILA. Damn you! Damn you a thousand times!

THE GOAT GOBLIN. Why do you refuse to recognise me?

MARI-GAILA. Because I've never seen you! Demon!

THE GOAT GOBLIN. Come and dance with me!

MARI-GAILA. I don't want anything to do with you!

THE GOAT GOBLIN. Jujurujú! I'll carry you through the air, higher than the sun and moon! Jujurujú!

MARI-GAILA. I despise you.

THE GOAT GOBLIN. Do you want me to carry you to the end of the road? I only need to blow once and you'll be there.

MARI-GAILA. I know.

THE GOAT GOBLIN. You've been walking all night and you're not even half-way there.

MARI-GAILA. Move out of the way Goat Goblin and let me get past!

MARI-GAILA *attempts to drag the cart but cannot. It appears excessively heavy, as if made of stone.* THE GOAT GOBLIN *again lets out his cry.*

THE GOAT GOBLIN. Jujurujú! You won't reach your door tonight. Do you want my help?

MARI-GAILA. What will it cost me?

THE GOAT GOBLIN. Nothing. We'll dance as we finish the journey.

MARI-GAILA. If that were all . . .

THE GOAT GOBLIN. No more, no less.

MARI-GAILA. I already have a wonderful lover, you know.

THE GOAT GOBLIN. Jujurujú! Then I'll leave you to it.

THE GOAT GOBLIN *laughs loudly and then disappears from the churchtower, riding off on the weathervane. We are now back to the moonlit path and the sound of the rustling cornfields.* MARI-GAILA *feels herself lifted off the ground by a sudden gust of wind. The wind increases as she is swept higher into the air, sighing in delight. She can feel* THE GOAT GOBLIN's *hairy rump under her skirt. To avoid falling, she stretches out her arms and seizes* THE GOAT GOBLIN's *twisted horns.*

THE GOAT GOBLIN. Jujurujú!

MARI-GAILA. Where are you taking me, Satan?

THE GOAT GOBLIN. For a dance.

MARI-GAILA. Where are we going?

THE GOAT GOBLIN. Over the moon.

MARI-GAILA. We're falling! I think I'm going to faint!

THE GOAT GOBLIN. Wrap your legs around me.

MARI-GAILA. God, you're hairy!

MARI-GAILA *faints and feels herself carried through the clouds. When she finally opens her eyes, after what seemed like a long ride over the moon, she finds herself at the door of her house. The moon, almost too full to be real, shines on the cart where* THE IDIOT's *face remains rigidly frozen.*

Scene Nine
SIMONIÑA *descends barefoot from the loft in her nightshirt. The sound of loud knocking echoes through the dark and empty kitchen.*

SIMONIÑA. There's someone at the door, father!

PEDRO GAILO. Knock . . . Knocking . . .

SIMONIÑA. Shall I ask who it is?

PEDRO GAILO. There's no harm in asking.

MARI-GAILA'S VOICE. Open up! Damn you!

SIMONIÑA. It's mother! She's come back! I told you
she would!

PEDRO GAILO. I wonder what's brought her back!

SIMONIÑA. Where are the matches?

PEDRO GAILO. I haven't got them.

MARI-GAILA'S VOICE. Come on, you dopey gits! Do you
plan to leave me out here staring at the moon all night?

SIMONIÑA. I'm looking for the matches.

MARI-GAILA. It's freezing out here!

SIMONIÑA. Give me a second to light the lamp.

The long, dark shadow of THE SEXTON *appears above the
cane screen. Beside the fireplace the brightly shining lamp swings
gently from side to side.* SIMONIÑA, *her nightshirt slipping
off her shoulders, lifts the bar off the door.* MARI-GAILA *is
standing in the moonlight looking dark and beautiful. The cart is
lying on its side in the middle of the road.*

MARI-GAILA. Talk about trying to wake the dead!

PEDRO GAILO. When people work hard all day they're
entitled to a good night's sleep!

MARI-GAILA. Why is it that the only thing that ever comes
out of your mouth is drivel? Go back to sleep and don't
bother waking up again!

PEDRO GAILO. You return to seek shelter in your own home
and that's all you can come out with? Harlot!

MARI-GAILA. You're giving me a headache!

PEDRO GAILO. Well, that's easily remedied by cutting off
your head!

MARI-GAILA. Go back to your Latin, this isn't you!

PEDRO GAILO. What about my self respect?

MARI-GAILA. What self respect?

PEDRO GAILO. You're nothing but a whore!

MARI-GAILA. If you don't shut that mouth of yours, I'm going to whack you across the face!

SIMONIÑA. Please, don't start fighting.

MARI-GAILA. All this ranting and raving's not going to get you anywhere now that we've lost our income!

SIMONIÑA. What's happened to the idiot, mother?

MARI-GAILA. He's dead and gone.

PEDRO GAILO. How? Was it sudden?

MARI-GAILA. An epileptic fit. So, that's goodbye to our daily bread!

PEDRO GAILO. We should be thankful that his suffering is over.

MARI-GAILA. I collected four silver coins in the past couple of days!

   MARI-GAILA *unties a knotted hankerchief with her teeth and tosses the coins into her hand so that they can be seen.* SIMONIÑA, *on seeing the shining silver, begins her lament.*

SIMONIÑA. The sun has gone from our door! The good old days are over! He left this world without a care for any of us!

PEDRO GAILO. We ought to let my sister Marica know.

MARI-GAILA. Simoniña can go in the morning . . .

SIMONIÑA. Mother of God! My aunt's going to hit the roof when I tell her! She'll go crazy!

MARI-GAILA. Don't say a thing. Just leave the cart at her door and come straight back.

SIMONIÑA. Why do I have to take the cart?

MARI-GAILA. Because I'm telling you to, stupid! There's no way we're paying for the funeral!

PEDRO GAILO. Or giving any explanations!

SIMONIÑA. But Aunt Marica might not agree to it.

MARI-GAILA. When she finds that cart on her doorstep, she won't have much choice.

PEDRO GAILO. Well, if we've made our minds up we'd better get it done before dawn.

MARI-GAILA. That's the first intelligent thing I've heard you say!

SIMONIÑA. I'm not going near my aunt's doorway unless I'm armed with an apronful of rocks.

PEDRO GAILO. Shut up, you silly bitch! She's your aunt and whatever happens, you're not to hit her!

MARI-GAILA. If she's rude, aim the rocks at the roof.

PEDRO GAILO. It won't come to that if you get there before dawn.

MARI-GAILA. I see you can talk sense from time to time.

PEDRO GAILO. If at all possible, we should avoid family rows. Simoniña, leave the cart at the door and come straight home, without saying a word to anyone.

SIMONIÑA. Mother should have dropped it off on her way back home.

PEDRO GAILO. These things are best left for men to decide.

MARI-GAILA. Shut up, drivel brain! Don't you think I thought of it?

PEDRO GAILO. I'm not suggesting you didn't. Men are just better at handling these things.

SIMONIÑA. Let's change the subject!

MARI-GAILA. I agree. Now go quickly while it's still dark and leave the cart at your aunt's door.

SIMONIÑA. I'm scared!

MARI-GAILA. Don't be so stupid!

SIMONIÑA. I'm petrified of the dead body!

MARI-GAILA. Go on! Take that cart away from here.

SIMONIÑA. But the path's pitch dark now!

MARI-GAILA. Well, that's how your mother got home.

PEDRO GAILO. Why don't you just do what we say, Simoniña?

SIMONIÑA. Please, come with me father!

PEDRO GAILO. I'll call out to you from the doorway.

MARI-GAILA. Why don't you just get on with it, you stupid child!

SIMONIÑA *puts on her skirt with trembling hands. She adjusts her apron over her head as a scarf and then walks out of the house, crossing herself and moaning softly. She begins dragging the dark cart through the moonlight.* THE IDIOT's *ashen and dishevelled head remains frozen in the same disturbing expression. The tiny childlike hands clasping the blanket glow like wax.* PEDRO GAILO *is kneeling in the doorway, his arms raised to Heaven as he attempts to encourage his daughter to keep going.*

PEDRO GAILO. Do as you're told! . . . You'll be back in no time! . . . Can you hear me? . . . Don't be afraid! . . . You've a full moon to guide you . . . Can you still hear me? . . .

SIMONIÑA'S FAR OFF VOICE. Keep talking to me, father!

Scene Ten
Dawn. A rose-coloured sky with birds singing. Scarecrows with lifeless outstretched arms protrude from the upper branches of nearby fig-trees. Two pigs are grunting around the cart outside MARICA

DEL REINO's *door. The shabby, balding old woman leans out of a window and shouts at the pigs.*

MARICA DEL REINO. Go on! . . . Get away! . . . Away I said, you greedy swines! . . . God save me! The pigs are round the cart! How could they leave it here without saying a word! Shameless souls! They could have knocked!

MARICA DEL REINO *rushes out of the kitchen armed with a broom. Her skirt isn't properly fastened and her breasts, like those of an old goat, hang out over her bodice.*

MARICA DEL REINO. Go on, you thieving swines! Clear out, you filthy scum! . . . There's nothing to be afraid of, my dear! You stay put! Oh God! They've eaten his face! The pigs have eaten his face! He's had it!

Hearing MARICA DEL REINO's *cries,* THE NEIGHBOURS *come running. Faces can be seen peering from the tiny windows at the top of the houses. A crowd of people gathers outside the old woman's house. They can be seen emerging from stables filled with noisy cattle. The screaming, witch-like woman whacks the skeletal pigs, who continue grunting around the cart.* SERENÍN DE BRETAL, *a wise old man, puts out the lamp at the entrance to the stable.*

SERENÍN DE BRETAL. What's the world coming to. I never thought I'd live to see the day when animals turned into savages and devoured Christian souls.

Standing at the top of the path surrounded by children, A PREGNANT WOMAN *crosses herself and spreads her arms protectively around her offspring. Her expression is that of a woman resigned to a slow death.*

THE PREGNANT WOMAN. Mother of God! Mother of God!

SERENÍN DE BRETAL. Do you know if the idiot was left out here all night?

AN OLD WOMAN AT A WINDOW. Maybe, maybe not.

THE PREGNANT WOMAN. Mother of God! Mother of God!

MARICA DEL REINO. They dragged him here last night

without a word, without a single knock on the door, not even a cry to wake me! This is their dirty work!

THE PREGNANT WOMAN. His mother called him to her!

MARICA DEL REINO. Look at his body! It's frozen stiff! His hands and face eaten by pigs! It turns my stomach to see such butchery! You're all witnesses! Devoured by pigs!

SERENÍN DE BRETAL. The pigs didn't know what they were doing.

THE OLD WOMAN AT THE WINDOW. Well, that's obvious!

MARICA DEL REINO. It makes me sick to see what's left of him! Poor little Laureano, abandoned at my door! Abandoned to die by uncaring scoundrels!

THE OLD WOMAN AT THE WINDOW. I'm surprised that he didn't cry out when they attacked him!

A GIRL. Maybe he did.

MARICA DEL REINO. It would have woken me.

THE PREGNANT WOMAN. I didn't sleep a wink all night.

THE OLD WOMAN AT THE WINDOW. It all sounds very strange to me!

SERENÍN DE BRETAL. What if he were already dead when the pigs attaccked him? There's no blood around! Surely the cart would be covered in blood if he'd been attacked alive! It wouldn't surprise me if the morning frost killed him, it can be fatal for anyone in his condition.

THE OLD WOMAN AT THE WINDOW. He was probably already dead when they brought him here!

SERENÍN DE BRETAL. Well then, you'll have to go to the authorities.

MARICA DEL REINO. If anyone's guilty they'll not go free!

THE OLD WOMAN AT THE WINDOW. They must have been very quiet!

MARICA DEL REINO. We, the righteous, must rise up against this outrage! Who's responsible for this, Laureano? If only the dead could speak!

SERENÍN DE BRETAL. Ssh! Keep quiet! Don't make any accusations you might regret. The dwarf died of natural causes. No one's stupid enough to destroy their livelihood.

MARICA DEL REINO. Are you implying that he died in my care?

SERENÍN DE BRETAL. All I'm saying is that it was God's will.

MARICA DEL REINO. Why all this secrecy then? Why leave him at my door without a word? He died in their thieving hands!

SERENÍN DE BRETAL. Well then, send him back to them. Do as they did.

THE OLD WOMAN AT THE WINDOW. It all seems very mysterious to me!

End of Act Two

Act Three

Scene One

The GAILOS' house. Husband and wife sit huddled in the smoky, rustic kitchen, like two silent shadows. A stone is thrown onto the roof. A CHORUS OF NOISY CHILDREN then begins singing outside the door.

THE CHILDREN.
    Mari-Gaila! Mari-Gaila!
    All your life you've dilly-dallied!
    Mari-Gaila! Mari-Gaila!
    We all know you've, whoops, miscarried!

MARI-GAILA. Ignorant bastards!

PEDRO GAILO. Watch it!

MARI-GAILA. Foul-mouthed rabble!

PEDRO GAILO. Don't encourage them!

MARI-GAILA. You deserve it!

PEDRO GAILO. Slut!

MARI-GAILA. Fool!

Silence. A witch-like shadow passes by the house and looks in through the door. It is ROSA LA TATULA, bent and toothless, carrying an empty sack and a staff. MARI-GAILA gets up and speaks to the old woman in a low voice. They both enter the house. MARI-GAILA begins singing.

ROSA LA TATULA. Have you any news for me, Pedro Gailo?

PEDRO GAILO. We're getting older, Tatula.

ROSA LA TATULA. I bet you can still break a heart or two.

MARI-GAILA. You're hoping! He's been screaming at me all evening like some hysterical lion. He even threatened to slit my throat!

ROSA LA TATULA. You know how men love to talk.

MARI-GAILA. Let's hope it's only talk!

MARI-GAILA sighs. She reaches out for the jug and fills a glass, savouring it with the tip of her tongue. She offers it at arms' length to her husband.

MARI-GAILA. Here, drink!

PEDRO GAILO. I want to receive communion.

MARI-GAILA. Drink from my glass.

PEDRO GAILO. I need to cleanse my conscience.

MARI-GAILA. Why are you refusing?

PEDRO GAILO. I've a dark sin hanging over me!

MARI-GAILA. I'm offering to share my glass with you.

PEDRO GAILO. My soul doesn't belong to you.

MARI-GAILA. Drink and forget about it.

PEDRO GAILO. Plague-ridden harlot!

MARI-GAILA. Just listen to him, Tatula!

PEDRO GAILO. Shameless whore!

MARI-GAILA. Drunken bastard!

The long, dark figure of THE SEXTON *heads towards the door. He stops on the threshold, terrified, his hair standing on end and his arms outstretched in the form of a cross.* MARICA DEL REINO, *covered in a large shawl, is dragging the cart towards the house.*

PEDRO GAILO. It's the end of the world, sister!

MARICA DEL REINO. I'm returning your gift.

MARI-GAILA. You're not leaving that corpse at my door.

MARICA DEL REINO turns her head without answering. She senses a shadowy evil presence behind her. SIMONINA,

*returning from the fountain, is standing in the middle of the road,
her hands firmly on her hips. At that moment she bears a striking
resemblance to her mother, Mari-Gaila.*

SIMONIÑA. Take your baggage out of here, aunt!

MARICA DEL REINO. You're in my way.

SIMONIÑA. I won't let you get past!

MARICA DEL REINO. I'll get past even if I have to crush
your skull while I'm at it.

SIMONIÑA. Father! Help!

PEDRO GAILO. Why are you deliberately making trouble
outside my house?

MARICA DEL REINO. He was your flesh and blood.

PEDRO GAILO. And yours, Marica.

MARICA DEL REINO. He didn't die in my care.

MARI-GAILA. He was alive when he left us, sister-in-law.

MARICA DEL REINO. Sister-in-law! How dare you call me
sister-in-law! It chokes me to hear it!

MARI-GAILA. Go on, speak up! I've nothing to be afraid of!

MARICA DEL REINO. Whore!

PEDRO GAILO. Show some respect for the dead by keeping
that mouth of yours firmly shut! I would have thought that
the presence of death would have prevented such a foul
outburst!

ROSA LA TATULA. You're frightening me!

SIMONIÑA. Smooth down your hair, father. It's looking a
bit wild.

PEDRO GAILO. It's that corpse out there crying out for a
decent burial that's responsible!

MARICA DEL REINO. Well, go on and arrange it then. He
didn't die in my care so the burial's not my problem!

MARI-GAILA. Witch!

MARICA DEL REINO. Whore!

PEDRO GAILO. Get out of here, Marica! Get away from my door! My nephew will have a funeral fit for an angel.

SIMONIÑA. I didn't realize my father was such a rich man!

MARI-GAILA. He's delirious!

MARICA DEL REINO. Let me through, Simoniña!

SIMONIÑA. Not past me.

MARICA DEL REINO. If you're not careful you're going to find this knife wedged between your ribs!

SIMONIÑA. Witch!

MARICA DEL REINO. And straight through your heart!

SIMONIÑA. Mother! Help!

MARI-GAILA. Let her get past, you stupid fool!

PEDRO GAILO. Simoniña, bring the corpse into the house. We'll wash him and lay him out in my best shirt so that he's fit to receive judgement in the presence of the Lord.

SIMONIÑA. Did you hear that, mother?

MARI-GAILA. I heard but I'm not saying a word.

ROSA LA TATULA. I don't know why you're arguing about it. If you leave the corpse at the door of the church for three days you'll make more than enough money for the funeral.

MARI-GAILA. He won't last for three days in this heat.

ROSA LA TATULA. He's been pickled in brandy.

PEDRO GAILO. We'll wash his face properly, shave his stubble and give him a crown of lilies. He died innocent and deserves the prayers of the angels.

MARI-GAILA. Pompous fool! Isn't it time you rang the bells for mass? Or do you expect them to go off on their own!

Blocking out the light from the doorway with his black cassock,
THE SEXTON *looks up to the sun to guess the time. He
then runs to the church jangling his keys.* THE CHORUS OF
NOISY CHILDREN *circle the house once more.*

THE CHILDREN.
    Mari-Gaila! Mari-Gaila!
    We all know with whom she tarried!
    Mari-Gaila! Mari-Gaila!
    We all know that she's miscarried!

Scene Two
MARI-GAILA *and* ROSA LA TATULA *are conversing
conspiratorially at the back of the house, beneath the magnificent
fig-tree where the scarecrow stands, a ragged cassock hung on two
brooms in the form of a cross.*

ROSA LA TATULA. We can talk out here.

MARI-GAILA. Carry on, then!

ROSA LA TATULA. Do you remember the future the cards
    once predicted for you?

MARI-GAILA. The infamous cards!

ROSA LA TATULA. They predicted love three times over.

MARI-GAILA. A deceptive prophecy!

ROSA LA TATULA. You saw it yourself.

MARI-GAILA. My luck hasn't changed.

ROSA LA TATULA. That's because you don't want it to . . .
    I've a message for you.

MARI-GAILA. What is it?

ROSA LA TATULA. A message from somebody who wants an
    answer.

MARI-GAILA. Did Séptimo Miau send you?

ROSA LA TATULA. Right first time. Now, what do you think he wants?

MARI-GAILA. Something beautiful.

ROSA LA TATULA. He wants to see you!

MARI-GAILA. What a devil! What did he say when he heard about the idiot?

ROSA LA TATULA. He questioned everyone there and then, like a judge. It's probably best if I tell you what really happened. The idiot died from an overdose of brandy which that poofter Miguelín forced down him.

MARI-GAILA. I should have known it was that thieving git! What did Séptimo say when he found out?

ROSA LA TATULA. Nothing. He just stood there silently rolling up a cigarette.

MARI-GAILA. Waiting for the right moment.

ROSA LA TATULA. I see you know how Séptimo works! Later he joined everyone for a drink, and once he had Miguelín well and truly drunk he jumped on him, shaved off his mole, ripped off his trousers and threw him out onto the road. You should have seen it!

MARI-GAILA. What did Ludovina say?

ROSA LA TATULA. She couldn't stop laughing!

MARI-GAILA. Do you think there's ever been anything between her and Séptimo?

ROSA LA TATULA. There may have been.

MARI-GAILA. Well, if there was, then there probably still is.

ROSA LA TATULA. Jealous?

MARI-GAILA. I don't care what they get up to!

ROSA LA TATULA. Séptimo only has eyes for you!

MARI-GAILA. One eye you mean.

ROSA LA TATULA. The fact that he wants to talk to you proves it.

MARI-GAILA. I'm just one of the many! . . .

ROSA LA TATULA. Is that your answer?

MARI-GAILA. I've not given you an answer yet.

ROSA LA TATULA. Well, that's what I'm waiting for.

MARI-GAILA. I need to think about it.

ROSA LA TATULA. The heart doesn't usually need to think twice.

MARI-GAILA. So they say . . .

ROSA LA TATULA. What shall I tell him?

MARI-GAILA. I don't want to play his games any more!

ROSA LA TATULA. You don't know what you're missing!

MARI-GAILA. A life on the road.

ROSA LA TATULA. Think of the money!

MARI-GAILA. Come rain or shine!

ROSA LA TATULA. Good food at roadside inns!

MARI-GAILA. Unnecessary problems!

ROSA LA TATULA. You'd live like a queen! Sparkling earrings and patterned stockings like these. Try them on and I'll tell him how good they look!

MARI-GAILA. Proper stockings?

ROSA LA TATULA. The best money can buy! The aristocracy call them rabbit hutches.

MARI-GAILA. How witty of them!

ROSA LA TATULA. Well, what's your answer?

MARI-GAILA. Give him my thanks.

ROSA LA TATULA. Is that all, Mari-Gaila?

MARI-GAILA. If he wants anything else, tell him to come and get it himself.

MARI-GAILA smiles thoughtfully, looking out towards the glimmering river. A caravan of Hungarians with bears and copper pots passes along the riverbank. MARI-GAILA begins singing.

MARI-GAILA.
   The messages you send I will not receive,
   Only your whispers will make me grieve.

ROSA LA TATULA. Séptimo wants to talk to you somewhere private.

MARI-GAILA. So we can say goodbye.

ROSA LA TATULA. Goodbye, only if you won't agree to anything else. Well, what do you say?

MARI-GAILA. What do you expect a woman in love to say?

ROSA LA TATULA. Will you go wherever he wants?

MARI-GAILA. I'll go!

ROSA LA TATULA. Swear it?

MARI-GAILA. I swear it.

ROSA LA TATULA. Give me a quick drink before I go off and tell him.

MARI-GAILA. Let's go in.

ROSA LA TATULA. Wait!

The old woman grabs MARI-GAILA by the arm. Two CIVIL GUARDS cross the road with a man in handcuffs. The two women watch in amazement from beneath the fig-tree, recognizing THE PILGRIM with the grey beard and stone pillow.

MARI-GAILA. They always pick on those least able to defend themselves!

ROSA LA TATULA. Don't be stupid! That's the Polish Count!

MARI-GAILA. Him! . . . I thought it was Séptimo.

ROSA LA TATULA. Séptimo keeps to his puppets.

MARI-GAILA. He's a crafty bastard!

ROSA LA TATULA. You've got to admire him!

MARI-GAILA. That's why I hate him!

Scene Three

San Clemente. The Romanesque church with its golden stones and the churchyard filled with greenery. Peace and fragrant breezes. The sun casts its early morning rays on the emerald river. SÉPTIMO MIAU is sitting on a wall in the churchyard. SIMONIÑA, kneeling by the cart in the shadows of the portico, is begging for money to pay for THE IDIOT'*s funeral. The grotesque waxen head of* THE IDIOT, *adorned with a crown of camellias, stands out against the white pillow. The rigid rotting corpse is covered in a blue shroud decorated with gold stars. On* LAUREANO'*s stomach, swollen like that of a pregnant woman, lies a pewter dish filled with copper coins. At the very top of this pile of black coins lies a shiny peseta.*

SÉPTIMO MIAU. Well, how's it going? Collected much money?

SIMONIÑA. A little!

SÉPTIMO MIAU. I don't think you realize what a goldmine you're burying!

SIMONIÑA. And I suppose you're the only one who does!

SÉPTIMO MIAU. Freaks are delicate commodities you know, they have to be handled with care.

SIMONIÑA. We were careful with him!

SÉPTIMO MIAU. Not careful enough! I don't see a cloth or painting here which will catch the eye. A freak like that could have been taken to the best fairs in Madrid!

SIMONIÑA. That's the kind of talk that sent my mother onto the streets!

SÉPTIMO MIAU. Your mother knows what she wants.

SIMONIÑA. Although you may not believe it.

SÉPTIMO MIAU. There's no need to get so worked up about it. If she'd have come to some arrangement with me she could have left all this misery behind.

SIMONIÑA. My mother's got her reputation to think of! She doesn't want to get involved with you.

SÉPTIMO MIAU. It would all have been legal and above board.

SIMONIÑA. Whoring? Legal?

SÉPTIMO MIAU. I'm talking about a simple understanding between two people who get together to make a living. All above board. I would have hired the cart and given her a good price for it. With two dogs trained to pull it, there's no knowing how much we could have made!

SIMONIÑA. Well, there's no point in talking about it now!

SIMONIÑA *sighs. Getting up from the stones on which she has been kneeling, she shoos away the flies that have gathered around the waxen head. A group of* PIOUS WOMEN, *with the scent of incense lingering in their mantillas, leave the church.*

SIMONIÑA. A little something for the burial!

AN OLD WOMAN. What a stench!

ANTHER OLD WOMAN. He's rotting!

BENITA THE SEAMSTRESS. When are you going to bury him?

SIMONIÑA. When we've collected enough money.

BENITA THE SEAMSTRESS. Just look at the stitching on the shroud! It hasn't even been tacked properly!

SIMONIÑA. It's good enough for the maggots.

BENITA THE SEAMSTRESS. Who made it?

SIMONIÑA. My mother.

BENITA THE SEAMSTRESS. It's not particularly well sewn!

SIMONIÑA. She's not a seamstress.

BENITA THE SEAMSTRESS. Couldn't she find any better thread for the braid?

SIMONIÑA. Why don't you stop finding faults with everything and just give me a coin.

BENITA THE SEAMSTRESS. I don't have one.

SIMONIÑA. Doesn't your needlework bring much money in?

BENITA THE SEAMSTRESS. Enough to live decently and don't you forget it.

SIMONIÑA. That won't stop people talking.

BENITA THE SEAMSTRESS. Maybe not but my reputation's intact.

SIMONIÑA. You long to be rich.

BENITA THE SEAMSTRESS. I may not be as well off as you but I'm respectable!

SIMONIÑA. You're obsessed with respectability!

BENITA THE SEAMSTRESS. It's what I hold in most esteem!

SIMONIÑA. Unfortunately!

BENITA THE SEAMSTRESS. What do you mean?

SIMONIÑA. Well, it's easy to be respectable while . . .

BENITA THE SEAMSTRESS. Holy Father! Is that the way for a child to talk!

SIMONIÑA. As I don't mix with the high and mighty, I don't know how ladies are expected to behave!

BENITA THE SEAMSTRESS. I'm going! I can't bring myself to listen anymore!

SIMONIÑA. But you've not given a thing!

BENITA THE SEAMSTRESS. And I don't intend to.

SIMONIÑA. Well, it's a good thing that we don't have to rely on you for charity!

PEDRO GAILO, *dressed in his cassock and surplice, appears at the door of the church. There is a strong smell of extinguished altar candles in the air. Golden rays of sunlight shine through the arched door into the shadows.*

PEDRO GAILO. Damn your gossiping!

SIMONIÑA. They talk to me, I reply.

PEDRO GAILO. You women are all the same.

SÉPTIMO MIAU. Whatever you say about women my friend, no party's complete without them! You shouldn't complain, because you've got one hell of a wife. We met on the way to a fair once and I couldn't help noticing her many talents. She had quite an ability for conning punters into parting with their money.

SIMONIÑA. Just listen to the way they all talk about mother. How can you be so stupid as to talk of killing her!

PEDRO GAILO. Shut your mouth, Simoniña!

SIMONIÑA. You just carry on believing all the malicious rumours you hear.

COIMBRA *jumps up on her hind legs and wags her tail as she dances around* THE SEXTON, *who watches her sullenly.* COIMBRA *irreverently sniffs the cassock and sneezes in a manner which resembles an old woman coughing.*

SÉPTIMO MIAU. Spit it out, Coimbra!

PEDRO GAILO. Damn you!

SÉPTIMO MIAU. Why don't you take her paw, my friend?

PEDRO GAILO. I know what you're up to!

SÉPTIMO MIAU. Do tell me, what are we up to?

PEDRO GAILO. The Devil's work!

SÉPTIMO MIAU. We live in a slanderous world, Coimbra.

SIMONIÑA. Oh! I suppose it was good deeds that left you half-blind!

SÉPTIMO MIAU. Is that what you believe, young lady?

SIMONIÑA. I believe in God.

SÉPTIMO MIAU *spits out his cigar butt, lifts his eye patch with his fingers and displays the eye which usually remains covered. He winks and then hides it again behind the eye patch.*

SÉPTIMO MIAU. There! Now you know I'm not a marked man!

SIMONIÑA. There must be some nasty reason why you keep it covered.

SÉPTIMO MIAU. Because it sees too much. It sees so much that it burns, therefore I have to keep it covered. It sees through walls and good intentions!

SIMONIÑA. Holy Mary! Only witches see as much as that.

PEDRO GAILO. Satan was expelled from the kingdom of God because he wanted to see too much.

SÉPTIMO MIAU. Satan rebelled because he wanted to know.

PEDRO GAILO. Seeing and knowing are both fruits of the same tree. The Devil wanted to keep an eye on eternity, he wanted to understand both the past and the future.

SÉPTIMO MIAU. And in the end, he got what he wanted.

PEDRO GAILO. He wanted to be as powerful as God but he went blind waiting for the time that never comes. Had he looked three times he could have been God!

SÉPTIMO MIAU. You're a very wise man, my friend.

PEDRO GAILO. I read a lot.

SÉPTIMO MIAU. We all should.

A dark, hunched, old woman can be seen approaching along the path through the cornfields. MIAU *leaves the churchyard whistling with* COIMBRA *at his side. He joins* ROSA LA TATULA *at the gate.*

SÉPTIMO MIAU. Did you talk to her?

ROSA LA TATULA. I told her I'd be back.

SÉPTIMO MIAU. How was she?

ROSA LA TATULA. She's crazy about you. I don't think she realizes how certain men treat their women!

SÉPTIMO MIAU. Maybe I will walk out on her one day, but then again, she may well walk out on me. At least she'll have seen something of the world!

ROSA LA TATULA. And suffered!

SÉPTIMO MIAU. Do you think she'll change her mind?

ROSA LA TATULA. The Devil looks after his own.

SÉPTIMO MIAU. She's one hell of a woman.

ROSA LA TATULA. Now, take the daughter. Twenty, but not an inch on her mother!

SÉPTIMO MIAU. Her mother's got a certain something.

ROSA LA TATULA. Despite everything, she still manages to keep the firm body and energetic passion of a young girl!

SÉPTIMO MIAU. I'm getting excited, Tatula!

ROSA LA TATULA. What a rogue!

SÉPTIMO MIAU. When did you arrange to see her next?

ROSA LA TATULA. When you decide on a place to meet.

SÉPTIMO MIAU. I don't know these parts very well. Is there a cane field around here?

ROSA LA TATULA. We all know what you're after!

The old woman scratches her grey mass of hair and gives him a toothless grin. SÉPTIMO MIAU *removes his eye patch and gazes across the green fields.*

Scene Four
*The sacred river of Roman history is emerald green, glimmering
with dream-like ripples. Copper-coloured cattle are drinking along
the bank. Young girls as fresh as summer cherries and old women
– their ochre colouring reminiscent of the figures in medieval
altar paintings – are bleaching their linen in the sun. The drowsy
afternoon produces an intense, resonant silence. MIGUELÍN EL
PADRONÉS silently peers over a hedge. He winks mischievously
and waves his arms to beckon over the various groups of people.
Distant voices are heard approaching.*

A GIRL. What is it, Padronés?

ANOTHER GIRL. Tell us your secret, fart-face.

MIGUELÍN. Come over here and take a look. This shouldn't
be missed!

A GIRL. What is it?

MIGUELÍN. A nest of lovebirds.

*The great patriarch, SERENÍN DE BRETAL, sowing wheat
with his sons and grandsons, tilts his cap to one side like an old
lawyer.*

SERENÍN DE BRETAL. Well! Well! Well, you scoundrel! So
that's the mystery! A couple fornicating!

THE VOICES OF YOUNG MEN AND WOMEN. Jujurujú!
Let's go and take a look!

A GIRL. You're a devil, Padronés!

*High up, on a piece of rocky ground covered in heather, the
silhouette of a shepherd, QUINTÍN PINTADO, can be seen.
He carries a sling and has a black greyhound by his side.*

QUINTÍN PINTADO. If you're lying Padronés, you'll need to
run faster than those legs will carry you. Because it'll be you
I'll be aiming at!

AN OLD WOMAN. Another devil!

QUINTÍN PINTADO. Where's the ceremony?

MIGUELÍN. In the brushwood.

QUINTÍN PINTADO. Jujurujú! Let's go and take a look.

MIGUELÍN. Send the greyhound after them!

QUINTÍN PINTADO. A royal hunt.

A VOICE. He's escaping.

ANOTHER VOICE. After him!

QUINTÍN PINTADO. There's no greyhound fast enough for
   that one.

A GIRL. Let him go. Men can do what they want. It's women
   who have to watch their reputations.

THE VOICES OF YOUNG MEN AND WOMEN. Jujurujú!
   It's the woman we want.

   *Young and old alike leave their work in the fields and come
   running over the fences. Those who are most daring cut across
   the green canefields at the edge of the river, bringing excited dogs
   with them. Some of the younger girls smile somewhat ashamedly.
   The eyes of the older women burn with anger.* MARI-GAILA *can
   be heard screaming as she runs out into the road, her skirt gripped
   by the dogs.*

A VOICE. Who was she fornicating with?

ANOTHER VOICE. The puppeteer!

MARI-GAILA. What do you think you're doing! You stupid
   bastards! . . .

A VOICE. Whore!

ANOTHER VOICE. We'll have you dancing in your petticoats!

AN OLD WOMAN. You're an insult to decent women!

A CHORUS OF VOICES. Make her dance in her petticoats! In
   her petticoats! In her petticoats!

MARI-GAILA. I hope it blinds you! Bastards! Bastards!
   Bastards!

MARI-GAILA, *pursued by the men and dogs, runs along the riverbank. She attempts to hold up her tattered skirt in an effort to prevent her white legs being seen.* MILÓN DE LA ARNOYA, *a ruddy, well-built farmer who is bringing his cart along the path, blocks her way. He emits a loud cry of satisfaction.* MARI-GAILA *stops and picks up a rock.*

MILÓN DE LA ARNOYA. Jujurujú!

MARI-GAILA. If anyone dares come near me, I'll give them this!

MILÓN DE LA ARNOYA. Drop that rock!

MARI-GAILA. I'll use it in self-defence!

MILÓN DE LA ARNOYA. Drop it!

MARI-GAILA. Don't come near me, Milón!

The brutish figure of MILÓN DE LA ARNOYA *leaps forward, shouting wildly. The rock hits him on the chest.* MARI-GAILA, *her eyes blazing, reaches for another, but the ruddy giant grabs her firmly.*

MILÓN DE LA ARNOYA. Jujurujú! She's mine!

A VOICE. Milón's got hold of her!

MARI-GAILA. Let me go, Milón! Ask me nicely and you can have it. Just let me go!

MILÓN DE LA ARNOYA. No.

MARI-GAILA. Fool! The day will come when it could well be your wife in my position!

MILÓN DE LA ARNOYA. My wife would never even think of doing anything like that.

MARI-GAILA. It's obvious you don't know your wife very well!

MILÓN DE LA ARNOYA. Shut up, you evil-minded bitch!

MARI-GAILA. Let me go and I'll give you a night you won't forget. Let me go!

MILÓN DE LA ARNOYA. Go on! Get out of here! You've done what you set out to do!

MARI-GAILA *runs from the giant's arms. Her hair is now wild and dishevelled and her breasts are uncovered.* THE SCREAMING CHORUS OF VOICES *rises to a fevered pitch.*

A VOICE. She's getting away!

ANOTHER VOICE. Stop her!

THE CHORUS OF VOICES. After her! After her!

QUINTÍN PINTADO. Leave her to me!

QUINTÍN PINTADO *sends his greyhound after the fugitive as he prepares to shoot from his sling. Surrounded by what sounds like an army of wooden clogs,* MARI-GAILA *stops.*

MARI-GAILA. You evil souls! Bastards from Hell!

QUINTÍN PINTADO. You're going to dance in your petticoats! Show off your body!

MARI-GAILA. Don't come near me, Caiaphas!

QUINTÍN PINTADO. We want to see a few of your hidden talents!

A SCREAMING CHORUS. Jujurujú!

MARI-GAILA. Ignorant pigs! Perverts from Hell! If I miscarry because of you, I'll make sure you're all locked away!

A VOICE. We're not stupid enough to fall for a trick like that!

ANOTHER VOICE. Dance in your petticoats!

QUINTÍN PINTADO. Show us that body of yours!

MARI-GAILA. Is that what you really want, you bastards? I'll dance in my petticoats and I'll dance naked!

A SCREAMING CHORUS. Jujurujú!

MARI-GAILA. But don't even think of laying a finger on me! You can stare until your eyes fall out but I won't have anyone touch me!

A SCREAMING CHORUS. Jujurujú!

MARI-GAILA rips open her bodice. Still trembling, she steps out of her loose petticoats. A trickle of blood runs down her shoulder. Although sullen and resigned, MARI-GAILA displays her naked whiteness to the golden river with majestic grace and elegance.

MARI-GAILA. Satisfied now!

A SCREAMING CHORUS. Jujurujú!

A VOICE. Lift her onto Milón's cart.

OTHER VOICES. Onto the cart!

QUINTÍN PINTADO. Let her dance on her throne!

A SCREAMING CHORUS. Jujurujú!

The cart, a fragrant mountain of hay led by two golden oxen and the ruddy brutish giant, rolls along the riverbank like the triumphant chariot of the Bacchae.

Scene Five
San Clemente. The chuchyard is shrouded by a damp green silence; the Romanesque stones of the church appear to glitter in the golden afternoon sun, while the cornfields murmur softly. The sexton's cassock sways gently beneath the portico. Beside the cart, a chorus of rustling mantillas. Two rowdy youths knock the sexton to one side as they run into the church and climb up to the belltower. The bells begin to toll madly. PEDRO GAILO jumps up in fright and steps on his cassock, his arms wide open.

PEDRO GAILO. Is there no respect for the Lord anymore!

MARICA DEL REINO. None whatsoever!

ROSA LA TATULA. It was two boys who rushed up there! Reckless savages!

SIMONIÑA. Father, go up and give them a good hiding!

PEDRO GAILO. Dear God, what insubordination!

MARICA DEL REINO. This is what comes of a lack of abstinence!

A VOICE IN THE CORNFIELDS. Pedro Gailo, they're bringing your wife naked, on a cart, for all to see!

PEDRO GAILO *falls onto his knees and begins beating his head against a tombstone. Above him the bells continue tolling wildly, merging with the approaching sound of the rustic Bacchanalean procession. The sexton's forehead hits the stones with a tomb-like echo.*

MARICA DEL REINO. That's the end of your reputation!

PEDRO GAILO. I wish the earth would swallow me up!

ROSA LA TATULA. What happened?

THE VOICE IN THE CORNFIELDS. They found her flat on her back, only she wasn't alone!

SIMONIÑA. They're lying! It can't be true!

THE VOICE IN THE CORNFIELDS. I didn't see it!

PEDRO GAILO. Neither did anyone else who still boasts a shred of decency!

ROSA LA TATULA. Too true! People shouldn't talk about such behaviour.

PEDRO GAILO *runs into the church, tripping over his cassock. He climbs up to the belltower, his arms flapping in the narrow stairway like the wings of a trapped bird. On reaching the top, he peers out from beneath the bells. The procession is now moving towards the church. A group of excited young men dance around the cart. Above them, MARI-GAILA stands white and naked, attempting to cover herself with hay. The tall, dark sexton comes out onto the roof. Tiles crack with every step he takes.*

A VOICE. Eunuch!

THE CHORUS.
    Mari-Gaila! Mari-Gaila!
    Once danced all night!
    Mari-Gaila! Mari-Gaila!
    Now naked in the light!

PEDRO GAILO. The Blessed Sacrament commands me to

await the adulteress at the door of the church where we were married!

PEDRO GAILO *stands on the edge of the roof and jumps off. He falls head first like a plunging black bird, his arms outstretched, his cassock ripped. For a few seconds he appears dead, then suddenly he gets up and limps to the door of the church.*

A VOICE. I thought you were dead!

ANOTHER VOICE. He must have nine lives!

QUINTÍN PINTADO. Jujurujú! He's left his horns on the ground!

THE SEXTON *emerges from the portico with a lit candle in one hand and a missal in the other. He looks unusually mysterious, almost delirious. With his cap to one side and the open missal in his hand, he walks over to the cart of triumphant sexuality. As if coming to welcome him, the naked woman rushes out into the road, covering her sex. THE SEXTON extinguishes the flame over her crossed hands and then strikes them with the holy book.*

PEDRO GAILO. He that is without sin among you, let him cast the first stone!

VOICES. Stupid cuckold!

OTHER VOICES. Eunuch!

The insults continue. Stones are thrown and fists are raised. The angry comments grow louder and more violent, developing into a bloodthirsty pagan chant.

AN OLD WOMAN. How can you call yourself a man!

THE SEXTON *turns away magnaminously. Squinting at the open missal, he begins reciting the following divine words in Latin.*

PEDRO GAILO. Qui sine peccato est vestrum, primus in illam lapidem mittat.

THE SEXTON *hands the extinguished candle to the naked woman and leads her by the hand along the portico and over*

*the tombstones. The Latin words work a miracle! A profoundly
religious emotion moves the crowd's consciences and calms
the savage rage previously witnessed on their faces. These old
childlike souls breathe an air of eternal life. They all either slip
away or advise restraint. The liturgical spirit of the Latin words
has descended from the miraculous heavens.*

SERENÍN DE BRETAL. Let's stop this and get out of here!

QUINTÍN PINTADO. I really should get back to my cattle.

MILÓN DE LA ARNOYA. What if there's trouble with
the law?

SERENÍN DE BRETAL. There won't be.

MILÓN DE LA ARNOYA. But supposing there is?

SERENÍN DE BRETAL. Then keep your mouth shut and
hope for the best!

*The golden sunset envelops the churchyard. MARI-GAILA,
now serenely naked, walks barefoot over the tombstones, sensing
the rhythm of life beneath a vale of tears. As she moves into the
shadow of the portico, the grotesque head of* THE IDIOT, *crowned
with camellias, appears to her the head of an angel. Led by her
husband, the adulteress takes refuge in the church, a sanctuary
of exquisite religious prestige which, in that superstitious and
miraculous world of rustic souls is conjured by the mysterious and
incomprehensible Latin of the DIVINE WORDS.*

End of play

Bohemian Lights

Esperpento

Workshop readings from this translation of *Bohemian Lights* were presented at the ICA, London by The European Stage Company on 23 March 1992, with the following cast:

MÁXIMO ESTRELLA	Donald Sumpter
DON LATINO OF HISPALIS	Nicholas le Prevost
A PRISONER	Stevan Rimkus
A JAILER	Tim Sable
Directed by	Lluís Pasqual

Characters

MAX ESTRELLA
His wife MADAME COLLET
and his daughter CLAUDINITA
DON LATINO OF HISPALIS
ZARATHUSTRA
DON GAY
A YOUNG BOY WITH A CREW CUT
THE CONCIERGE'S LITTLE GIRL
TIGHT ARSE (VENANCIO)
A YOUNG BARMAN (CRISPÍN)
ENRIQUETA THE STREET WALKER
THE KING OF PORTUGUESE PIMPS (GORITO)
A DRUNKARD (ZACARÍAS)
The Young Modernistas – DORIO DE GADEX
                          RAFAEL DE LOS VÉLEZ
                          LUCIO VERO
                          MÍNGUEZ
                          GÁLVEZ
                          CLARINITO
                          PÉREZ
CAPTAIN PITITO, of the mounted police patrol
A NIGHT WATCHMAN
THE VOICE OF A NEIGHBOUR
TWO POLICEMEN
SLICK-BACK SERAFÍN
A JAILER
A PRISONER
THE PORTER OF A NEWSPAPER OFFICE
DON FILIBERTO, the Editor-in-Chief of the *Popular Paper*
THE HOME SECRETARY (PACO)
DIEGUITO, His Secretary
A SECURITY ATTENDANT (FERNÁNDEZ)
AN OLD HEAVILY MADE UP TART
and THE MOLE
AN UNKNOWN YOUNG MAN
THE MOTHER OF THE DEAD CHILD (ROMUALDA)
THE PAWNBROKER
THE POLICEMAN

THE CONCIERGE
A BRICKLAYER
AN OLD WOMAN
THE RAGWOMAN
THE RETIRED OFFICER
LOCAL INHABITANTS
SEÑORA FLORA THE CONCIERGE
CUCA THE NEIGHBOUR
BASILIO SOULINAKE
A FUNERAL SERVICE COACHMAN
TWO GRAVEDIGGERS
RUBÉN DARÍO
THE MARQUIS OF BRADOMÍN
PAY PAY THE POSER
PACONA, an old newspaper seller
CROWDS
POLICE
DOGS
CATS
A PARROT

The action takes place in an absurd, brilliant and hungry
Madrid.

Scene One

Dusk. An attic with a small, narrow, sunlit window. Portraits, engravings and autographs are scattered along the walls, held in place by drawing pins. Lifeless conversation between a blind man and a tired, sad, fair-haired woman. The blind man is a mannered Andalusian, a poet of odes and madrigals, MÁXIMO ESTRELLA. As the woman is French she is known in the community as MADAME COLLET.

MAX. Read me Buey Apis's letter again.

MADAME COLLET. Be patient, Max.

MAX. He could have waited until I was dead and buried.

MADAME COLLET. He'll go long before you do.

MAX. Collet, it's going to be hard for us without my regular income from journalism! How else am I expected to earn a meagre living, Collet?

MADAME COLLET. Another door will open.

MAX. Death's. We could commit collective suicide.

MADAME COLLET. Death doesn't frighten me. But we do have a daughter to consider, Max!

MAX. And what if Claudinita agrees to my collective suicide plan?

MADAME COLLET. She's too young!

MAX. Young people have also been known to commit suicide, Collet.

MADAME COLLET. Not because they're sick of life. Young people die for romantic reasons.

MAX. In other words, they kill themselves for loving life too much. It's a shame about Claudinita. With a peseta worth of coal we could set sail for eternity.

MADAME COLLET. Don't give up. Another door will open.

MAX. Name me one newspaper which would be prepared to employ a blind man?

MADAME COLLET. You could write a novel.

MAX. And if I don't find a publisher?

MADAME COLLET. Oh! Don't belittle yourself, Max. Everyone recognizes your talent.

MAX. I'm a has-been! Read me Buey Apis's letter.

MADAME COLLET. You can't possibly use that letter as an example.

MAX. Read it.

MADAME COLLET. It's not an easy letter to read.

MAX. Then read it slowly.

MADAME COLLET, *her face betraying dejection and resignation, carefully reads out the letter in a low voice. Outside, the sound of furious sweeping can be heard. The doorbell rings.*

MADAME COLLET. Claudinita, put down that broom and see who's at the door.

THE VOICE OF CLAUDINITA. It's always Don Latino.

MADAME COLLET. God help us!

THE VOICE OF CLAUDINITA. Should I slam the door in his face?

MADAME COLLET. He amuses your father.

THE VOICE OF CLAUDINITA. You can smell the brandy from here!

MÁXIMO ESTRELLA *sits up in a spirited manner, his full grey-flecked beard spread out across his chest. His blind head, framed in curls, has a classically archaic feel, recalling known statues of Hermes.*

MAX. Wait, Collet! I've recovered my sight! I can see! Oh,

how I see! Wonderfully! Moncloa looks beautiful! The only corner of France in this bleak plateau we call Madrid! We must return to Paris, Collet! We must! We must relive those times!

MADAME COLLET. You're hallucinating, Max.

MAX. I can see, I can see clearly!

MADAME COLLET. But what do you see?

MAX. The world!

MADAME COLLET. Can you see me?

MAX. I have no need to see the things I can touch!

MADAME COLLET. Sit down. Let me close the window. Try to get some sleep.

MAX. I can't!

MADAME COLLET. Your poor head!

MAX. I'm dead! It's night again.

He leans back into the armchair. The woman closes the window, and the attic is plunged into shadow, lit by a single shaft of setting sunlight. The blind man begins to sleep while the woman, a sad spectral figure, sits in a chair folding up Buey Apis's letter. A cautious hand pushes the door which opens with a seemingly endless creak. An asthmatic bespectacled old man enters, wearing a peaked cap, leading a small dog and carrying a briefcase filled with illustrated magazines. It is DON LATINO OF HISPALIS. *Behind him stands a young girl with unkempt hair, dressed in a tattered skirt and slippers:* CLAUDINITA.

DON LATINO. And how is our genius feeling today?

CLAUDINITA. He's waiting for the money from a couple of books which some swine had agreed to sell for him.

DON LATINO. Child, can you not draw on a somewhat more select vocabulary to describe this intimate friend of your father's, this great man who calls me brother? What language, Claudinita!

MADAME COLLET. Have you brought the money, Don Latino?

DON LATINO. Madame Collet, this is most unlike you. You have always shown such intelligence and understanding over these matters. Max has already disposed of the money in an irreproachable manner.

MADAME COLLET. It can't be possible. Is this true, Max?

DON LATINO. I pray, do not wake him from the arms of Morpheus!

CLAUDINITA. Father, what do you have to say about all this?

MAX. You can all go to Hell!

MADAME COLLET. Well my dear, your generosity has left us yet again with no supper!

MAX. Latino, you're such a cynic.

CLAUDINITA. Don Latino, pay up or you won't know what's hit you.

DON LATINO. You should get those claws trimmed, Claudinita.

CLAUDINITA. I'll scratch your eyes out.

DON LATINO. Claudinita!

CLAUDINITA. Sponger!

DON LATINO. Do something, Max.

MAX. How much did you get for the books, Latino?

DON LATINO. Three pesetas, Max! Three measly pesetas! It doesn't bear thinking about! I was cheated!

CLAUDINITA. You shouldn't have sold them!

DON LATINO. I couldn't agree with you more, Claudinita. They took me for a fool. But we can still do something about it.

MADAME COLLET. Fat chance!

DON LATINO. Max, if you follow me back to that charlatan bookseller and we create something of a disturbance, you might be able to get another ten pesetas out of him. You're better at these kind of things.

MAX. We'd have to return the money he gave us.

DON LATINO. A few empty gestures should suffice. Here Maestro, one relies on the art of rhetoric.

MAX. Do you really think so?

DON LATINO. But of course!

MADAME COLLET. Max, you shouldn't go out.

MAX. The fresh air will help wake me up. The heat's unbearable in here.

DON LATINO. It's certainly cooler outside.

MADAME COLLET. Max, you'll get into a terrible fight with nothing to show for it!

CLAUDINITA. Father, please don't leave!

MADAME COLLET. Max, I'll find something or other we can pawn.

MAX. It's daylight robbery and I won't put up with it. Latino, where did you take the books?

DON LATINO. To Zarathustra's.

MAX. Claudinita, fetch my hat and walking stick!

CLAUDINITA. Should I, mother?

MADAME COLLET. Let him have them!

DON LATINO. Madame Collet, we'll put up a fight, you'll see.

CLAUDINITA. Sponger!

DON LATINO. I find your dulcet tones quite overpowering, Claudinita!

MÁXIMO ESTRELLA *leaves, leaning on the shoulder of* DON LATINO. MADAME COLLET *gives a sigh of exhaustion while her daughter nervously removes the pins from her hair.*

CLAUDINITA. Well, I hope you realize where all this will end: somewhere in Tight Arse's tavern.

Scene Two
ZARATHUSTRA's *cave-like bookshop along Calle Consegos. Randomly stacked piles of books litter the floor and cover the walls. Four sordid illustrations from a serialized story are pasted over the glass plates of a door. In the 'cave' the cat, the parrot, the dog and the bookseller are having a literary gathering. The repellent puppet-like* ZARATHUSTRA, *a hunched figure with a face reminiscent of rancid bacon and with a green, serpent-like scarf wrapped around his neck, is at once sharply distant and painfully immediate. Enveloped in the torn stuffing of a tiny chair, his feet buried in rags and wrapped like vines around the brazier stand, he minds the shop. A mouse sticks his prying snout through a hole.*

ZARATHUSTRA. Don't think I can't see you, thief!

THE CAT. Meow! Meow!

THE DOG. Woof! Woof!

THE PARROT. Long live Spain!

MAX ESTRELLA *and* DON LATINO OF HISPALIS *are at the door. The poet removes his arm from the folds of his cloak and raises it majestically, in perfect coordination with his classical blind head.*

MAX. Is this, Poland, the way to greet a stranger?

ZARATHUSTRA. What do you want?

MAX. Now that's over with, I'd like to make it perfectly clear that I don't like the way you do business.

ZARATHUSTRA. It's nothing to do with you.

MAX. True, but you have dealt with my associate Don Latino of Hispalis.

ZARATHUSTRA. What's he complaining about? There was nothing wrong with the money he got from me!

DON LATINO *interrupts like a cowardly dog barking between his master's legs.*

DON LATINO. The Maestro isn't happy with the agreed amount. He wants the arrangement severed.

ZARATHUSTRA. Too late for that now. A moment ago it would still have been possible . . . but not any more. I just sold the bundle intact, made a couple of pesetas. The buyer left just as you came in.

Whilst saying all this, the bookseller removes the bundle of books which are still lying on the counter and carries them to a murky backroom signalling to DON LATINO as he does so. He reappears.

DON LATINO. A wasted journey, Maestro. This one doesn't miss a trick.

MAX. Zarathustra, you're a thief.

ZARATHUSTRA. Such insults hardly befit a poet, Don Max.

MAX. I'm going to crack your head open.

ZARATHUSTRA. Don Max, remember who you are.

MAX. Imbecile!

A tall, lean, sunburnt man has entered the 'cave'. He is dressed in a rough linen suit with canvas sandals and a flat cap. He is the eccentric DON PILGRIM GAY, a writer who has produced a chronicle of his wandering life in old-fashioned but lively Spanish, under the pseudonym of DON GAY PILGRIM. He politely greets everyone without coming further than the door.

DON GAY. Salutem plurimam!

ZARATHUSTRA. How were your travels, Don Gay?

DON GAY. Excellent.

DON LATINO. Where have you been?

DON GAY. I've just returned from London.

MAX. You've come all the way from London so that
Zarathustra can skin you alive?

DON GAY. Zarathustra is a good friend.

ZARATHUSTRA. Were you able to do all the work you
wanted?

DON GAY. Every last bit of it. My dear friends, in the British
Museum during these past two months I have succeeded
in copying by hand the only known print of *The Knight
Palmerin of Constantinople*.

MAX. Were you really in London?

DON GAY. I spent two months there.

DON LATINO. And how was the Royal Family?

DON GAY. I didn't spot them at the quay as I was leaving.
Maestro, are you acquainted with London, the contemporary
Babylon?

MAX. I am, Don Gay.

ZARATHUSTRA *moves to and from the backroom carrying a
burning candle. The greasy candlestick trembles in the puppet's
hands. He walks silently, his steps muted by the rags which are
wrapped around his feet. His hand, enclosed in a black mitten,
waves the candle over the bookshelves. Only half of his face can
be seen: the rest remains in shadow, giving the appearance that
his nose is folded over one ear. The parrot tucks his beak under
a wing. A group of armed policemen pass by with a man in
handcuffs. A YOUNG BOY WITH A CREW CUT, waving a
flag, rides past on a stick, causing something of a disturbance.*

THE BOY. Long live Spain!

THE DOG. Woof! Woof!

ZARATHUSTRA. A fine state Spain's in!

*The three visitors, sad visionaries standing in front of the counter
like three birds perched on a branch, temporarily put their
troubles aside as they discuss literary matters. They ramble on,
indifferent to the group of policemen, the cries of the boy with
the crew cut, the howls of the dog, and the barrage of complaints
from the puppet whose business it is to exploit them. These are
intellectuals, without a penny between them.*

DON GAY. One shouldn't be afraid to admit it. There's no
country to compare with England. There, religious sensibility
is expressed with such dignity and decorum that the families
held in most esteem are indisputably the most religious.
If Spain were capable of such religious standards, she'd
be saved.

MAX. We'll pray for her! Here, the real puritans are the
demagogues of the extreme Left. Perhaps, they're the new
breed of Christians, although they don't yet realize it.

DON GAY. My dear gentlemen, in England I found myself
a convert to the iconoclastic faith, to a true Christianity of
prayers and hymns, free from the perverse worship of illusory
relics. And to see the idolatry of this land!

MAX. When it comes to religion Spain is like an African tribe.

DON GAY. Maestro, we must reshape our idea of religion,
using as our focus the idea of God as Man. Our Christian
revolution must have its birth in the rhetoric of the Gospels.

DON LATINO. A greater rhetoric than Lenin's.

ZARATHUSTRA. Without religion, business transactions
could never be trusted.

DON GAY. Maestro, we must establish the Independent
Church of Spain.

MAX. With our Vatican city in El Escorial.

DON GAY. Perfect!

MAX. An infallible fortress.

DON LATINO. You will end your days lecturing in
Theosophy.

MAX. We must resurrect Christ the King.

DON GAY. In all my travels across the globe I have found that
great nations only emerge when there is a national church at
their side. Political development is worthless if it is deprived
of a religious conscience, one with a guiding ethic superior to
man-made laws.

MAX. I agree, illustrious Don Gay. The misery and great
moral affliction of the Spanish people resides in the lack
of sensibility with which they face the great enigmas of life
and death. For them, Life is a watery stew: Death, an ugly
old hag masked in a sheet who smiles obscenely: Hell, a
simmering cauldron filled with boiling oil where sinners are
fried like anchovies: Heaven, a scandal-free bazaar where,
with the prior permission of the priest, virtuous young virgins
may give assistance. This despicable country transforms
every elevated concept into the type of fairytale told by
sanctimonious seamstresses. Its religion successfully reduced
to the puerile chatter of senile biddies who dissect the cat
when it dies on them.

ZARATHUSTRA. And what can you tell us about these butch
viragos known as suffragettes?

DON GAY. You can't really categorize all of them as butch
viragos. Distinguished friends, do you know how much it
cost me to live in London? Three pence, which doesn't even
come to forty centimos. A pittance! And I lived like a Lord,
here you couldn't even live like that for three pesetas.

DON LATINO. Max, let's go and die in England. Don Gay,
give me the address of this grand hotel.

DON GAY. Saint James's Square. Don't you know it?
The Queen Elizabeth Guest House. Most reputable. As I
mentioned before, there's no comparison with what you can
get here for twice the price. In the morning they give you

tea with milk and bread with real butter. Sugar is a little scarce. But for dinner there's a meat casserole, sometimes even herrings. Cheese, tea. . . . Most days I'd ask for a glass of beer which was ten centimos. Everything was very clean, with soap and hot water in the washroom at no extra cost.

ZARATHUSTRA. It is true that the English like to wash a lot. I've noticed it myself. Every now and then one or two of them drop in here and they always look very scrubbed. People from other countries don't tend to feel the cold the way we Spaniards do.

DON LATINO. I couldn't agree with you more. I'm moving to England. Why ever did you leave that paradise, Don Gay?

DON GAY. I need the Spanish sun. It's my rheumatism, you see.

ZARATHUSTRA. Our sun is the envy of all foreigners.

MAX. What would happen to this land of ours if it clouded over? What would we Spaniards become? Perhaps a little sadder and somewhat less fiery. . . . Perhaps a trifle sillier, although I'm not so sure.

THE CONCIERGE'S LITTLE GIRL *peeps through the main door. Her hair is tied back in pigtails, her stockings have fallen down to her ankles and she has a hungry look about her.*

THE LITTLE GIRL. Do you know if the latest instalment of *The Dead Woman's Son* has come out yet?

ZARATHUSTRA. It's being distributed.

THE LITTLE GIRL. Do you know whether Alfred marries at the end?

DON GAY. And why do you want to know, sweetie?

THE LITTLE GIRL. I don't give a shit either way. It's Señorita Loreta, the Colonel's wife, who's asking.

ZARATHUSTRA. Well child, you can tell that lady from me that what the characters in the novel choose to do is their secret, especially when it's a question of weddings and deaths.

MAX. Be careful Zarathustra, you may be forced by Royal Decree to tell all.

ZARATHUSTRA. What would be the point in having the novel if everyone went around telling each other the plot.

THE LITTLE GIRL *runs out, jumping over puddles with her matchstick legs.* THE VISIONARY PILGRIM *is in a corner chatting to* ZARATHUSTRA. MÁXIMO ESTRELLA *and* DON LATINO OF HISPALIS *leave in the direction of* TIGHT ARSE's *tavern on Calle Montera.*

Scene Three
TIGHT ARSE's *tavern: gaslight; a zinc-topped counter; a dark lounge filled with tables and benches; card-players and whispered conversations.* MÁXIMO ESTRELLA *and* DON LATINO OF HISPALIS, *shadows in a dark corner of the room, toast each other with glasses of wine.*

THE YOUNG BARMAN. Don Max, Her Ladyship the Tango Tart was here looking for you.

A DRUNKARD. Ugh!

MAX. I don't know who you mean.

THE YOUNG BARMAN. Enriqueta the Street Walker.

DON LATINO. And since when does that tart go around with a title?

THE YOUNG BARMAN. Ever since she inherited the estate of her late father – who, God rest his soul, is still alive and well.

DON LATINO. Very funny!

MAX. Did she say whether she'd be back?

THE YOUNG BARMAN. She walked in, looked around,

asked for you, and then turned and bounced out again, licking her lips as she went. Talk of the Devil! Look, over there by the door!

ENRIQUETA THE STREET WALKER, *a youngish tart with a squint in one eye, known also as a newspaper and flower seller, lifts a patterned green scarf over her dark head adorned with gypsy combs.*

ENRIQUETA THE STREET WALKER. Lilies! Lilies! Don Max, I've got a message for you from my mother. She's ill and needs the money you owe her for the lottery ticket.

MAX. Give her back the lottery ticket and tell her to go to Hell.

ENRIQUETA THE STREET WALKER. Thank you most kindly, Sir. Is there anything else?

The blind man takes out a rather worn wallet. Flicking vaguely through its contents, he pulls out the lottery ticket and promptly throws it on the table. It lies unfolded between the wine glasses, its number clearly discernible beneath the flickering blue gaslight. ENRIQUETA THE STREET WALKER *wastes no time in reaching out for it.*

DON LATINO. This one is a winner!

ENRIQUETA THE STREET WALKER. Don Max despises money.

THE YOUNG BARMAN. Don't let her escape, Don Max.

MAX. I'll do what I want, boy. Go and ask the boss for the box of cigars.

THE YOUNG BARMAN. It's a lucky number, Don Max, symmetrical sevens and fives.

ENRIQUETA THE STREET WALKER. It's a definite prizewinner, there's no doubt about it! But you've got to cough up three pesetas and this gentleman's staying mum. My good man, I take my leave. If you want a lily, it's on the house.

MAX. Hold on a minute.

ENRIQUETA THE STREET WALKER. There's a doddering widower pining for me.

MAX. Let him pine a little longer. Boy, go and pawn this cloak for me.

ENRIQUETA THE STREET WALKER. They'll not give you a thing for that old bundle of rags. Ask Tight Arse for three pesetas.

THE YOUNG BARMAN. Give him a verse or two and he'll slip you the money. He thinks you're the new Castelar.

MAX. Fold up the cloak and get out of here.

THE YOUNG BARMAN. How much should I ask for it?

MAX. Take whatever they offer.

ENRIQUETA THE STREET WALKER. They won't want it.

DON LATINO. Shut up, you silly cow.

MAX. Go on boy, as quick as you can.

THE YOUNG BARMAN. On, on, on, on, on! To the breach; to the breach, Don Max!

MAX. You know your classics.

ENRIQUETA THE STREET WALKER. If they're reluctant to accept the cloak tell them it belongs to a poet.

DON LATINO. The Poet Laureate of Spain.

THE DRUNKARD. An exclusive mind!

MAX. I've never had any real talent. Mine's been an absurd existence!

DON LATINO. What you lack is the talent of knowing how to live.

MAX. If I die tomorrow my wife and daughter will be left relying on pennies from heaven.

*He gives a hollow cough, his beard shaking. His feverish eyes
look sad and glazed, betraying an excess of alcohol.*

DON LATINO. You shouldn't have pawned the cloak.

ENRIQUETA THE STREET WALKER. He's taking his
time. Anyway, are you buying, Don Max?

MAX. Order whatever you please, Your Ladyship.

ENRIQUETA THE STREET WALKER. I'll have a Rute
brandy.

DON LATINO. A classy drink.

ENRIQUETA THE STREET WALKER. As befits the lowly
wife of the King of Portuguese Pimps. Don Max, I can't
hang around any longer. My husband is outside trying to
catch my attention.

MAX. Tell him to come in.

*A lean, dirty tramp, known also as a newspaper seller, walks
in through the door, a wide smile distorting his pox-scarred face.
Like a dog who is trying to rid itself of fleas, he begins maniacally
shaking his shoulders. He is* THE KING OF PORTUGUESE
PIMPS, *the roguish accomplice of Her Ladyship* ENRIQUETA
THE STREET WALKER.

ENRIQUETA THE STREET WALKER. Manolo, come on
in!

THE KING OF PORTUGUESE PIMPS. Get out here.

ENRIQUETA THE STREET WALKER. Why? Scared of
losing your crown? Enter incognito, you great big dick!

THE KING OF PORTUGUESE PIMPS. Enriqueta, you're
asking for a good kick up the arse.

ENRIQUETA THE STREET WALKER. I'd like to see
you try it!

THE KING OF PORTUGUESE PIMPS. She only calls me the
King of Portuguese Pimps to try and put me down! There's

no stopping that tongue of hers since she went to Lisbon and found out how to make real money. The name's Gorito, at your service gentlemen. I don't think it's right to be known by my morganatic wife's silly nickname.

ENRIQUETA THE STREET WALKER. Shut your gob, dickhead!

THE KING OF PORTUGUESE PIMPS. Are you coming?

ENRIQUETA THE STREET WALKER. Give me a chance to drink this Rute. Don Max is paying.

THE KING OF PORTUGUESE PIMPS. What are you and the poet up to?

ENRIQUETA THE STREET WALKER. A bit of business.

THE KING OF PORTUGUESE PIMPS. Well make it quick.

ENRIQUETA THE STREET WALKER. I'm waiting for Tight Arse over there to pour it out.

TIGHT ARSE. What did you just call me, slagbag?

ENRIQUETA THE STREET WALKER. Sorry sweetie!

TIGHT ARSE. The name's Venancio.

ENRIQUETA THE STREET WALKER. And a lovely name it is too! Go on, pour me a Rute. And give my husband a glass of water, he's looking a bit flushed.

MAX. Venancio, don't ever compare me to that romantic fool Castelar again. Castelar was an idiot! Another round.

DON LATINO. I'm all for Castelar and I'm all for another round.

TIGHT ARSE. You're all too dogmatic. Castelar is the pride of Spain, a great orator. You might not all be aware of this, but my father helped him get where he is today.

ENRIQUETA THE STREET WALKER. Never!

TIGHT ARSE. My father was barber to Don Manuel Camo. Huesca's pride and glory.

THE DRUNKARD. An exclusive mind!

TIGHT ARSE. Shut it, Zacarías!

THE DRUNKARD. Did I say anything offensive?

TIGHT ARSE. You might have done!

THE DRUNKARD. Well, I've had a decent education you know.

ENRIQUETA THE STREET WALKER. A product of the Sacred Brothers' School! In the same class as my father!

THE DRUNKARD. Who's your father?

ENRIQUETA THE STREET WALKER. An MP.

THE DRUNKARD. I was educated abroad.

ENRIQUETA THE STREET WALKER. Do you travel incognito? You wouldn't happen to be Prince Jaime, the Carlist pretender to the throne?

THE DRUNKARD. You've obviously seen my photo!

ENRIQUETA THE STREET WALKER. Of course! Why are you not wearing the customary flower in your lapel?

THE DRUNKARD. Why don't you stick one in there for me.

ENRIQUETA THE STREET WALKER. My pleasure, it's on the house.

THE KING OF PORTUGUESE PIMPS. I thought you were a gentleman, Zacarías! Think very carefully before you touch her! Enriqueta is my property.

ENRIQUETA THE STREET WALKER. Shut it, fuckface!

THE KING OF PORTUGUESE PIMPS. Then watch it, slagbag!

ENRIQUETA THE STREET WALKER. This is none of your business, shitface.

THE YOUNG BARMAN *rushes in, breathless and excited. He*

has a bloody hankerchief tied around his forehead. For a moment everybody is visibly moved. Their differences are temporarily forgotten as they respond unanimously to the situation.

THE YOUNG BARMAN. There's trouble on the streets!

THE KING OF PORTUGUESE PIMPS. Long live the proletariat!

THE DRUNKARD. I'll drink to that! We voted for action at the union meeting last night.

ENRIQUETA THE STREET WALKER. You must have been caught in the thick of it, Crispín!

THE YOUNG BARMAN. This was some fascist bastard from the Property Protection League trying to be clever!

TIGHT ARSE. Watch your language, boy! Even we Republicans realize that property is sacred. The Property Protection League is made up of members from every walk of life. We're talking about decent family men, so try to get your facts right for a change!

A crowd of noisy agitators runs along the centre of the street waving banners. A couple of rowdy workers dressed in simple cotton shirts, neck-scarves and espadrilles enter the bar. They are accompanied by lively women with matted, tied-back hair.

THE KING OF PORTUGUESE PIMPS. Enriqueta, my blood is boiling! If you're not feeling particularly political you can wait here.

ENRIQUETA THE STREET WALKER. Dickhead, I'd follow you to the ends of the earth. Honorary Red Cross nurse reporting for duty!

TIGHT ARSE. Drop the shutters, Crispín! Anybody on the lookout for trouble had better leave now.

THE FLOWER SELLER *and* HER PIMP *join the other customers pushing their way to the door. A* GROUP OF WORKERS *rushes past outside the tavern. The sound of metal shutters crashing down resounds through the streets.*

THE DRUNKARD. Long live the heroes of the second of May!

MAX. How much did they pay you for the cloak, boy?

THE YOUNG BARMAN. Nine pesetas!

MAX. Take what I owe you, Venancio. And you, My Ladyship, hand over the lottery ticket!

DON LATINO. The bird has flown!

MAX. Carrying off my dreams of riches! Where do you think we could find that tart?

TIGHT ARSE. She'll be out there where the action is.

THE YOUNG BARMAN. She always ends up at the Modernistas' rendezvous.

MAX. Latino, lend me your eyes so that we can go out in search of Her Ladyship the Tango Tart.

DON LATINO. Max, give me your hand.

THE DRUNKARD. An exclusive mind!

A VOICE. Death to the Property Protection League! Lynch the bastards!

Scene Four

Night. MÁXIMO ESTRELLA *and* DON LATINO OF HISPALIS *stagger arm-in-arm along a deserted, gravelled street. Broken street lamps. Closed doors and windows. A faint, flickering green glow from the street lamps. The moon high above the rooftops divides the pavement. Occasional footsteps. Epic trotting. Roman soldiers – the sound of a police patrol. Shadows of policemen. The echo of the patrol dies away. The Modernistas' rendezvous, a late night café. A ray of light from its partly opened door splits the pavement in two. The wandering philosophers* MAX *and* DON LATINO, *two drunkards who've taken leave of their senses, totter beneath the shimmering glow of the street lamps.*

MAX. Where are we?

DON LATINO. There's no sign on this street.

MAX. I keep stepping on broken glass.

DON LATINO. The honourable masses have done a very good job of destroying the city.

MAX. Where are we heading?

DON LATINO. Just follow me.

MAX. Take me home.

DON LATINO. The Modernistas' haunt is still open.

MAX. I'm tired of drinking and running around in circles.

DON LATINO. A quick coffee will cheer you up.

MAX. It's cold, Latino.

DON LATINO. The sharp night air! . . .

MAX. Lend me your coat.

DON LATINO. Poetic delirium once again!

MAX. I'm left with no cloak, no money, and no lottery ticket!

DON LATINO. We'll find that street walking tart around here.

The tart in question appears beneath a street lamp: a tawdry, unkempt figure with smudged make-up, screeching out in vulgar tones.

ENRIQUETA THE STREET WALKER. 5775! Get your lucky number here! The winner's drawn tomorrow! Up for grabs! Up for grabs! Number 5775!

DON LATINO. You've turned to advertising!

ENRIQUETA THE STREET WALKER. I'll buy you a coffee.

DON LATINO. Thank you, my dear.

ENRIQUETA THE STREET WALKER. You too, Don Max, whatever you want. Here we all are together again, three sad drop-outs! Don Max, a quick flash of my tits. It's on the house.

MAX. Give me the lottery ticket and go to Hell.

ENRIQUETA THE STREET WALKER. Don Max, tell me first whether you've got the money to pay for it in that old wallet of yours.

MAX. You're a true daughter of our Conservative Government!

ENRIQUETA THE STREET WALKER. If I had as much money as this Government, I'd be made!

DON LATINO. I'd be happy with just the interest on it!

MAX. The Revolution is as unavoidable here as in Russia.

DON LATINO. We won't live to see it!

MAX. Well then, we haven't very long left.

ENRIQUETA THE STREET WALKER. Did you get as far as Cibeles? There was quite a scene between the demonstrators and the Property Protection League. We really let them have it.

DON LATINO. All scabs deserve what's coming to them.

ENRIQUETA THE STREET WALKER. I couldn't agree with you more! When you get a free minute Don Latino, come and find me and we'll start putting the world to rights.

MAX. Pass over that winning number, Enriqueta.

ENRIQUETA THE STREET WALKER. Hand over the cash and you get the dream ticket.

MAX. You'll get the money when I get the merchandise.

ENRIQUETA THE STREET WALKER. Well, Enriqueta doesn't quite see it like that!

The door to the café opens further. From the inside, bringing with them the stale stench of cooking oil, emerge the key figures of the Modernista Parnassus, a group of second-rate writers comprising of RAFAEL DE LOS VÉLEZ, DORIO DE GADEX,

LUCIO VERO, MÍNGUEZ, GÁLVEZ, CLARINITO *and*
PÉREZ. *A number of them are tall, thin and melancholy; others
are livelier, with shining eyes and full faces. The bright, ironic,
lisping* DORIO DE GADEX *greets* MAX *in his customary
exaggerated manner.*

DORIO DE GADEX. All hail Maestro! Hail to thee, father
and masterful magician!

MAX. Good evening, Don Dorio!

DORIO DE GADEX. Maestro, have you never feared the
people's cries for freedom?

MAX. It is like the majestic roar of the sea! I am with the
people!

DORIO DE GADEX. And I am not!

MAX. Because you are an idiot!

DORIO DE GADEX. Let us be civil, Maestro! You are no
more one of the people than I am! You are a poet, and we
poets are members of the privileged classes. As Ibsen once
said, something subtle and equivocal lurks below the surface
of all art, a secret which the mob cannot see.

MAX. Don't bore me with Ibsen!

PÉREZ. I didn't know that you'd become a theatre critic,
Don Max.

DORIO DE GADEX. Shut up, Pérez!

DON LATINO. Only geniuses are permitted to speak.

MAX. I feel at one with the people. I was born to be a leader
of men, but I debased myself by perpetrating translations and
churning out verses. At least they're better than the ones you
modernistas manage to produce!

DORIO DE GADEX. Maestro, present yourself to the Spanish
Royal Academy.

MAX. Don't joke about it, idiot. I've written enough! But
our narrow-minded press boycotts my work. They detest me

for my defiance and my talent. I refuse to please everyone.
Buey Apis sacks me as if I were a servant! The Academy
of Writers pretends I don't exist! I am the primary poet
of Spain! The primary poet! The primary poet! And I am
starving! I don't feel embarrassment at having to beg for
alms! And nothing can strike me down! I am truly immortal!
I will outlive the stuffy Academy of Writers. Death to
Maura!

THE MODERNISTAS. Death to Maura! Death to Maura!
Death to Maura!

CLARINITO. Maestro, we the younger generation of writers,
will force your nomination through.

DORIO DE GADEX. Now Goofy Galdós is dead, there'll be a
place in the Academy for you.

MAX. They'd rather give it to some third-rate travel writer
than pass it on to me.

DORIO DE GADEX. Maestro, have you read *The Latest
Adventures of the Streetwise Dwarf*? A real masterpiece! We
were up till dawn yesterday singing it aloud at the Puerta del
Sol! It was the show of the season!

CLARINITO. Just imagine, even the Police arrived to
break us up!

ENRIQUETA THE STREET WALKER. It was better than
seeing the best bullfighter in action!

DON LATINO. You should offer the Maestro an audition.

DORIO DE GADEX. Don Latino, don't say another word.

PÉREZ. I hope you too will join us, Don Latino.

DON LATINO. I've a deep voice, like a grunting pig.

DORIO DE GADEX. A true classicalist.

DON LATINO. And what would a true classicalist be doing
amongst a group of modernista nightingales? Come on boys,
let's get to it!

DORIO DE GADEX, *an ugly, comic, hunched figure, stretches*

out his arms. In the moonlight they resemble the plucked wings of a chicken.

DORIO DE GADEX. The Streetwise Dwarf.

THE MODERNISTA CHORUS. Begin! Begin! Begin!

DORIO DE GADEX. A cowardly liar who loved to boast.

THE MODERNISTA CHORUS. A liar! A liar! A liar!

DORIO DE GADEX. He wanted to rule the world.

THE MODERNISTA CHORUS. The world! The world! The world!

DORIO DE GADEX. A true Tartuffe, a rogue through and through.

THE MODERNISTA CHORUS. Through and through! Through and through! Through and through!

DORIO DE GADEX. He had no brain to speak of.

THE MODERNISTA CHORUS. No brain! No brain! No brain!

DORIO DE GADEX. Absolutely nothing inside his head.

THE MODERNISTA CHORUS. His head! His head! His head!

DORIO DE GADEX. Quite frankly he'd be better off dead.

THE MODERNISTA CHORUS. Dead! Dead! Dead!

A noisy interruption. Loud trotting; Roman soldiers – alias a mounted police patrol – appear through a side street, the moonlight shining on their helmets and swords. The sound of a bugle calling the men to attention. The café door slams shut. CAPTAIN PITITO of the mounted police patrol stands up in his stirrups.

CAPTAIN PITITO. It's beyond belief that you intellectuals should be the ones causing such a commotion! You'll leave the illiterate masses with nothing to do.

MAX. Eureka! Eureka! It is he! Mighty Mouth himself! Great and powerful Caesar, leader of mounted men, speak to me in the language of your forefathers!

CAPTAIN PITITO. Get this drunkard down the station!

MAX. Leader of mounted men, I too am fluent in slang.

CAPTAIN PITITO. Night watchman! Night watchman!

A NIGHT WATCHMAN. I'm coming!

CAPTAIN PITITO. Lock up this drunkard!

THE NIGHT WATCHMAN *approaches, gasping for breath and reeking of brandy; his lantern and pike sway as he walks.* CAPTAIN PITITO *spins his horse around. Sparks fly from the horseshoes. The noisy trotting of the disappearing patrol echoes through the streets.*

CAPTAIN PITITO. Night watchman, he's your responsibility now.

A NIGHT WATCHMAN. Should I give him the cold water treatment?

CAPTAIN PITITO. You'd be better off giving him a good thrashing.

A NIGHT WATCHMAN. Leave it to me!

DON LATINO. Buy him a drink, Max. It's the only way to get through to these country bumpkins.

MAX. I'm broke.

DON LATINO. You've nothing left?

MAX. Absolutely nothing!

A NIGHT WATCHMAN. Get moving!

MAX. I'm blind.

A NIGHT WATCHMAN. And what do you expect me to do about it?

MAX. Are you a faith healer?

A NIGHT WATCHMAN. I am the law!

MAX. It isn't quite the same thing.

A NIGHT WATCHMAN. But it could be. Get moving!

MAX. How many times do I need to tell you? I'm blind.

A NIGHT WATCHMAN. You're an anarchist, just like these long-haired layabouts. Wind! Wind! And more wind!

DON LATINO. A great big north wind!

A NIGHT WATCHMAN. Get back!

THE MODERNISTAS. Let's follow the Maestro! Let's follow the Maestro!

A NEIGHBOUR. Pepee! Pepee!

A NIGHT WATCHMAN. Go on! Get out of here! I don't want any trouble!

He knocks at the door of the café with his pike. THE COOK, a fat man wearing a white apron, peers out. He asks what's going on and then disappears again, muttering to himself. A few seconds later TWO SLEEPY POLICEMEN emerge, fastening up their belts.

A POLICEMAN. What's the problem?

A NIGHT WATCHMAN. This one here needs to be taken down to the station.

A SECOND POLICEMAN. We're on relief duty, so we'll have to drop him at HQ.

A NIGHT WATCHMAN. He just needs to sleep it off.

A NEIGHBOUR. Pepee! Pepee!

A NIGHT WATCHMAN. Duty calls! I'm coming! He's all yours.

BOTH POLICEMEN. Step back please, gentlemen.

DORIO DE GADEX. We are going with him.

A POLICEMAN. This drunkard could be Don Mariano de Cavia for all I care! And there's a poet if ever I saw one! The more he drinks the better he writes!

A SECOND POLICEMAN. He gets a bit boring at times!

DON LATINO. And rude!

A POLICEMAN. Who asked for your opinion? Do you know him, by any chance?

DON LATINO. We're friends.

A SECOND POLICEMAN. Are you all journalists?

DORIO DE GADEX. God forbid!

ENRIQUETA THE STREET WALKER. They're merchant bankers.

A POLICEMAN. There's no law preventing you from following your friend, but I won't stand for any nonsense. I've got a lot of respect for talent, you know.

A SECOND POLICEMAN. Let's get going.

MAX. Latino, lend me your hand. My dear officers of the law, I hope you'll find it in your hearts to forgive me for being blind!

A POLICEMAN. That's enough politics for one day.

DON LATINO. Where are we heading?

A POLICEMAN. Straight to Police HQ.

A SECOND POLICEMAN. Definitely the place to be.

MAX. Death to Maura! Death to all Conservatives!

THE MODERNIST CHORUS. Death! Death! Death!

MAX. Death to Maura! Hang the bastard!

A POLICEMAN. That's enough! That drunken poet had better watch his step! He's asking for it!

A SECOND POLICEMAN. They'll knock him senseless – and that's a shame, 'cos he seems a talented man.

Scene Five
The hallway of Police HQ. Shelves filled with files. Benches along the walls. A table with dirty dressed-sheepskin briefcases. The airless

room is filled with the nauseating stench of stale tobacco smoke.
Sleepy policemen. Plain-clothes detectives. Bowler hats, truncheons,
wide collars, gaudy rings, prominent hairy moles. A shoddy old man
– all wig and cotton sleeves – writes; a young man with greased-
back hair – the cool I've-seen-it-all type smothered in aftershave
– paces up and down dictating, cigar in mouth. Those who work
under him call him DON SERAFÍN, *but he is more disrespectfully*
known as SLICK-BACK SERAFÍN. *A slight commotion.* MAX
ESTRELLA *bursts in shouting, a bare-headed, laughing madman.*
A sighing and pleading DON LATINO *leads him by the arm.*
Behind them, peering police helmets. THE MODERNISTAS
have gathered in the corridor – their pipes, bow-ties and long hair
prominent beneath the poor light of a small oil lamp.

MAX. I took the liberty of detaining these officers of the law!
  They were out getting sloshed in some disreputable joint so I
  asked them to accompany me here.

SLICK-BACK SERAFÍN. Watch what you say, Sir.

MAX. I'm not at fault, Mr Policeman.

SLICK-BACK SERAFÍN. Inspector.

MAX. It's all the same.

SLICK-BACK SERAFÍN. Your name, please?

MAX. My name is Máximo Estrella, my pseudonym Manque
  Max. I have the honour of not being a member of the
  Academy.

SLICK-BACK SERAFÍN. You're going too far. Constables,
  why was this man arrested?

A POLICEMAN. For causing a public disturbance and
  shouting communist slogans. He's had a bit too much
  to drink!

SLICK-BACK SERAFÍN. Your profession?

MAX. Temporarily unemployed.

SLICK-BACK SERAFÍN. Where have you worked?

MAX. Nowhere.

SLICK-BACK SERAFÍN. But you have worked?

MAX. Free men and singing birds do not work. Yet am I not humiliated, abused, imprisoned, searched, and interrogated?

SLICK-BACK SERAFÍN. What's your address?

MAX. This needs to be written in italics. A palace, on the corner of Calle San Cosme.

A SHORT CONSTABLE. You mean a tenement block. Before we were married my wife rented a poky room in that same building.

MAX. Wherever I choose to live is always a palace.

A SHORT CONSTABLE. I wouldn't know.

MAX. Because you bureaucratic arseholes don't know a thing, not even how to dream!

SLICK-BACK SERAFÍN. You are officially under arrest!

MAX. Whatever you say! Latino, can you see a bench anywhere around here where I could lie down for a quick kip?

SLICK-BACK SERAFÍN. You don't come here to sleep.

MAX. But I'm really sleepy!

SLICK-BACK SERAFÍN. You are insulting my authority! Are you aware of who I am?

MAX. Slick-Back Serafín!

SLICK-BACK SERAFÍN. If you ever call me that again, I'll knock your teeth out!

MAX. I'm sure you'll find a way of keeping yourself in check! I am the primary poet of Spain! I know people in every newspaper! I even know the Home Secretary. We were at school together!

SLICK-BACK SERAFÍN. The Home Secretary does not associate with vagrants.

MAX. Little do you know.

SLICK-BACK SERAFÍN. How dare you insult Don Paco in my presence! I won't put up with it! Don Paco is like a father to me!

MAX. I don't believe it. Let me ring and ask him.

SLICK-BACK SERAFÍN. You can ask him from the cell.

DON LATINO. My dear Inspector, please show a little more consideration! This is a matter concerning the literary reputation of our country! This is Spain's Victor Hugo!

SLICK-BACK SERAFÍN. Shut up.

DON LATINO. Please forgive my interruption.

SLICK-BACK SERAFÍN. If you want to stay with him, we can provide you with a bed for the night!

DON LATINO. Thank you Inspector!

SLICK-BACK SERAFÍN. Constables, take this drunkard to cell two.

A POLICEMAN. Start walking!

MAX. I refuse.

SLICK-BACK SERAFÍN. Then drag him there.

ANOTHER POLICEMAN. Let's be having you, grandad!

MAX. They're trying to kill me! They're trying to kill me!

A MODERNISTA VOICE. Butchers!

DON LATINO. We're talking about a country's literary reputation!

SLICK-BACK SERAFÍN. No more protests. Now, get out of here.

ANOTHER MODERNISTA. Long live the Inquisition!

SLICK-BACK SERAFÍN. Silence! Or I'll have you all arrested!

MAX. They're trying to kill me! They're trying to kill me!

THE POLICE. Dirty wino! Bloody drunks!

THE GROUP OF MODERNISTAS. We must go to the Press!

> *They all rush out: floating scarves, smouldering pipes, romantic manes. An explosion of voices and blows from behind the cell door.*

SLICK-BACK SERAFÍN. Those fresh-faced modernista fools must think we're still at school!

Scene Six
The prison. A basement cell, poorly lit by a small oil lamp. A human form stirs in the shadows. Shirt, muffler, espadrilles. He walks around talking to himself. Suddenly, the door opens. MAX ESTRELLA, pushing and stumbling, is sent rolling to the back of the cell. The door slams shut.

MAX. Bastards! Mercenaries! Cowards!

THE JAILER. Oi, shut it or I'll cuff you!

MAX. Cretin!

> *The other inmate emerges from the darkness. Once he is lit it becomes clear that he is handcuffed, and his face covered in blood.*

THE PRISONER. Good evening!

MAX. I'm not alone?

THE PRISONER. So it seems.

MAX. Who are you, comrade?

THE PRISONER. An outcast.

MAX. From Barcelona?

THE PRISONER. From all over.

MAX. An outcast! . . . Only Catalan workers would use such a term to paraphrase their struggle. An outcast, when coming from the likes of you is incitement. Your time is coming.

THE PRISONER. You can see further than most. Barcelona is a web of hatred and destruction. I am a Catalan worker and I'm proud of it!

MAX. Are you an anarchist?

THE PRISONER. I am what the law has made me.

MAX. We are of the same church.

THE PRISONER. You wear a cravat.

MAX. A halter of horrendous servility! I'll remove it so we can talk.

THE PRISONER. You are not a member of the proletariat.

MAX. I am the pain of a bad dream.

THE PRISONER. There's something enlightening about you. You talk as if you were from another era.

MAX. I am a blind poet.

THE PRISONER. That's no small misfortune! In Spain hard work and intelligence have always been despised. Here money is everything.

MAX. We should install an electric guillotine on the streets of Madrid for public consumption.

THE PRISONER. That's not enough. The revolutionary objective must be the destruction of wealth, as in Russia. It's not enough to just behead the rich – some heir or other will appear. And even when one does away with inheritance, the dispossessed continually plot to get back what they believe is theirs. We must demolish the old order, and that will only come with the destruction of wealth. Industrial Barcelona must be burnt to the ground, so that a new nation with enlightened concepts of ownership and labour can emerge from its ashes. In Europe, there is no crueller, more exploiting employer than the Catalan. Even world-wide, his only rival is the Spanish-American colonialist. Barcelona must perish if it is to be saved!

MAX. I'm rather fond of Barcelona!

THE PRISONER. Yes, yes, I remember Barcelona!

MAX. I owe her the brief moments of pleasure I have experienced during the dark hours of my blindness: every day an employer is killed, some days even two . . . It is some comfort.

THE PRISONER. You don't count the workers who fall.

MAX. Workers multiply prolifically, somewhat like rabbits. Employers, on the other hand, breed slowly, like elephants and other powerful prehistoric beasts. Saul, we must spread our new philosophy across the world.

THE PRISONER. My name is Matthew.

MAX. But I baptise you Saul. I am a poet, the alphabet is therefore at my disposal. Listen to what I am about to say and remember it well when you are free. A really good hunt can put the price of employers' hides higher even than Calcutta ivory.

THE PRISONER. That's what we're working towards.

MAX. On the other hand, we could think about doing away with the proletariat; with no proletariat there'd be no exploitation.

THE PRISONER. By destroying the city we would destroy the bourgeois business interests.

MAX. I agree. Barcelona must be destroyed like Carthage and Jerusalem. Alea jacta est! Give me your hand.

THE PRISONER. I'm handcuffed.

MAX. Are you young? I can't see you.

THE PRISONER. I'm young. I'm thirty.

MAX. What are they accusing you of?

THE PRISONER. It's a long story. They branded me an undesirable . . . I refused to leave the textile factory to go and fight for King and country. I organized a riot and the boss denounced me. I was imprisoned. I have been around all over looking for work. And now I'm passing through, everywhere I turn a cross against my name. I know what Fate's got in store for me. A couple of shots in the back of the head for 'attempting to escape'. And it's going to get worse.

MAX. What are you afraid of?

THE PRISONER. They would enjoy torturing me.

MAX. Pigs!

THE PRISONER. I know how they work.

MAX. Bastards. And then they wonder why everyone goes on about the Inquisition!

THE PRISONER. One night as I'm walking along a deserted street, our beloved officers of the law, having been paid seven extra pesetas, will do away with me. And the idle rich will call it justice!

MAX. The infamous Hispanic cruelty. It's common to rich and poor alike.

THE PRISONER. Rich and poor alike!

MAX. Rich and poor alike! Matthew, where could we find a bomb that would rid Spain of its plague-ridden lands?

THE PRISONER. Distinguished poet, who sees so much, can't you see a raised fist of defiance?

The cell door opens. THE JAILER, *with the smug air of a bully, orders the handcuffed prisoner to accompany him.*

THE JAILER. Oi! You, Catalan. Line up!

THE PRISONER. I'm ready.

THE JAILER. Well, get moving. You, sunshine, are going for a nice, brisk walk.

With resigned strength, THE PRISONER *turns to* THE BLIND MAN *and brushes his chin against his shoulder. He says goodbye in a low voice.*

THE PRISONER. My time has come . . . I don't think we'll see each other again . . .

MAX. This is terrible!

THE PRISONER. They're going to kill me. . . . What will the malicious press print tomorrow?

MAX. Whatever they're told to print.

THE PRISONER. Are you crying?

MAX. With helplessness and rage. Hold me, brother.

They embrace. THE JAILER *and* THE HANDCUFFED MAN *leave. The cell door is shut again.* MAX ESTRELLA *fumbles around, searching for the wall. He sits down against it in a cross-legged position usually associated with oriental meditation. The blind poet's posture suggests an overwhelming silent grief. From outside, the sound of voices and galloping horses.*

Scene Seven

The offices of The Popular Paper. *A low room with a tiled floor. In the centre a long black table, surrounded by empty chairs. Immediately in front of each chair faded files and stacks of paper, their whiteness accentuated by the bright, green, circular glow emitted by the single bulb framed in a frilled lampshade. At one end, a bald man wearing a frayed jacket is smoking and writing: claw-like fingers, ink-stained nails; the long-suffering editor with the perpetually miserable countenance. This practical and mythical man relights his cigar. The partition door opens and the screech of a doorbell cuts through the silence.* THE PORTER *appears – a stumpy, sour-faced old man with a moustache and beer gut, looking like one of those dashing colonels who always manage to fall off their horses during a parade. It is an amazing, uncanny resemblance.*

THE PORTER. Don Latino of Hispalis is here with a few of his cronies. They're asking for the Executive Director himself. I told them that you were the only one around. Will you see them, Don Filiberto?

DON FILIBERTO. Tell them to come through.

He continues writing. THE PORTER *leaves. The green partition door remains swinging, like that of a seedy gambling saloon.*

THE MODERNISTA BRIGADE *enter; long hair, pipes, old coats and the odd cloak. The bald editor pushes his glasses onto his forehead, picks up his cigar, and puts on an air of importance.*

DON FILIBERTO. Gentlemen and good people, come through! Pray tell me, what can I and the paper do for you?

DON LATINO. We've come to protest against a catastrophic police outrage! Max Estrella, the great poet, although not universally accepted as such, has been arrested and brutally mistreated in a basement cell of the Ministry of Misgovernment.

DORIO DE GADEX. Long live the Inquisition!

DON FILIBERTO. Good God! Could it possibly be that our great poet is drunk?

DON LATINO. One glass too many is hardly justification for this gross violation of Human Rights.

DON FILIBERTO. Max Estrella is also a friend of ours. Good God! If our Executive Director isn't here by now, he won't return. . . . You gentlemen must know how a newspaper is run. The Executive Director must always, by nature, be a tyrant! . . . Without consulting him I cannot print your protests in our editorial column. I don't know the paper's policy with regard to the Police Department. . . . As for your version of events, well, quite frankly, I find it a little hard to believe.

DORIO DE GADEX. It's disgusting, Don Filiberto!

CLARINITO. Sheer cowardice!

PÉREZ. Shameful!

DON LATINO. It doesn't bear thinking about!

DORIO DE GADEX. Back to the Middle Ages!

DON LATINO. Dorio, my son, don't embarrass us!

DON FILIBERTO. The passion of youth! 'Divine treasure'

as our beloved Nicaraguan poet, Rubén Darío, once called it! 'Youth, divine treasure! You go never to return!' I also read, you know. Sometimes I rather admire the modernista geniuses. The Executive Director jokes that I've been infected. Have any of you read the story that I published in *Sphere Magazine*?

CLARINITO. I have, Don Filiberto! I've read it and admired it.

DON FILIBERTO. What about you, Dorio my friend?

DORIO DE GADEX. I never read my contemporaries, Don Filiberto.

DON FILIBERTO. Dorio my friend, I wouldn't want to imply that you don't read the Classics either!

DORIO DE GADEX. Our extraordinary brains, Don Filiberto, ooze out of our heads. They can be seen dripping onto our collars.

DON FILIBERTO. Any comments regarding the residue on my clothing can be equally applied to yours.

DORIO DE GADEX. You have a lethal tongue, Don Filiberto!

DON FILIBERTO. Which finds inspiration in your comments!

DORIO DE GADEX. I could never aspire to such a lofty mission!

CLARINITO. Dorio, don't resort to lavatory humour.

DON FILIBERTO. Dorio, my friend, I am used to these witty exchanges. It's all part of being a journalist. And here I'm not referring to the journalism of today. In the past I have joked with the liveliest of politicians; my remarks have been quoted by the most illustrious of journalists; references have been made to my charming repartee, my definition of journalism quoted per se. Do you know it? Just in case you don't, I'll take the liberty of repeating it for you. 'The journalist is a hack parliamentarian, Congress a large editorial office and each editorial office a small Congress.'

Journalism is an escapade, like politics. They are the same circle in different spheres. If you had a working knowledge of Karma's theories, I could explain it all theosophically.

DORIO DE GADEX. I think Don Latino's dabbled in it. We've never bothered.

DON LATINO. Dabbled in it! I think that's something of an understatement! I don't think you know the story behind my pseudonym. I am named Latino after the baptismal waters of our beloved church and for being a pain on the streets of the Latin Quarter of Paris, and Hispalis after the Andalusian lands of Spain where I was born. In the language of the occult, Latino becomes transformed into a mysterious magical word, onital. If I recall correctly, you, Don Filiberto, also like to dabble in the occult.

DON FILIBERTO. Let's not confuse things. This is rather too serious for that. I am a theosophist!

DON LATINO. I know not who I am!

DON FILIBERTO. I can quite believe it.

DORIO DE GADEX. One of Madrid's many vagrants.

DON LATINO. Dorio, don't squander your wit, everything is expendable. Between friends it's safer to offer a cigarette. So come on, pass me a ciggie!

DORIO DE GADEX. I don't smoke.

DON FILIBERTO. You must have some vices!

DORIO DE GADEX. I like to rape servant girls.

DON FILIBERTO. Is it fun?

DORIO DE GADEX. It has its moments, Don Filiberto.

DON FILIBERTO. You must be a father several times over?

DORIO DE GADEX. I make them have abortions.

DON FILIBERTO. A childkiller to boot!

PÉREZ. A man of many talents.

DORIO DE GADEX. Shut up Pérez, this doesn't concern you! Don Filiberto, your humble servant is a Neo-Malthusian.

DON FILIBERTO. Do you mention it on your CV?

DORIO DE GADEX. I've got a huge fluorescent sign at home announcing it to the world.

DON LATINO. Thus, with silly chit-chat, we Spaniards attempt to forget our hunger and our politicians.

DORIO DE GADEX. And our appalling plays and our actors and our tram system and our street paving.

PÉREZ. You are incorrigible!

DORIO DE GADEX. Pérez, shut up and listen.

DON FILIBERTO. Spain may find herself without bread but wit and good humour will always remain.

DORIO DE GADEX. Don Filiberto, who would you say is our number one comic?

DON FILIBERTO. You disrespectful individuals will probably claim it's Don Miguel de Unamuno.

DORIO DE GADEX. No, Sir! Our number one comic is King Alfonso XIII.

DON FILIBERTO. He has the joie de vivre of the people of Madrid and the conservatism of the Bourbons.

DORIO DE GADEX. He is our very best cómic, Don Filiberto. The best! King Alfonso has broken all records by appointing García Prieto Prime Minister.

DON FILIBERTO. Here, my young friend, you must keep such irreverent opinions to yourself. Our newspaper finds inspiration in Don Manuel García Prieto. I am perfectly aware of the fact that he is not a brilliant man, or a particularly good orator, but he is a conscientious politician. Now, let's get back to the case of our friend Manque Max. I could telephone the Home Secretary's private office. I know someone there who used to cover court cases for us. I'll ask to be put through. Good God! Manque Max is one of the Maestros after all, he deserves some consideration. What do these gentlemen leave for the bullies and louts? Yobs with flick knives! Was Manque Max in his usual state by any chance?

DON LATINO. Illuminated.

DON FILIBERTO. How deplorable!

DON LATINO. He didn't step over the bounds of decency. I was with him. Just imagine! We've been friends since our Paris days. Do you know Paris? I travelled to Paris at the same time as the abdicated Queen, Isabel. I even defended her in my writings. I translated a couple of books for the Garnier publishing house. I was financial editor of the *Hispano-American Money Magazine*. A great journal! And all of this under my pseudonym, Don Latino of Hispalis.

The telephone rings. DON FILIBERTO, *the bald, catarrh-ridden journalist, that practical and mythical man found in all editorial staff, asks to be put through to the private section of the Home Office. Silence. Then muttering, light laughter, a whispered joke.* DORIO DE GADEX *sits himself down in the Executive Director's chair, lifts his well-worn boots onto the table, and sighs loudly.*

DORIO DE GADEX. I am going to write the back page article, annotating the speech of our esteemed leader. 'All our country's great forces are dead.' These words were uttered only yesterday by our distinguished Prime Minister, Don Manuel García Prieto, Marquis of Alhucemas, in a stunning oratorical outburst. The House, captivated by his performance, applauded the profound importance of his concept; a profundity equalled only by that other notable remark, 'The hazardous reefs are slowly disappearing from view': And summed up in his supreme declamation, 'Cry God for Freedom, Progress, Spain and Saint James!'

DON FILIBERTO *puts down the receiver and makes his way into the centre of the room, covering his bald head with his yellow, ink-stained hands – the hands of a diligent skeleton on the biblical Day of Judgement!*

DON FILIBERTO. You've taken this joke too far! Get your feet off that table! I've never seen such rude behaviour!

DORIO DE GADEX. Then you've obviously never stepped into the American Senate.

DON FILIBERTO. Look at the dust on my files!

DORIO DE GADEX. That is the philosophy lesson of the day. Remember man that thou art dust and unto dust thou shalt return!

DON FILIBERTO. You couldn't even quote it in Latin! You're nothing but a group of insolent children!

CLARINITO. Don Filiberto, the rest of us have been on our best behaviour.

DON FILIBERTO. You've all had a good laugh at his jokes, and as far as I'm concerned that constitutes insolence. You laugh at anything! Nothing is sacred, nothing worthy of respect. Even our greatest contemporary writers and politicians become prattling windbags in your eyes! Maura . . .

DORIO DE GADEX. The King of Toerags!

DON FILIBERTO. Benlliure, a dozen-a-day sculptor!

DORIO DE GADEX. I couldn't have put it better myself.

DON FILIBERTO. Cavestany, a poet of cheap jingles!

DORIO DE GADEX. Who has to resort to do-it-yourself guides to writing before he can put pen to paper.

DON FILIBERTO. And my poor boss, probably nothing but a misguided idiot!

DORIO DE GADEX. He married into money.

DON FILIBERTO. As far as you're all concerned, there's

nothing great in our country, nothing worthy of admiration.
I feel sorry for all of you! You're nothing but silly fools with
no sense of patriotism!

DORIO DE GADEX. Patriotism is a luxury we can't afford.
Wait till we get a car, Don Filiberto.

DON FILIBERTO. You can't be serious for a moment!
There's even one member of your group, someone you all
refer to as Maestro, who dares to shout, 'Long live triviality!'
And not in a café or amongst friends, but in the Ateneo
Theatre! And that just can't be allowed! You don't believe
in anything; you're cynical and destructive. We should be
thankful that there is a section amongst the youth of today
who are quite unlike yourselves, a group of committed young
people full of patriotic spirit.

DON LATINO. If you're referring to those stupid little boys
in the Property Protection League, I'm afraid I can't agree.
At least these modernistas, call them pompous vagrants if you
will, have never sunk to the depths of community policing.
Let each be judged according to his merits. By the way, I
heard that one of these Property Protection League tinpot
policeboys was killed this afternoon. Do you know anything
about it?

DON FILIBERTO. Hardly a boy. He was approaching sixty.

DON LATINO. Well, let's hope someone's got the sense to
bury him. One more corpse, one less corpse, it's only the
undertaker who cares!

Suddenly the telephone rings. DON FILIBERTO *picks up the
receiver and begins a pantomime of nods, whispers and shouts.
Whilst listening, his receiver to his ear and his head twisted
to one side, he glances across the room, his eyes resting on the
young Modernistas. When he hangs up, his face betrays the open
expression of an impeccable conscience. The theosophist begins to
appear in his quiet smile, in the ivory pallor of his temples, in the
broad roundness of his bald head.*

DON FILIBERTO. The order has already been given to set
our friend Max Estrella free. Please advise him not to drink.

He is a talented man and could certainly do much more than he manages at present. Now, get out and let me work. I have to get the paper finished on my own, alone and unaided.

Scene Eight

The private Secretariat of His Excellency the Home Secretary. The smell of Havana cigars, appalling paintings, a rather tacky appearance of provincial luxury. The room recalls both an office and a seedy gambling joint. Suddenly a telephone urinates loudly in the silent, bureaucratic lap. And DIEGUITO GARCÍA – *known as* DON DIEGO DEL CORRAL *in the various legal journals – takes three leaps and pounces on the receiver, bringing it up to his ear.*

DIEGUITO. Who is this?

. . .

I've already given the order to set him free.

. . .

My pleasure! My pleasure!

. . .

An alcoholic!

. . .

Yes . . . I know his work.

. . .

How unfortunate!

. . .

It won't be possible. We haven't any spare money!

. . .

I'll certainly let him know. Let me make a note of it.

. . .

My pleasure! My pleasure!

MAX ESTRELLA *appears at the door, pale and bruised; his tie is loose, disdain and derangement are written all over his face. Behind him,* A SECURITY ATTENDANT *is buttoning up his breeches.*

THE SECURITY ATTENDANT. Stop where you are, Sir.

MAX. Don't lay a finger on me.

THE SECURITY ATTENDANT. Please leave as quickly and as quietly as possible.

MAX. Tell the Home Secretary I'm here to see him.

THE SECURITY ATTENDANT. He can't be seen.

MAX. That may be the case, but I presume he can be heard.

THE SECURITY ATTENDANT. Please leave, Sir. These are not visiting hours.

MAX. Just tell him I'm here.

THE SECURITY ATTENDANT. I've had my orders . . . so let's leave it shall we, Sir.

DIEGUITO. Fernández, let the gentleman through.

MAX. At last! Someone who speaks the same language!

DIEGUITO. Manque Max, my friend. I do hope you'll forgive me, I can only spare a few minutes. The editor of *The Popular Paper* called me about you. You're obviously liked there. You seem to be loved and admired all over. Should you ever need me, you know where I am. Don't forget now . . . Who knows! . . . I'm a real romantic when it comes to journalism . . . I hope to write something myself one day . . . I've been toying with the idea of a spontaneous piece for sometime now. Something light, bubbly and fiery. I'm counting on you for a bit of guidance. Goodbye Maestro! I sincerely regret that our meeting should have arisen from such an unfortunate situation!

MAX. That is precisely what I've come to complain about. You have a police force made up of second-rate riff-raff!

DIEGUITO. You find a little of everything, Maestro.

MAX. Let's not argue about it. I want the Home Secretary to hear what I have to say. I also mean to use the occasion to thank him personally for securing my release.

DIEGUITO. His Excellency the Home Secretary doesn't know anything about this.

MAX. Well then, I'll make it my duty to inform him.

DIEGUITO. His Excellency the Home Secretary is incredibly busy at the moment. Nevertheless I will go in and see him.

MAX. And I'll go with you.

DIEGUITO. That's out of the question!

MAX. I'll make a scene!

DIEGUITO. You're out of your mind!

MAX. Yes, out of my mind! Because I've been ignored and cast aside. The Home Secretary is a friend of mine from the old days. I want to hear him say that he does not know me! Paco! Paco!

DIEGUITO. I shall tell him you're here.

MAX. I can do it myself. Paco! I am a ghost from the past!

HIS EXCELLENCY THE HOME SECRETARY *opens his office door and peers out in his shirt sleeves; his flies are undone, his waistcoat unbuttoned, and his glasses hang from the end of a string like two absurd eyeballs dancing on his belly.*

THE HOME SECRETARY. What's all this noise, Dieguito?

DIEGUITO. Home Secretary, I'm afraid I couldn't stop it.

THE HOME SECRETARY. Who is this man?

MAX. A friend from the old days. Don't you recognize me, Paco? Have I changed that much? Are you sure you don't know who I am? I'm Máximo Estrella!

THE HOME SECRETARY. But of course! Of course! Of course! Are you blind?

MAX. As were Homer and Belisarius.

THE HOME SECRETARY. An accident, I suppose . . .

MAX. Definitely and irreversibly. A gift from Venus.

THE HOME SECRETARY. Christ! Why haven't you come to see me before now? I so rarely see your work in the papers.

MAX. I've been forgotten! You were sensible to leave the literary profession for politics. In the Arts you can't even make enough to eat. The Arts are nothing but bright colours, rags, and hunger!

THE HOME SECRETARY. There's no doubt about it. The Arts don't get the recognition they deserve. Nevertheless, they are a valuable commodity. Max, my friend, I must get back to work. Leave a note with this young man stating what you need . . . You've come a little late.

MAX. I've come in my own time. I'm not here to ask for anything. I've come to demand satisfaction and punishment. I try to earn a living by writing poetry but it's a miserable existence. You probably think I'm an alcoholic. Luckily I am! If it weren't for the drink, I'd have shot myself years ago. Paco, your hired assassins have no right to slap me or spit at me, and I've come to ask that you punish the contemptible louts, thus offering the Goddess of Justice some satisfaction!

THE HOME SECRETARY. My dear friend Max, I don't know anything about this. Dieguito, what happened?

DIEGUITO. There's been some trouble on the streets. The congregation of groups has been forbidden, the Maestro here got somewhat excited . . .

MAX. I was arrested for no reason and tortured as in the days of the Inquisition. Look at the marks on my wrists.

THE HOME SECRETARY. What does the Police report state, Dieguito?

DIEGUITO. More or less what I've just told you, Sir . . .

MAX. They're lying! I was unjustly arrested by a mounted warrior, after asking him whether he knew the Greek language of his forefathers.

THE HOME SECRETARY. Well, if you want my opinion it's the question that seems unjust. How could you possibly expect a simple policeman to speak ancient Greek!

MAX. He was an officer.

THE HOME SECRETARY. It wouldn't have made a difference if he'd been a general. You're not entirely blameless! You've always been a bit on the wild side and the years haven't done anything to mellow that! I can't help feeling a little envious of your inexhaustible sense of humour!

MAX. My life is perpetually dark. I've been blind for a year now. I dictate and my wife writes, but it doesn't work.

THE HOME SECRETARY. Your wife is French, isn't she?

MAX. My wife is a saint with atrocious spelling. I have to dictate each word, letter by letter. I lose track of my ideas. It's mortifying! If there was bread in the house I doubt that this damned blindness would be so painful. A blind man sees the world so clearly. Eyes are but credible deceivers. Goodbye Paco! Max Estrella is not quite the tiresome friend who's fallen on hard times.

THE HOME SECRETARY. Máximo, hold on a minute. Don't go. Since you've come, let's talk. You bring back memories of an important, perhaps even the happiest period of my life. How distant it all seems now! We used to study together. You lived along Calle del Recuerdo, Memory Lane. You had a sister. I was in love with her. I even wrote poems for her!

MAX.
    Memory Lane,
    Helena's window,
    Where I saw
    The dark girl standing!
    Memory Lane,

Wandering Minstrels,
A ladder of moon
Which I caught
To climb up!

THE HOME SECRETARY. You've got an amazing memory! I can hardly believe it! What happened to your sister?

MAX. She entered a convent.

THE HOME SECRETARY. And your brother Alex?

MAX. He died!

THE HOME SECRETARY. What about the others? You were quite a family.

MAX. I think they're all dead!

THE HOME SECRETARY. You haven't changed at all! . . . Max, I don't want to offend you, but while I'm here I could arrange some sort of pension for you.

MAX. Thank you!

THE HOME SECRETARY. Does that mean you accept?

MAX. I've no alternative!

THE HOME SECRETARY. Dieguito, make a note of this. Where do you live, Max?

MAX. I hope you've got plenty of spare ink my young Maestro, this is quite an address. 23a Calle Bastardillos, Inside Staircase, Attic B. Please note that if you need a thread to guide you through the labyrinth, don't ask the concierge, she bites.

THE HOME SECRETARY. God, how I envy your sense of humour!

MAX. The world is mine, everything smiles at me. I don't have a care in the world.

THE HOME SECRETARY. I wish I was in your shoes!

MAX. Paco, don't be such a fool!

THE HOME SECRETARY. Max, each month you'll get the pension brought to you. Now goodbye! A final embrace!

MAX. Take this finger and try not to get so sentimental.

THE HOME SECRETARY. Goodbye, Genius and Anarchy!

MAX. I came to ask amends for an affront to my dignity. I wanted some kind of just punishment for the bastards who arrested me. Clearly, I didn't achieve either aim. You offered me money and I accepted because I too am a bastard. I couldn't leave this world without sinking to the depths of depravity at least once. I have truly earned your embrace, Home Secretary!

MÁXIMO ESTRELLA, *his head held high and his arms spread out like a cross, moves forward like a ghostly apparition; his eyes stare ahead, tragic in their blind tranquillity.* THE HOME SECRETARY, *fat, greasy and badly-groomed, responds with that well-known gesture usually associated with the character actor of an old French melodrama. They embrace. A tear rests in* THE HOME SECRETARY's *eye as they pull apart. He deposits some banknotes into the Bohemian's hand as he squeezes it.*

THE HOME SECRETARY. Goodbye! Goodbye! Please believe me when I say that I won't forget this moment.

MAX. Goodbye Paco! I thank you in the name of two wretched women!

THE HOME SECRETARY *presses an electric bell. The sleepy* SECURITY ATTENDANT *enters.* MÁXIMO ESTRELLA, *using his stick to try and locate the door, is making his way towards the balcony at the far end of the room.*

THE HOME SECRETARY. Fernández, accompany this gentleman to a cab.

MAX. My dog is probably waiting for me at the door.

THE SECURITY ATTENDANT. There is an elderly gentleman waiting for you in the lobby.

MAX. Don Latino of Hispalis: my dog.

THE SECURITY ATTENDANT *guides the Bohemian out by the arm. He leads him clumsily out of the office, glancing sideways in an attempt to fathom the expression on the Home Secretary's face – the stale expression of an old character actor playing out the great recognition scene.*

THE HOME SECRETARY. My dear Dieguito, there you had a man who lacked willpower! He had everything: looks, wit and eloquence. His conversation was colourful, brilliant and spellbinding.

DIEGUITO. What a striking image!

THE HOME SECRETARY. No question about it, he was the most talented member of our generation!

DIEGUITO. You wouldn't believe it to look at him now – in the middle of the gutter, stinking of brandy and greeting every pimp and prostitute he comes across in French.

THE HOME SECRETARY. Twenty years! A lifetime! And now out of the blue this Bohemian ghost reappears! I was able to save myself from such disaster by renouncing the pleasurable occupation of verse composition. Dieguito, you can't really understand what I'm talking about because you weren't born a poet.

DIEGUITO. Thank God!

THE HOME SECRETARY. Ah Dieguito! You'll never know what it means to be part of the illusory world of Bohemia! You were born a bureaucrat, you are not part of the world of dreams. But I am!

DIEGUITO. Do you regret it, Don Francisco?

THE HOME SECRETARY. I think I probably do.

DIEGUITO. Would His Excellency the Home Secretary care to change places with the poet, Manque Max?

THE HOME SECRETARY. The law graduate Don Diego del

Corral has put on the ceremonious robes of duty. Now, could you please suspend this interrogation for a moment and try to think of a way of accounting for the money we've just given Máximo Estrella.

DIEGUITO. We'll take it from the police funds.

THE HOME SECRETARY. How ironic!

THE HOME SECRETARY *sinks into an armchair in front of the fireplace, which throws a flickering light onto the carpet. He lights a quality cigar and asks for the official Government newspaper* The Gazette. *He puts on his glasses, flicks through the newspaper, places it over his face and falls asleep.*

Scene Nine

A café, lengthened by misty mirrors. Marble-topped tables. Red couches. At the far end of the room, the counter. Behind it the bust of a fair-haired man stands out amidst the various refreshments. The café has a piano and a violin. Shadows and music float amidst the hazy smoke and the faint flicker of arc lamps. The multiplying mirrors reflect a hive of activity. The background is an absurd geometric maze, presenting the café as a mirage of distortion. The monotonous beat of the music; lights in the depths of the mirror; the veil of smoke pierced by the trembling flicker of the arc lamps. The two figures who enter, MANQUE MAX *and* DON LATINO, *are automatically absorbed into this poetic atmosphere.*

MAX. Where are we?

DON LATINO. The Café Colón.

MAX. See if Rubén's here. He usually sits in front of the musicians.

DON LATINO. There he is, looking like a miserable pig.

MAX. Let's go and sit with him, Latino. When I die, the sceptre of poetry will pass to this negro.

DON LATINO. Don't ask me to be your executor.

MAX. He is a great poet!

DON LATINO. Well, I can't see why.

MAX. Then you're not fit to be Maura's barber!

By cutting through the chairs and marble-topped tables, they reach the corner where the silent RUBÉN DARÍO *sits. Faced with* MAX ESTRELLA's *spectral presence, the bitterness of life reaches through to him; with the egoistic gesture of an angry child, he closes his eyes and downs his glass of absinth wine in one. The mask of this idol is finally lit by a sour smile as the blind man stops at the table.* MAX *raises his arm with the grand gesture of a majestic statue.*

MAX. Hail, beloved brother, though less in years greater in worth!

RUBÉN. How delightful! It's been so long since I last saw you. What have you been up to?

MAX. Nothing!

RUBÉN. How delightful! You're not often in here?

MAX. This is a rather expensive café. I can't afford such luxuries. From now until Judgement Day, it's taverns and bars for me.

RUBÉN. Max, let's enjoy life, and forget Death's dark lady while we can.

MAX. Why?

RUBÉN. Let's not mention her!

MAX. You fear her and I long for her! Rubén, I will carry any messages you choose to give me across the River Styx. I've come here to shake your hand for the last time, guided by the distinguished Don Latino of Hispalis, a man who despises your poetry as if he were a member of the Royal Academy of Writers!

DON LATINO. My dear Max, please don't exaggerate!

RUBÉN. Is this gentleman Don Latino of Hispalis?

DON LATINO. We have met before, Maestro! Many years ago we were both journalists on the *Hispano American Money Magazine*.

RUBÉN. I don't have much of a memory, Don Latino.

DON LATINO. I was the financial editor, we saw quite a lot of each other in Paris.

RUBÉN. I had forgotten.

MAX. But you've never been to Paris!

DON LATINO. My dear Max, how many times do I have to ask you not to get carried away. Sit down and invite us to dinner. Today Rubén, our friend, this great poet is known as Magnificent Max!

RUBÉN. How delightful! Max, we must escape from this Bohemian life!

DON LATINO. This is a man of substance, with taxpayers' money up his sleeve!

MAX. This afternoon I was forced to pawn my cloak and now I'm inviting you to dinner. Dinner with the very best champagne, Rubén!

RUBÉN. How delightful! Following the example of Saint Martin of Tours you share your cloak with me, transfigured into dinner. How delightful!

DON LATINO. Waiter! The menu! I consider it a little extravagant to order French wines. After all gentlemen, we must think of tomorrow!

MAX. I'd rather we didn't!

DON LATINO. I'll second your opinion if we take poison along with the coffee, brandy and cigars.

MAX. You miserable bourgeois bastard!

DON LATINO. My dear Max, let's come to an arrangement. I'll drink modestly, a small beer say, and you can let me have what a heavy drinking session would have cost in cash.

RUBÉN. Watch your manners, Don Latino.

DON LATINO. Your humble servant is no poet. I do more than write poetry to earn a living.

RUBÉN. I too indulge in celestial matters.

DON LATINO. I do beg your pardon! Because, Sir, even if I find myself reduced to the ignominy of selling serialized stories, I remain an avid supporter of the spiritual and the magical.

RUBÉN. So do I!

DON LATINO. I recall that you were trying to educate yourself in that field.

RUBÉN. I have sensed the Elements as Consciences.

DON LATINO. Undoubtedly! Undoubtedly! Undoubtedly! Consciences, Willpower and Authority!

RUBÉN. Sea and Earth, Fire and Wind. Divine Monsters. Divine possibly because they are Eternities!

MAX. Nothing is eternal.

DON LATINO. And the fruit of Nothing: the Four Elements symbolized by the four gospels. The Creation, which is plurality, only begins in the Quaternary. But from the Trini-Unity comes the Number. This is why the Number is sacred!

MAX. Shut up, Pythagoras. I suppose this is what you learnt during those intimate moments with Madame Blavatsky of the Theosophical Society.

DON LATINO. Max, these jibes are intolerable! You are a profoundly irreligious, Voltairian cynic! Madame Blavatsky is an extraordinary woman, and you should not laugh in such a despicable manner at the reverence she inspires. You could well find yourself punished by the retribution of Karma. This wouldn't be the first time it's happened!

RUBÉN. The wonders of the Universe! Luckily we neither see them nor understand them. Without this ignorance, life would be a constant barrage of fear.

MAX. Do you believe, Rubén?

RUBÉN. I believe!

MAX. In God?

RUBÉN. And in Christ!

MAX. And in the flames of Hell?

RUBÉN. And in the harmony of the Spheres!

MAX. Rubén, you're a fraud!

RUBÉN. A little naive, perhaps!

MAX. Is it just a pose?

RUBÉN. No!

MAX. For me there is nothing beyond the final grimace. If there is anything, I'll come back and tell you.

RUBÉN. Shut up, Max. Let's not sever the bonds of our friendship!

MAX. Rubén, don't forget this meal. And now, let's mingle the wine with the roses of your poetry. We are listening.

RUBÉN *tremulously withdraws into himself, his expression that of an idol evoking mysteries and unknown horrors.* MAX ESTRELLA *extends his arm out somewhat emphatically.* DON LATINO *refills the glasses.* RUBÉN *emerges from his meditation with the insurmountable sadness usually associated with Aztec sculptures.*

RUBÉN. I'll see if I can remember 'A Pilgrimage to Santiago de Compostela' . . . It is my latest composition.

MAX. Has it been published? If it has, I will have read it – but from your lips it will sound new.

RUBÉN. I may not remember it.

A YOUNG MAN *is writing at the adjacent table. The open book and the stack of paper in front of him suggests that he is translating. He leans shyly towards* RUBÉN DARÍO.

THE YOUNG MAN. Maestro, if you get stuck, I could prompt you.

RUBÉN. How delightful!

MAX. Where has it been published?

THE YOUNG MAN. I read it in manuscript form. It was to be published in a journal which died before it was ever born.

MAX. Are you referring to Paco Villaespesa's journal?

THE YOUNG MAN. I was his secretary.

DON LATINO. An excellent post.

MAX. You have nothing to be jealous of, Latino.

THE YOUNG MAN. Can you remember it, Maestro?

RUBÉN nods with the reverence of a priest, and after wetting his lips in the glass, begins reciting in a slow, rhythmic, almost lethargic manner, paying particular attention to the differentiation of the consonants.

RUBÉN.
    The path was reaching its end,
    And in the corner, behind a dark door,
    We divided stale bread
    With the Marquis of Bradomín!!!

THE YOUNG MAN. But that's the end of the poem, Maestro.

RUBÉN. The time has come to drink to our infamous friend.

MAX. He has gone from this world!

RUBÉN. He has returned to his village to prepare for death. His farewell letter inspired this poem. Let us drink to the health of an exquisite sinner!

MAX. Let's drink!

He raises his glass. Delighting in the aroma of the absinth wine, he sighs, evoking the distant sky of Paris. The piano and violin begin a well-known operetta melody. The café's clientele tap out the beat on their glasses with teaspoons. After drinking, the three exiles are heard chatting excitedly in French. They emphatically recall the lights of the divine and mortal feast that is: Paris! Cabarets! Magic! And to the rhythm of their dialogue, their spiritual father, the limping PAUL VERLAINE, marches past.

Scene Ten

A path through a park. A clear distant sky. Intense moonlight.
Mounted police patrols. A car rolls past silently and luminously.
Young sluts and old hags with painted mask-like faces prowl
through the clandestine shadows of the branches, attempting to
make money through immoral means. A number of sleeping figures
are scattered on the park benches. MAX ESTRELLA and DON
LATINO walk beneath the shadows of the path. The spring scent
of lilies permeates the night's humidity.

AN OLD HEAVILY MADE-UP TART. Handsome! Oi! . . .
  Handsome! Wanna join me in here for a bit?

DON LATINO. I might consider it if you put your teeth
  back in.

AN OLD HEAVILY MADE-UP TART. Gissa fag then!

DON LATINO. I'll give you *The Spanish Correspondence*
  Magazine instead so that you can educate yourself. There's a
  letter in it written by Maura.

AN OLD HEAVILY MADE-UP TART. He knows where he
  can stuff it!

DON LATINO. Jews don't like to stuff anything anywhere.

AN OLD HEAVILY MADE-UP TART. Keen, aren't you!
  Hold on a minute, and I'll call a friend. Mole! Mole!

  THE MOLE *appears, a young tart dressed in white stockings,*
  an apron, a shawl, and espadrilles. She stops in the shadows of
  the flower bed, laughing shamelessly.

THE MOLE. Well, take a look at these spring chickens!
  There'll be no street walking for me tonight.

AN OLD HEAVILY MADE-UP TART. They'll set us up in
  the Ritz.

THE MOLE. Just throw me a couple of coins and a single
  peseta for the bed. Now you can't get any fairer than that!

AN OLD HEAVILY MADE-UP TART. Miserable sods!
  Come on, gissa fag!

MAX. Have a cigar.

AN OLD HEAVILY MADE-UP TART. Very funny!

THE MOLE. Grab hold of it, stupid.

AN OLD HEAVILY MADE-UP TART. I'll grab it all right!
It's a quality cigar, this one!

THE MOLE. Let me have the odd puff.

AN OLD HEAVILY MADE-UP TART. This one is all mine.

THE MOLE. For the King of Portuguese Pimps.

AN OLD HEAVILY MADE-UP TART. No fear, dribble
brain! I'll use it to bribe the Health Inspector!

THE MOLE. And what about you two arty astronomers? In
the mood for something daring?

*The two tarts have moved cautiously and clandestinely out of
the shadows of the path.* THE OLD HEAVILY MADE-UP
TART *now stands beside* DON LATINO OF HISPALIS;
THE MOLE *beside* MANQUE MAX.

THE MOLE. Go on, have a good look up my nice clean
petticoats!

MAX. I'm blind.

THE MOLE. You must see something!

MAX. Nothing!

THE MOLE. Go on, have a feel. I'm nice and firm.

MAX. It's like marble!

THE YOUNG TART, *laughing provocatively, grabs the poet's
hand and guides it across her shoulders, pressing it against her
breast.* THE OLD HAG's *white chalk mask cracks as she gives
a toothless grin in a pathetic attempt to tempt* DON LATINO.

AN OLD HEAVILY MADE-UP TART. Come along with me,
handsome. Let's leave your friend and The Mole to it. Come
on! Don't be shy. If a copper comes along we can always buy
him off with this Havana cigar.

Smiling, the white spectral hag leads him away. The sound of whispering. They disappear in amongst the trees. A grotesque parody of the Garden of Armida. MANQUE MAX and the other whore remain, two solitary figures at the edge of the path.

THE MOLE. Go on, grab hold of my tits . . . don't be shy . . . You're supposed to be a poet!

MAX. How did you know?

THE MOLE. It's the biblical mane. Am I wrong?

MAX. No, you're not wrong.

THE MOLE. If I could be arsed to tell you the story of my life, you'd have some real material there. Now, tell me: what do you think of me?

MAX. You're a nymph!

THE MOLE. And you've got a very posh voice! Your mate has gone off with the Gossip. So, come on, gimme me your hand. Let's go somewhere dark and secluded and I'll show you a good time.

MAX. Just drop me off at a park bench where I can wait for that Hispalic pig.

THE MOLE. What d'you mean?

MAX. An Hispalic is a Sevillian.

THE MOLE. It might be where you come from, but I'm from the other side of town.

MAX. How old are you?

THE MOLE. Well, I don't really know.

MAX. And is this your regular nocturnal patch?

THE MOLE. Sort of.

MAX. At least it's an honourable way of earning a living!

THE MOLE. You've no idea how hard I work. I have to watch what I do. The Gossip talked to me about going to work in a brothel. A really classy joint! But I didn't want to go . . .

I didn't fancy lying flat on my back. I always save my best assets for the blokes who know how to treat a girl. Why don't you have a go?

MAX. I haven't the time.

THE MOLE. Go on. If you don't try, you'll never know what you can do. I could really grow to like you.

MAX. I'm a poet with no money.

THE MOLE. Are you by any chance the one who wrote that song about Joselito the bullfighter?

MAX. I'm the one!

THE MOLE. Really?

MAX. Really.

THE MOLE. Recite it . . .

MAX. I don't remember it.

THE MOLE. That's 'cos you didn't have anything to do with it in the first place. Anyway, jokes apart, what have you written?

MAX. The verses about Espartero.

THE MOLE. And do you remember them?

MAX. I can recite them like a true flamenco singer.

THE MOLE. I bet you can't!

MAX. If only I had a guitar!

THE MOLE. Can you play it?

MAX. I'm not blind for nothing, you know.

THE MOLE. I could grow to like you a lot!

MAX. I don't have any money.

THE MOLE. Just pay for the bed and we'll call it quits. If you're satisfied with my services and decide to invite me to breakfast, I won't refuse.

MÁXIMO ESTRELLA, *with the sensitive touch of a blind man, runs his fingers along her moon-shaped face, her neck, and her shoulders.* THE TART *giggles contentedly. She removes a gypsy comb from her gathered hair and begins to comb her ringlets. She is growing more and more sleepy.*

THE MOLE. Do you really want to know what I look like? I'm very dark and very ugly!

MAX. I would never have guessed! You don't seem a day older than fifteen.

THE MOLE. Whatever you say. Three years since I first became a woman. Enough talking, let's go. There's a decent house nearby.

MAX. Are you going to keep your promise?

THE MOLE. Which one? Saving my best assets for the bloke who knows how to treat a girl? You don't seem like much of a goer but you know what to do with your hands! Leave my face alone and move onto my body.

MAX. Do you have black hair?

THE MOLE. Yes!

MAX. You smell of flowers.

THE MOLE. Because I've been selling them.

MAX. What colour eyes do you have?

THE MOLE. Guess!

MAX. Green?

THE MOLE. Clever! Just like Pastora Imperio the dancer. To look at me you'd think I was a gypsy.

The amber glow of a lit cigarette and the asthmatic cough of DON LATINO *emerge from the darkness. The sound of a distant mounted police patrol echoes through the streets. A car's headlights. The lantern of a night watchman. The hinges of an iron gate. A clandestine shadow. The chalk-like face of another prostitute. Endless shadows.*

Scene Eleven

A street in the older, Austrian section of Madrid. The garden wall of a convent. An upper class residence. The lights of a tavern. A distressed group of neighbours are standing on the pavement. A bare-breasted woman with a hoarse voice carries a dead child in her arms, a bullet through its head. MAX ESTRELLA and DON LATINO stop suddenly.

MAX. There's broken glass around here too.

DON LATINO. There must have been quite a fight!

MAX. Bastards! . . . The lot of them! . . . And we poets more than anyone!

DON LATINO. One lives on miracles!

THE MOTHER OF THE DEAD CHILD. Idiots! Cowards! I hope the fires of Hell burn out your entrails! Idiots! Cowards!

MAX. What's going on, Latino? Who's crying? Who's screaming as if her world were coming to an end?

DON LATINO. A poor woman carrying a dead child in her arms.

MAX. Her tragic voice frightens me!

THE MOTHER OF THE DEAD CHILD. Mercenaries! Murderers of children!

THE PAWNBROKER. She's a little upset, and doesn't really know what she's saying.

THE POLICEMAN. The authorities will take it all into consideration.

THE LANDLORD OF THE TAVERN. Accidents are unavoidable in the necessary restoration of law and order.

THE PAWNBROKER. That anarchic rabble destroyed my shop window.

THE CONCIERGE. Why didn't you pull down the metal shutters?

THE PAWNBROKER. I was away when the riot began. I just hope they agree to pay for any damages to private property.

THE LANDLORD OF THE TAVERN. People who loot establishments which serve the public good have no sense of patriotism.

THE MOTHER OF THE DEAD CHILD. Butchers of my beloved child!

A BRICKLAYER. The people are hungry.

THE PAWNBROKER. And recklessly arrogant.

THE MOTHER OF THE DEAD CHILD. Idiots! Cowards!

AN OLD WOMAN. Be careful, Romualda!

THE MOTHER OF THE DEAD CHILD. Let them kill me as they did my innocent babe!

THE RAGWOMAN. As innocent as they come! That must be taken into consideration!

THE LANDLORD OF THE TAVERN. You'll be saying there was no warning siren next.

THE RETIRED OFFICER. I heard it.

THE MOTHER OF THE DEAD CHILD. Liar!

THE RETIRED OFFICER. My word is sacred.

THE PAWNBROKER. The grief is driving you crazy, Romualda.

THE MOTHER OF THE DEAD CHILD. Murderers! To look at you is to see hangmen!

THE RETIRED OFFICER. The forces of authority must be unrelenting.

THE BRICKLAYER. Especially when it comes to the poor. People like us are killed to protect the business interests which bleed us dry.

THE LANDLORD OF THE TAVERN. We're talking about people who pay their taxes.

THE PAWNBROKER. Honest businessmen don't bleed
anyone dry.

THE CONCIERGE. Do you think we complain just for the
sake of it!

THE BRICKLAYER. The life of a worker means nothing to
this Government.

MAX. Latino, take me out of this inferno.

*The sound of shots is heard. The group, aware of the impending
danger, moves away frightened and confused. The hoarse cries of
the mother can be heard above all the confusion. On hearing the
shots she presses the dead child closer to her breast.*

THE MOTHER OF THE DEAD CHILD. Cursed rifles! Use
your bullets to kill me too!

MAX. Her voice cuts through me.

THE MOTHER OF THE DEAD CHILD. You're so cold, my
darling!

MAX. The tragic anger in her voice. I've never heard anything
like it!

DON LATINO. It's all a bit too theatrical for my liking.

MAX. Idiot!

The lantern, pike and cloak of A NIGHT WATCHMAN *appear
along the pavement, accompanied by the sound of wooden clogs.*

THE PAWNBROKER. Night watchman, what happened?

A NIGHT WATCHMAN. A prisoner attempting to escape.

MAX. Latino, I can't even scream any more . . . The rage
inside here is killing me! My mouth is filled with poison.
That dead man knew what was coming . . . And yet he did
not fear death. Torture was his only fear . . . During these
wretched times the legacy of the Inquisition still clouds the
history of Spain. Our life is a Dantesque Inferno of shame
and anger. I am dying of hunger and yet I am content,
content at not having played a part in this tragic masquerade.

Did you hear these people's comments? You unscrupulous bastard! You're just like them. No, worse! Worse because you don't have a peseta to your name and yet you promote appalling literature published in instalments. Latino, miserable procurer of pulp fiction, take me to the viaduct. One quick jump and you could be reborn as a new man.

DON LATINO. Max, don't over-excite yourself!

Scene Twelve

The corner of a steep, narrow street with a baroque church in the background. A clear moon over the dark bells. DON LATINO and MAX ESTRELLA are sitting on the steps of a doorway philosophizing. During their conversation dawn breaks. The sound of birds on the roof of the church. The distant dawn light. The night watchmen have already left but all doors remain closed. The concierges are beginning to get up.

MAX. It must be near dawn.

DON LATINO. It is.

MAX. And so cold!

DON LATINO. Let's take a walk.

MAX. Help me, I can't get up. I'm numb with cold!

DON LATINO. It's no more than you deserve for pawning your cloak!

MAX. Lend me your overcoat, Latino.

DON LATINO. Max, you're out of your mind!

MAX. Help me up.

DON LATINO. Come on, you lazy old reactionary.

MAX. I can't move my legs!

DON LATINO. This is quite a performance!

MAX. Imbecile!

DON LATINO. Come to think of it, your face is looking
   rather odd!

MAX. Don Latino of Hispalis, grotesque personae par
   excellence! I shall immortalize you in a novella!

DON LATINO. In a tragedy, Max.

MAX. Our tragedy is no longer a tragedy.

DON LATINO. But it has to be something!

MAX. An Esperpento.

DON LATINO. Stop twitching, Max!

MAX. I'm freezing to death!

DON LATINO. Come on, get up! Let's go for a walk.

MAX. I can't.

DON LATINO. Stop this farce. Let's get going.

MAX. Breathe on me. Where have you gone, Latino?

DON LATINO. I'm right beside you.

MAX. Now that you've been transformed into an ox, I can't
   recognize you. Breathe hard on me, illustrious ox from
   Bethlehem's stable. Bellow, Latino! You are the bell-ox and
   if you bellow hard enough Buey Apis, the Sacred Bull will
   appear. We shall fight with him in the bullring.

DON LATINO. You're beginning to frighten me. This joke
   isn't funny anymore.

MAX. The avant-garde are deceiving themselves. It was Goya
   who invented the Grotesque. Our classical heroes have gone
   to Calle Álvarez Gato; Cat's Alley.

DON LATINO. You're completely drunk!

MAX. Classical heroes reflected in concave mirrors give us the
   Grotesque or Esperpento. The tragic sense of Spanish life can
   only be rendered through an aesthetic that is systematically
   deformed.

DON LATINO. Rubbish! Don't be so pompous!

MAX. Spain is a grotesque deformation of European civilization.

DON LATINO. It may well be, but I'm not getting involved!

MAX. In a concave mirror, even the most beautiful images become absurd.

DON LATINO. I agree. But I do enjoy looking at myself in the hall of mirrors in the Calle Álvarez Gato.

MAX. So do I. Distortion ceases to be distortion when subjected to a perfect mathematic. My present aesthetic approach consists in the transformation of all classical norms with the mathematics of a concave mirror.

DON LATINO. And where is this mirror?

MAX. At the bottom of an empty wine glass.

DON LATINO. Most ingenious! I take my hat off to you!

MAX. Latino, let's distort forms of expression in the same mirror that distorts our faces and contorts the whole miserable life of Spain.

DON LATINO. We'll go to the Calle Álvarez Gato.

MAX. Let's go and see what kind of palace we can rent. Prop me up against the wall. Shake me!

DON LATINO. Don't twitch.

MAX. It's a nervous twitch. I don't even realize I'm doing it!

DON LATINO. And you expect me to believe that!

MAX. Lend me your overcoat.

DON LATINO. What was that?

MAX. I can't feel my hands anymore. My fingertips are frozen. I'm very ill!

DON LATINO. You're trying to fool me so that you can laugh at me.

MAX. Imbecile, take me to the door of my house and let me die in peace.

DON LATINO. You of all people should know that no one will be up at this time.

MAX. Just knock!

DON LATINO OF HISPALIS, *turning his back on* MAX, *begins to kick the door. The echo rebounds through the steep, deserted, narrow streets; as if responding to a certain provocation, the church clock under the weathercock strikes five times.*

MAX. Latino!

DON LATINO. What now? Stop pulling faces!

MAX. If only Collet were awake! . . . Help me up so that I can call her.

DON LATINO. Your voice will never reach up there.

MAX. Collet! I'm bored to death!

DON LATINO. What about me?

MAX. Latino, I think I'm beginning to see again. How did we get to this funeral? Such an apotheosis belongs only in Paris. We must be at Victor Hugo's funeral! Latino, how did we come to preside over such an affair?

DON LATINO. Stop hallucinating, Max.

MAX. It's incredible how well I see.

DON LATINO. You know, this isn't the first time you've done this.

MAX. Who are we burying, Latino?

DON LATINO. It's a secret between ourselves.

MAX. The sun's shining so brightly on the funeral hearse!

DON LATINO. If everything you say wasn't one big joke it would have some theosophical significance. . . . If I presided

over a funeral, I would be the corpse. All these wreaths do
seem to suggest that you must be the corpse.

MAX. Allow me to oblige. To calm your fear, let me lie here
in wait. I am the corpse! What will the malicious press print
tomorrow? The same question the Catalan outcast was asking
himself.

MÁXIMO ESTRELLA *lies down against the door. A stray
dog, running in a zig-zag, crosses the steep, narrow street. He
stops in the middle, lifts a hind leg and urinates. His bleary eyes,
like those of a poet, are raised up to the sky's remaining star.*

MAX. Latino, prepare for the Gloria.

DON LATINO. If you don't put a stop to this macabre joke, I
am leaving.

MAX. I'm the one who's leaving. Forever!

DON LATINO. Get up, Max. Let's move on.

MAX. I'm dead.

DON LATINO. You're frightening me! Max, let's go. Stand
up, and stop twitching, you silly bastard! Max! Max!
Damned fool! Say something!

MAX. Dead people can't talk.

DON LATINO. I'm definitely leaving.

MAX. Goodnight!

DON LATINO OF HISPALIS *blows on his numbed fingers
and walks around, holding himself erect under his dirty overcoat.
With a grumpy cough he returns to* MAX ESTRELLA's *side.
He attempts to prop him up as he whispers in his ear.*

DON LATINO. Max, you're very drunk. It would be a crime
to leave this wallet on you so that somebody could steal
it. Max, I'll take care of your wallet, you can have it back
tomorrow.

Finally, from behind the door, the screeching voice of CUCA

THE NEIGHBOUR *is heard. The echo of steps in the hall.*
DON LATINO OF HISPALIS *creeps away into an alley.*

THE VOICE OF CUCA THE NEIGHBOUR. Señora Flora!
Señora Flora! Someone must have nailed you to the bed!

THE VOICE OF SEÑORA FLORA THE CONCIERGE. Who
is it? Hold on a minute until I find the box of matches.

CUCA THE NEIGHBOUR. Señora Flora!

SEÑORA FLORA THE CONCIERGE. I'm on my way!
Who is it?

CUCA THE NEIGHBOUR. You're a bit on the slow side this
morning! Who do you think it is? It's me, Cuca, I'm on my
way to the laundry!

SEÑORA FLORA THE CONCIERGE. Finally! The bloody
matches! Is it time already?

CUCA THE NEIGHBOUR. It's time all right and well past it!

*The tired steps of a woman in slippers are heard. A murmur of
voices. The grating of a lock, followed by the appearance of two
women in the hollow of the door. The first is grey haired, lively
and as lean as a greyhound, with a bundle of clothes propped
up on her hip; the second is a buxom figure, with a red flannel
underskirt, a frayed scarf across her shoulders, matted hair and
slippers. The Bohemian's body slips, remaining motionless over
the threshold as the door opens.*

CUCA THE NEIGHBOUR. Jesus Christ! A dead man!

SEÑORA FLORA THE CONCIERGE. It's Don Max the
poet, drunk as a skunk.

CUCA THE NEIGHBOUR. He's the colour of wax!

SEÑORA FLORA THE CONCIERGE. Cuca, for Christ's
sake, keep an eye on things for a minute while I run up and
tell Madame Collet.

SEÑORA FLORA THE CONCIERGE *begins climbing the
stairs, her slippers flapping with each step. She can be heard
swearing. Once alone* CUCA *appears visibly afraid. She touches*

*the Bohemian's hands and then leans over to peer at the half-open
eyes, beneath his pale forehead.*

CUCA THE NEIGHBOUR. Good Lord! He's not drunk! This
is death, it couldn't be clearer. Señora Flora! Señora Flora!
I can't stay a minute longer! I've already wasted enough of
the day! I'm leaving this to the authorities, Señora Flora! It's
death all right!

Scene Thirteen
*A funeral wake in an attic. MADAME COLLET and
CLAUDINITA, dishevelled and gaunt, weep for the deceased who
is now lying in a narrow coffin, between four candles, shrouded
in a sheet. The shiny tip of a nail, splintering one of the planks,
protrudes onto the deceased's unprotected temple. The outside of the
coffin is covered in black mourning cloth. Inside, the rough pine
boards are covered by a kitsch, yellowing mat. The coffin rests
between two corners of the tiled floor. The two women weeping at
either side receive the reflection of the candles on their crossed hands.
DORIO DE GADEX, CLARINITO and PÉREZ, leaning
against the wall, are three funeral puppets standing to attention.
Suddenly the mourners are disturbed by the irritating screech of the
doorbell.*

DORIO DE GADEX. The undertaker will be here at four.

CLARINITO. It can't be four already.

DORIO DE GADEX. Do you happen to have a watch,
Madame Collet?

MADAME COLLET. Don't let them take him from me yet!
Don't let them take him!

PÉREZ. It can't possibly be the undertaker.

DORIO DE GADEX. Not one of us has a watch! We're a
wealthy lot, make no mistake about it!

CLAUDINITA *stumbles wearily to answer the door. Voices and
the cough of* DON LATINO OF HISPALIS *are heard – the
familiar cough of tobacco and brandy.*

DON LATINO. The genius is dead! Don't cry, my child! He has died and yet he has not died! Genius is immortal! Comfort yourself, Claudinita, with the fact that you are the daughter of Spain's leading poet! It should be a consolation to know that you are the daughter of Victor Hugo! An illustrious orphan! Let me embrace you!

CLAUDINITA. You're drunk!

DON LATINO. I may look it. I'm not even surprised to hear that I look it. But it's grief!

CLAUDINITA. Your breath reeks of brandy!

DON LATINO. It's grief! The effects of grief, scientifically corroborated by the Germans!

DON LATINO *staggers to the door; his briefcase filled with magazines. His small tailless and earless dog trails between his matchstick legs. His glasses are resting over his forehead as he wipes his droopy eyes with a filthy handkerchief.*

CLAUDINITA. He's rat-arsed!

DORIO DE GADEX. For the funeral. You can always count on Don Latino!

DON LATINO. Max, my brother, though less in years . . .

DORIO DE GADEX. Greater in worth. Great minds think alike.

DON LATINO. Exactly! I couldn't have put it better myself.

DORIO DE GADEX. The Maestro said it before we did.

DON LATINO. Madame Collet, you are a most distinguished widow! And in the midst of your intense grief, you should feel proud to have been the companion of Spain's leading poet! He died poor as Genius should! Max, have you no longer a word for your faithful dog? Max, my friend, though less in years, greater in . . .

DORIO DE GADEX. Worth!

DON LATINO. Idiot! You could at least have let me finish!

Young Modernistas, the Maestro is dead and yet you address one another as if you were equals in the Hispano-American Parnassus! I took a bet with this cold corpse as to which one of us would be the first to undertake the final journey. And as usual, he won! We made the same bet so many times. Do you remember, brother? You died of hunger, as in time I and all worthy Spaniards shall! They slammed every door in your face and you took revenge by starving to death! Well done! Let this shame fall on every bastard in the Academy! In Spain talent remains a crime!

DON LATINO *leans over and kisses the dead man's forehead. At the foot of the coffin, between the endless flicker of the candles, the small dog shakes his stumpy tail. MADAME COLLET raises her head painfully, and looks at the three puppets lined up against the wall.*

MADAME COLLET. For God's sake, take him out into the hall!

DORIO DE GADEX. We'll have to get him some smelling salts. He can barely stand!

CLAUDINITA. Just let him sleep it off! I detest him!

DON LATINO. Claudinita! Spring flower!

CLAUDINITA. If father hadn't gone out yesterday, he'd still be alive!

DON LATINO. Claudinita, this is an unjust accusation! Grief is driving you to distraction!

CLAUDINITA. Bastard! Always interfering!

DON LATINO. I know that you love me really!

DORIO DE GADEX. Don Latino, let's take a walk around the corridor.

DON LATINO. Yes, let's go! This scene is simply too painful!

DORIO DE GADEX. Well then, let's not prolong it unnecessarily.

DORIO DE GADEX *pushes the drunken old man towards*

the door. The small dog jumps over the coffin and follows them, knocking over one of the candles. In the row of puppets pinned to the wall there is now a suggestive hollow space.

DON LATINO. I'll treat you to a couple of glasses of red wine. What do you say?

DORIO DE GADEX. Don Latino, as I'm sure you're aware, I'm an easy man to please.

They disappear into the dark red shadows of the long sad corridor, with the cat at the foot of the jug and the scarlet reflections on the tiles. CLAUDINITA *watches them leave, her eyes burning with anger. She then breaks into hysterical tears and bites at the handkerchief that she has been squeezing in her hands.*

CLAUDINITA. He gives me the creeps! I can't bear to look at him! That man is father's murderer!

MADAME COLLET. For God's sake, child! Don't say such things!

CLAUDINITA. He's the real murderer. I detest him!

MADAME COLLET. The dreaded moment was inevitable, and we knew it. . . . The sad realization of his blindness killed him. . . . He couldn't work and now he's at peace.

CLARINITO. Now everyone will start recognizing his talent, you'll see.

PÉREZ. He no longer casts a shadow.

MADAME COLLET. Without the acclaim of you younger men, who also struggle from one misery to another, he would have been alone in his final years.

CLAUDINITA. More alone than he was!

PÉREZ. The Maestro was a rebel like ourselves.

MADAME COLLET. Max, my poor friend, you alone killed yourself! You alone, without a thought for these two wretched women! All your life you've worked to kill yourself!

CLAUDINITA. Father was so good!

MADAME COLLET. He was his own worst enemy!

A tall, bald, buttoned-up man appears at the door. He has the long red beard of a Jewish anarchist and envious eyes protruding from the stiff head of an obstinate buffalo. He is an untrustworthy German journalist, listed in police files as a Russian anarchist and known by the false name of BASILIO SOULINAKE.

BASILIO. Peace to you all!

MADAME COLLET. I'm sorry Basilio, I can't even offer you a chair!

BASILIO SOULINAKE. Oh! Don't worry about me. Don't give it a second thought. Madame Collet, I won't allow it. Forgive me please for arriving a little late, as late as the army as you Spaniards would say. In the tavern where a number of us immigrant Slavs eat, I've just been given the news that my friend Máximo Estrella has died. Tight Arse's young barman passed me the newspaper. Was it very sudden?

MADAME COLLET. He collapsed! He took no care of himself.

BASILIO SOULINAKE. Who certified him dead? Doctors in Spain are very good, as good as the best elsewhere in the world. Spaniards however, lack an internationally recognized authority. This is not the case in Germany. I studied medicine for ten years and yet I am not a doctor. On entering this room, my first impression was that I was in the presence of a sleeping man, not a dead man. And with respect to this first impression I am, as the Spaniards would say, as obstinate as you can get. Madame Collet, yours is a serious responsibility. My friend Max Estrella is not dead! He displays all the characteristics of an interesting case of catalepsy.

MADAME COLLET and CLAUDINITA scream with joy as they embrace each other. Their eyes liven up, their hands flutter nervously, and the curls resting on their foreheads bounce from side to side. SEÑORA FLORA THE CONCIERGE, arrives panting. Heavy breathing and flapping slippers announce her arrival.

SEÑORA FLORA THE CONCIERGE. The funeral hearse has arrived! Are there enough of you to carry the late deceased downstairs? If not, my husband can come up.

CLAUDINITA. Thanks, we can manage.

BASILIO SOULINAKE. My dear concierge, please inform the funeral service coachman that the burial has been postponed. And may the wind blow favourably on him. Isn't that how you Spaniards would put it?

MADAME COLLET. Ask him to wait! . . . You could be mistaken, Basilio.

SEÑORA FLORA THE CONCIERGE. The pavement is filled with top hats and frock coats – and, unless I'm mistaken, a very posh funeral hearse! What a crazy world! You'd think it was the funeral of a politician! I didn't think the deceased was that important! Madame Collet, what shall I tell the coachman? Because his type won't wait! He says he's got another trip out to the Calle Carlos Rubio.

MADAME COLLET. Oh, Jesus! I don't know what to do.

SEÑORA FLORA THE CONCIERGE. Cuatro Caminos is quite a way, and time's getting on!

CLAUDINITA. Let him go! We don't want him back!

MADAME COLLET. If he can't wait . . . Undoubtedly . . .

SEÑORA FLORA THE CONCIERGE. It'll cost you double. Is it really worth keeping the corpse in the house for a couple more hours. Let them take him away, Madame Collet!

MADAME COLLET. What if he's not dead?

SEÑORA FLORA THE CONCIERGE. Not dead! You haven't left the room so you don't notice the stench.

BASILIO SOULINAKE. Señora, would you be so kind as to tell me whether you have ever studied medicine at a university? If you have I will shut my mouth and say nothing more. But if you have not, then I will refrain from entering into an argument and simply state that he is not dead but merely cataleptic.

SEÑORA FLORA THE CONCIERGE. Not dead? He's dead and rotting!

BASILIO SOULINAKE. Señora, without a university education you cannot discuss such matters. Democracy does not exclude technical categories. You should at least know that, Señora Concierge!

SEÑORA FLORA THE CONCIERGE. Hold on a minute! Are you saying he's not dead? Pity you can't change places! Madame Collet, do you have a mirror? Stick it in front of his mouth and you'll soon see he's not breathing.

BASILIO SOULINAKE. That is not scientific proof! As you Spaniards are always saying, I'm very glad to see you well. Isn't that how you put it?

SEÑORA FLORA THE CONCIERGE. You came here to hold a conference and distress these poor women with a hoax. They've enough worry already what with their grief and their debts.

BASILIO SOULINAKE. Do carry on talking, Señora Concierge. As you can see, I am not interrupting you.

THE FUNERAL SERVICE COACHMAN *appears at the door: the red nose of a drunkard, an old top hat decorated with ribbon, a frayed mourning coat, a cotton wig, and black breeches.*

THE FUNERAL SERVICE COACHMAN. It's gone four o'clock and I've got another customer waiting at the Calle Carlos Rubio!

BASILIO SOULINAKE. Madame Collet, I'll assume full responsibility because I've studied cases of catalepsy in German hospitals. Your husband, and my friend and companion, Max Estrella, is not dead!

SEÑORA FLORA THE CONCIERGE. My dear gentleman, try not to make a scene. Madame Collet, where do you keep your mirror?

BASILIO SOULINAKE. That is an anti-scientific experiment!

THE FUNERAL SERVICE COACHMAN. Just put a lit

match to his thumb. If it burns to the end, he's as dead as my grandfather. Please forgive me if I've been disrespectful!

THE FUNERAL SERVICE COACHMAN *props his whip against the wall and strikes a match. Kneeling beside the coffin, he uncrosses the hands of the deceased and holds up a yellowing palm. He places the burning match on the tip of the thumb. It continues flickering before finally burning out. CLAUDINITA lets out an agonized scream, rolls her eyes and begins to beat her head against the wall.*

CLAUDINITA. My father! My father! My beloved father!

Scene Fourteen

A plot in the East Madrid cemetery. A cold evening. A biting wind. An aggressively sterile evening light illuminates the gravestones. TWO GRAVEDIGGERS are patting down the earth of a grave. They stop work for a moment, lighting the cigarette butts taken from behind their ears with a spark from their tinderboxes. They sit and smoke at the foot of a grave.

THE FIRST GRAVEDIGGER. This one here was a writer.

THE SECOND GRAVEDIGGER. Not much of a funeral!

THE FIRST GRAVEDIGGER. The papers claimed that he was a talented man.

THE SECOND GRAVEDIGGER. Talent doesn't count for much in Spain. Filth and corruption get rewarded, as does everything else which is vaguely rotten.

THE FIRST GRAVEDIGGER. Things aren't that bad!

THE SECOND GRAVEDIGGER. Well, take a look at that poser with the earring over there!

THE FIRST GRAVEDIGGER. What about him?

THE SECOND GRAVEDIGGER. Lives like a king, even though he's the biggest shit around. Look at him flirting with the Councillor's widow.

THE FIRST GRAVEDIGGER. Councillor! You mean bureaucratic bastard!

THE SECOND GRAVEDIGGER. You said it. Can you imagine a woman in her position losing her head over someone like that?

THE FIRST GRAVEDIGGER. That's the problem with women, they're all blind.

THE SECOND GRAVEDIGGER. The triumph of vice over virtue! It's the same everywhere.

THE FIRST GRAVEDIGGER. Do you know her? Is she good for a laugh?

THE SECOND GRAVEDIGGER. She's well-built in all the right places, if that's what you mean. Just watch her arse move as she walks! Not bad at all!

THE FIRST GRAVEDIGGER. Some bastards have all the luck!

Two slow moving shadows, friends from MÁXIMO ESTRELLA'S funeral cortège, appear through a path filled with tombstones and crosses. They creep forward, talking in hushed voices, like two souls filled with a religious respect for death. One is an old gentleman with a snow-white beard and a Spanish cloak wrapped around his shoulders. He is the Celtic MARQUIS OF BRADOMÍN. The other is the dark, intense RUBÉN DARÍO.

RUBÉN. It is unnerving but appropriate that after all these years we should meet in a cemetery!

THE MARQUIS. On consecrated land. If one calls it that, my dear Rubén, our meeting acquires a different significance.

RUBÉN. How right you are. Neither cemetery nor necropolis. Such names denote a sad and terrible coldness, like the study of grammar. Marquis, what does the word necropolis suggest to you?

THE MARQUIS. Academic pedantry.

RUBÉN. For me, necropolis is the end of everything. It evokes the irreparable and the monstrous – dying without hope in a hotel room. And consecrated ground? Consecrated ground harbours a certain light.

THE MARQUIS. A golden dome – and beneath it, my dear Rubén, there religiously resounds the strange and terrible trumpet!

RUBÉN. Death would be desirable, Marquis, if it were not for the terror of the unknown. I would have been happy three thousand years ago in ancient Athens!

THE MARQUIS. I would not exchange my Christian baptism for the smile of a cynical Greek. Despite my sins, I expect eternal life.

RUBÉN. How delightful!

THE MARQUIS. Perhaps life in Greece was more serene . . .

RUBÉN. They were the only men who knew how to sanctify it!

THE MARQUIS. We sanctify death. Life is no more than an instant. Death is the only truth. And of all deaths, I prefer the Christian death.

RUBÉN. The delightful philosophy of a Spanish nobleman! How delightful! Marquis, let's speak no more of her!

They walk around in silence. THE GRAVEDIGGERS, *who have now finished patting down the earth, take turns drinking from their jug. The black outlines of the two figures stand out against the wall of white gravestones.* RUBÉN DARÍO *and* THE MARQUIS OF BRADOMÍN *stop before the dark patch of earth over the grave.*

RUBÉN. Marquis, how did you come to be a friend of Máximo Estrella?

THE MARQUIS. Max was the son of a Carlist captain who died at my side during the war. Did he tell another story?

RUBÉN. He claimed that you had both fought together in the Mexican revolution.

THE MARQUIS. What an imagination! Max was born thirty years after my trip to Mexico. Do you know how old I am? I've almost reached a century. My dear poet, my days shall soon be over.

RUBÉN. Are you eternal, Marquis?

THE MARQUIS. That's what I'm afraid of, but patience!

The dark shadows of THE GRAVEDIGGERS – *glimmering hoes over their shoulders – move towards the path of tombs. They approach.*

THE MARQUIS. Could these be philosophers, like those at Ophelia's grave?

RUBÉN. Marquis, have you ever known an Ophelia?

THE MARQUIS. All adolescent girls are Ophelias. That creature was a willing woman, my dear Rubén. But the prince, like all princes, was a little slow on the uptake!

RUBÉN. Don't you love the divine William?

THE MARQUIS. During my period of literary flirtation, I chose him as my mentor. He is exquisite! With a shy philosopher and an unbelievably silly girl he miraculously created the most beautiful of tragedies. In our Spanish theatre, my dear Rubén, Hamlet and Ophelia would become two comic characters. A shy boy and a silly girl! Just imagine what the glorious Quintero brothers would have done with them!

RUBÉN. There's a little of Hamlet in all of us.

THE MARQUIS. In you, who continues to have luck with the ladies, perhaps. But I, burdened with age, am nearer to being the skull of Yorick.

THE FIRST GRAVEDIGGER. If you're looking for the way out gentlemen, just follow us. It's closing time.

THE MARQUIS. Rubén, how would you feel about staying here?

RUBÉN. Horrible!

THE MARQUIS. Well then, we'd better follow these two.

RUBÉN. Marquis, should we return tomorrow to place a crucifix over our friend's grave?

THE MARQUIS. Tomorrow! By tomorrow we'll both have forgotten this Christian intention.

RUBÉN. Perhaps!

They linger in silence, following THE GRAVEDIGGERS *who stop at the corner of each path of graves to wait for them.*

THE MARQUIS. I'm too old to walk any faster.

THE FIRST GRAVEDIGGER. You don't have to apologize, Sir.

THE MARQUIS. In a couple of years I'll complete my century.

THE SECOND GRAVEDIGGER. You must have seen a fair number of funerals!

THE MARQUIS. Unless you've been at this for a couple of years, probably more than you. Are there many people dying at this time of year?

THE FIRST GRAVEDIGGER. There's no shortage of work. Young and old alike.

THE SECOND GRAVEDIGGER. Falling leaves mean an autumn harvest.

THE MARQUIS. Do they pay you for each funeral?

THE FIRST GRAVEDIGGER. They pay us a daily wage of three pesetas, come what may. With the cost of living what it is at the moment, that's barely enough to eat. We manage to pick up a bit extra here and there. But all in all, poverty.

THE SECOND GRAVEDIGGER. It's all a question of luck. Either you've got it or you haven't.

THE FIRST GRAVEDIGGER. Some families who lose a loved one pay us a couple of pesetas to take care of the grave. Others promise to pay but never do. Most of the families pay for the first couple of months, but you're lucky if one in a hundred keeps it up for a whole year. Sorrow never lasts.

THE MARQUIS. Have you never known an inconsolable widow?

THE FIRST GRAVEDIGGER. Not one! But that's not to say there isn't one.

THE MARQUIS. Have you never heard of Artemisia and Mausolus?

THE FIRST GRAVEDIGGER. I can't speak for anyone else, but I certainly haven't.

THE SECOND GRAVEDIGGER. We see so many women around here, that it's not always possible to recognize them.

They walk very slowly. RUBÉN, now pensive, scribbles a few words onto an envelope. They arrive at the creaking wrought-iron gate. The kind MARQUIS brings an ivory hand from beneath his cape and hands some coins to the gravediggers.

THE MARQUIS. You may not know your mythology but you are both stoic philosophers. May you live to see many more funerals.

THE FIRST GRAVEDIGGER. At your service. Much obliged!

THE SECOND GRAVEDIGGER. Same here. If there's anything we can do for you, Sir . . .

They remove their caps to show their appreciation before moving away. A smiling MARQUIS OF BRADOMÍN wraps himself up in his cloak. RUBÉN DARÍO keeps his hand on the envelope on which he has written a number of lines. Coming forward from behind the shelter of a high wall, the old MARQUIS's coach approaches the cemetery gate.

THE MARQUIS. Is that a poem, Rubén? Would you like to read it to me?

RUBÉN. When I've polished it. It's still rather a monstrosity.

THE MARQUIS. My dear Rubén, poems should be published at every stage: from what you would refer to as the monstrous stage through to their definitive form. They would then acquire the same value as the proofs of etchings. Are you sure that you wouldn't like to read it to me?

RUBÉN. Tomorrow, Marquis.

THE MARQUIS. The word tomorrow should never be uttered to a man of my age standing at the gate of a cemetery. Well, let's climb into the coach. We still have to visit a bandit. I want you to help me sell the manuscript of my *Memoirs* to a publisher. I need the money. I've been ruined since I carried out the disastrous idea of retiring to the Bradomín estate. It wasn't women that proved the end of me, despite the fact that I loved them to distraction. It was agriculture!

RUBÉN. How delightful!

THE MARQUIS. My *Memoirs* will be published after my death. I intend to sell them as if I were selling my own skeleton. Let us assist one another.

Scene Fifteen

TIGHT ARSE's *tavern. Darkness broken by the flickering gas lamp.* DON LATINO OF HISPALIS *stands stammering in front of the counter, persistently offering to buy* PAY PAY THE POSER *a drink. He stumbles and falls, annoying everyone around him.*

DON LATINO. Drink up, my friend! You can't imagine the sorrow that fills my heart! Drink up! I downed it all in one!

PAY PAY THE POSER. That's because you have no class.

DON LATINO. Today we have buried Spain's leading poet! Four friends turned up at the cemetery. That was it! Not one bastard turned up from the Learned Establishment! What do you think of that, Venancio?

TIGHT ARSE. Whatever you say, Don Latí.

DON LATINO. Genius shines with its own light! Isn't that right, Poser?

PAY PAY THE POSER. Absolutely, Don Latino.

DON LATINO. I've taken upon myself the burden of publishing his writings! A reputable task! I am the literary executor! He has bequeathed us a social novel with the stature of *Les Miserables*. I am the executor! And thus the royalties from his entire works will pass on to the family. And I don't care if I'm ruined while attempting to publish them! Such are the obligations of friendship! Like the nocturnal pilgrim, my immortal hope does not look to the earth for fulfilment. Gentlemen, not one representative from the Learned Establishment! At least there were four friends, four extraordinary personalities! The Home Secretary, Bradomín, Rubén and yours truly. Isn't that right, Poser?

PAY PAY THE POSER. The entire Royal Family could have been there for all I care.

TIGHT ARSE. Don't you think you're taking things a bit far by claiming that the Government was officially represented at Don Max's funeral. If you spread that around you're going to find yourself head high in shit!

DON LATINO. I'm not lying! The Home Secretary was at the cemetery. We even said hello!

THE YOUNG BARMAN. It must have been the Phantom!

DON LATINO. Shut up, you silly fool! Didn't President Maura call in on the family of Gallo the Matador to pay his respects?

PAY PAY THE POSER. José Gómez, alias 'Gallito', was a star who died fighting majestically in the arena. He was the king of the bullring.

TIGHT ARSE. What about Juan Belmonte alias 'Terremoto', the human earthquake?

PAY PAY THE POSER. An intellectual!

DON LATINO. Another round, boy! This is the saddest day of my life! I lost a friend who was like a brother to me, a Maestro! This is why I am drinking, Venancio.

TIGHT ARSE. Your bill is rocketing, Don Latí. You'd better check to see if you've got enough money on you. Just in case!

DON LATINO. I've got enough money to buy you and your entire tavern.

He pulls out a handful of notes from the inner pockets of his overcoat and throws them over the counter, under the devious glance of PAY PAY THE POSER *and to the visible astonishment of* VENANCIO. THE YOUNG BARMAN *bends down to pick up a note which has fallen between the old man's muddy legs. The young* STREET WALKER, ENRIQUETA, *hidden in a corner of the dive, removes the scarf from her forehead and sits up, her eyes fixed on the counter.*

THE YOUNG BARMAN. Has somebody left you their fortune, Don Latí?

DON LATINO. Somebody who owed me a few pesetas finally paid up.

TIGHT ARSE. You call that a few.

ENRIQUETA THE STREET WALKER. There's thousands!

DON LATINO. Do I owe you anything?

ENRIQUETA THE STREET WALKER. Of course you bloody well do! You cashed in on that lottery ticket I sold you.

DON LATINO. That's not true.

ENRIQUETA THE STREET WALKER. Number 5775.

THE YOUNG BARMAN. That's the number Don Max had!

ENRIQUETA THE STREET WALKER. In the end he didn't want it and Don Latí took it. And the mean bastard hasn't bothered to hand over my share of the takings.

DON LATINO. I'd forgotten!

ENRIQUETA THE STREET WALKER. You've got a terrible memory.

DON LATINO. I'll give it to you.

ENRIQUETA THE STREET WALKER. I'm sure you will.

DON LATINO. You can count on my boundless generosity.

THE YOUNG BARMAN *slips behind his boss and slyly pulls his apron while pretending to be otherwise engaged.* TIGHT ARSE *locks the till and joins the young man in the dark corner where the animal hides are stored. They whisper and gesture maniacally, whilst keeping an eye and ear on the group at the counter.* ENRIQUETA THE STREET WALKER *winks at* DON LATINO.

ENRIQUETA THE STREET WALKER. Don Latí, you could set me up for life with that cash!

DON LATINO. I'll buy you a flat.

ENRIQUETA THE STREET WALKER. Now, that's a man talking!

DON LATINO. Crispín, my son, a glass of anisette for the lady.

THE YOUNG BARMAN. It's on the way, Don Latí!

DON LATINO. Are you going to confession?

ENRIQUETA THE STREET WALKER. Don Latí, you are a dear sweet man! One in a million! Now, stop pinching my bum!

PAY PAY THE POSER. Be careful, Don Latino, a certain woman of ill repute has her eyes on your money.

ENRIQUETA THE STREET WALKER. We split the lucky ticket fifty fifty! Don Latí paid one and a half pesetas and I matched it.

DON LATINO. This is daylight robbery, Enriqueta!

ENRIQUETA THE STREET WALKER. What are you afraid of? Can't you stop pinching my bum? You're worse than a mad dog on heat!

PAY PAY THE POSER. This isn't the woman for you.

ENRIQUETA THE STREET WALKER. I'd have him in his grave before the week was out.

DON LATINO. We'd soon see about that.

PAY PAY THE POSER. You need a woman with a little less energy.

ENRIQUETA THE STREET WALKER. You'd be better off with my mother. But mother is a respectable widow – if you wanted anything out of her, you'd have to make a trip up the altar.

DON LATINO. I'm an apostle of free love.

ENRIQUETA THE STREET WALKER. Move in with me and mother. You can be the respectable gentleman lodger we advertised for in the local paper. Our previous lodger moved on only yesterday, leaving a room which would suit you perfectly. Where are you going, Don Latí?

DON LATINO. I'm off to see a man about a bicycle. I'll be back. Don't worry darling, wait for me here.

ENRIQUETA THE STREET WALKER. Don Latí, I'm a very jealous woman. I'll go with you.

TIGHT ARSE *stops whispering to the young man and takes two strides back to the counter. He grabs the drunken old man by the collar in the doorway.* DON LATINO *blinks, contorts his face and lets his arms fall to his side like those of a puppet.*

DON LATINO. Don't be so rough!

TIGHT ARSE. You and I have something to discuss. The deceased left quite a debt here. You can check the bills later but I suggest you make a payment now.

DON LATINO. Why?

TIGHT ARSE. Because you're too clever for your own good and we both know it.

PAY PAY THE POSER *moves towards them, swaying as he walks. He allows them to see that he has a knife hidden up his sleeve. He coughs and scratches his head, moving his cap to one side.* ENRIQUETA *wraps the shawl over her shoulder and clandestinely opens a small flick knife.*

PAY PAY THE POSER. Here we all are, our eyes popping out of their sockets as we take a good long look at all this money.

ENRIQUETA THE STREET WALKER. Don Latí will walk out into the street on my arm.

PAY PAY THE POSER. No way!

TIGHT ARSE. You, egghead, had better put that knife away and stop looking for trouble.

PAY PAY THE POSER. Don Latí, you must have pulled a job off at the bank!

DON LATINO. Of course.

ENRIQUETA THE STREET WALKER. Go and scratch your balls, fart-face! Don Latí hit the jackpot with his share of the lottery ticket 5775. I sold it to him!

TIGHT ARSE. Crispín and I were witnesses. Isn't that right?

THE YOUNG BARMAN. That's right.

PAY PAY THE POSER. Bullshit!

PACONA, *an old whore, known also as a newspaper seller, enters the tavern with a bundle of printed papers. She drops a copy of* The Madrid Herald *on the counter and then leaves as she entered, snooping around in silence. Only when she is at the door, looking up at the stars, does she begin her cry again.*

PACONA. *Madrid Herald*! Early edition! Get your *Herald*! Mysterious death of two women on the Calle Bastardillos! Read all about it! *Herald*!

DON LATINO *breaks away from the group and moves towards the counter in a sly, inquisitive manner. He opens out the newspaper, holding it under the circular spot of the gas lamp, and stutters through the headlines which the reporter uses to prepare for his story of the events on the Calle Bastardillos. The others look at him in contempt, as if he were a senile old man.*

DON LATINO. 'Coal Fumes. Two Women Gassed. According to a neighbour. Dona Vicenta Knows Nothing. Crime or Suicide? Mystery Continues!'

THE YOUNG BARMAN. Check if the paper gives the women's names, Don Latí.

DON LATINO. I'm looking.

PAY PAY THE POSER. Don't try too hard, pea brain!

ENRIQUETA THE STREET WALKER. Let's go, Don Latí.

THE YOUNG BARMAN. I bet you those two women are Don Máximo's wife and daughter!

DON LATINO. That's absurd! Why would they kill themselves?

TIGHT ARSE. They were having a rough time!

DON LATINO. They were used to it. There could only be one logical explanation. Grief at the loss of such a distinguished figure!

TIGHT ARSE. And just when you could have given them a hand.

DON LATINO. I intended to! I have a heart of gold, Venancio!

TIGHT ARSE. It's a crazy world!

DON LATINO. A grotesque esperpento!

THE DRUNKARD. An exclusive mind!

End of play

Silver Face

Characters

DON JUAN MANUEL MONTENEGRO
His sons – DON MIGUEL otherwise known as SILVER
            FACE
            DON PEDRITO
            DON ROSENDO
            DON MAURO
            DON GONZALITO
            DON FARRUQUIÑO
SABELITA, god-daughter to Don Juan Manuel Montenegro
THE ABBOT OF LANTAÑON
His sister DOÑA JEROMITA
THE SEXTON (BLAS DE MÍGUEZ)
THE SEXTON'S WIFE
THEIR LAZY DAUGHTER (GINERA)
A CHORUS OF ILLBRED CHILDREN
FUSO NEGRO, a madman
DON GALÁN, servant to Don Juan Manuel Montenegro
A group of five herdsmen – PEDRO ABUÍN
                            RAMIRO DE BEALO
                            MANUEL TOVÍO
                            MANUEL FONSECA
                            SEBASTIÁN DE XOGAS
THE OLD MAN OF CURES (QUINTO PIO)
and A SHEPHERD
PICHONERA THE MUTTERER
LUDOVINA, the innkeeper
and A WHORE AT ANOTHER INN
A TRAVELLER FROM MARAGATERIA
A PENITENT
THE BLIND MAN OF GONDAR
A SPANIARD RECENTLY RETURNED FROM
AMERICA
THE DEACON OF LESÓN
A GOSSIPY OLD WOMAN
A VOICE IN A CHIMNEY
OLD WOMEN
SCREAMS AND INSULTS
PROCLAMATIONS

THE CRIES OF WOMEN
THE DRONING CHANT OF PIOUS WOMEN
BLASPHEMOUS CURSES AND SHRIEKS
THE DIVINE LIGHT OF THE HOLY EUCHARIST

Act One

Scene One

A clear dawn sky. A distant village community in the hills of Lantaño. High on the rocks, the ruins of a castle. On the greener ground, an estate belonging to The Marquis of Bradomín. A group of herdsmen – MANUEL TOVÍO, MANUEL FONSECA, PEDRO ABUÍN, RAMIRO DE BEALO and SEBASTIÁN DE XOGAS – are resting beneath the shelter of the famous rocks. Their horses are scattered nearby, grazing on the sacred grass of these Celtic lands. In the distance, a wild mountain cow protests loudly as A SHEPHERD attempts to lead her to market.

PEDRO ABUÍN. Livestock from Lantaño has always had the right to pass through Lantañon.

RAMIRO DE BEALO. Not any more. The mayors lost the case and it's not worth contesting it.

PEDRO ABUÍN. That remains to be seen.

RAMIRO DE BEALO. Don't get into legal disputes with powerful dynasties.

PEDRO ABUÍN. Arrogant lot! Their power wouldn't amount to much if we all joined against them. Talk about tyranny! They're worse than the King!

SEBASTIÁN DE XOGAS. And there's no shortage of kings who've ended up with a noose around their necks.

RAMIRO DE BEALO. In other countries.

MANUEL FONSECA. The Montenegros are men without hearts!

PEDRO ABUÍN. We'll live to see this dynasty of degenerate bastards thrown out of house and home and reduced to begging for food and shelter. Mightier men have fallen!

MANUEL TOVÍO. In the meantime though, they deny us the right to pass through the Lands of Lantañon. The age we live in is so unjust!

Small groups of herdsmen and tradesmen from Cures, Tres Cures,

*Taveirós and Nigrán weave their way through the mountain
paths. A herd of cows, goaded by prods and shouts, stumbles
dangerously along the Celtic ridges. The voices of the herdsmen
and the barking of the dogs produces an epic sound which
resounds through the crystal-clear morning sky.*

PEDRO ABUÍN. Stop, my friends!

DISTANT VOICES. What is it?

PEDRO ABUÍN. It looks as if the inhabitants of Lantañon
now have the power to deny access to those travelling to the
fair at Viana. Are you happy about that?

THE OLD MAN OF CURES. If there's a law that says
so! . . .

PEDRO ABUÍN. There isn't one and Don Juan Manuel
doesn't have the power to stop us passing through!

THE OLD MAN OF CURES. You're expecting too much.

SEBASTIÁN DE XOGAS. I wouldn't go as far as that
but I think it's worth discussing. In accordance with past
agreements we have the right to cross the lands of Lantañon.
That was the arrangement reached with our forefathers.

RAMIRO DE BEALO. It's not worth the trouble. Don Juan
Manuel won the lawsuit he had with the mayors.

PEDRO ABUÍN. It was an unfair decision! If we all agreed to
travel together, what would those silly pieces of paper prove?

THE OLD MAN OF CURES. When a judge makes a
decision, good or bad, right or wrong, those who stand
against it can never win. That's the way it is, that's the way
it's always been and that's the way it will always be!

PEDRO ABUÍN. Writ or no writ, Montenegro doesn't own us.
We have our rights!

THE OLD MAN OF CURES. Arrogance doesn't win lawsuits.

SEBASTIÁN DE XOGAS. What are you going to do? Move
your cattle by boat?

THE OLD MAN OF CURES. We'll go to the gates of the estate and ask Don Juan Manuel's permission.

PEDRO ABUÍN. He's too arrogant to listen to us!

THE OLD MAN OF CURES. We should all go and convince him of our claim. There's strength in numbers.

PEDRO ABUÍN. And if he refuses? What then?

THE OLD MAN OF CURES. We'll just have to wait until he calms down. You're proposing we unite against the court's decision. That's what you're saying, is it? I'm saying we negotiate, we compromise to avoid trouble. Time will tell who was right.

RAMIRO DE BEALO. We've nothing to lose by going there.

MANUEL TOVÍO. If we catch him at a bad time, he'll throw us out before we know what's hit us.

PEDRO ABUÍN. Well if he shouts obscenities at me, I'll shout them back!

THE OLD MAN OF CURES. That won't get you very far!

A distant SHEPHERD standing alone against a protruding crag helps the delegation of men by making circles with his staff in the age-old lichen growing on the rockface.

THE SHEPHERD. Others have already tried your idea. And what did they get out of it? Abuse! I went on friendly terms. And what did I receive? Insults! He listened to what I had to say, pulled at his beard, and then told me to ask my wife to come and plead on my behalf!

MANUEL FONSECA. No doubt he planned to discuss it with her in bed.

THE SHEPHERD. I wish someone would discuss putting an end to him!

RAMIRO DE BEALO. He's a powerful man.

THE SHEPHERD. Well, take him your best cow.

PEDRO ABUÍN. He's probably done it already.

RAMIRO DE BEALO. Go to Hell!

PEDRO ABUÍN. We need to make a decision, my friends. I think we should take our cattle through Lantañon. But all of us must be agreed. If, as they say, there was a time when the houses of the rich and mighty were burned down, that time could return.

THE SHEPHERD. Let's go before we waste any more time. That grey-haired wolf may still be alone in his cave.

PEDRO ABUÍN. What do you all think? Do you think we should stay together and defend our right to cross this land?

THE OLD MAN OF CURES. As a man with the wisdom that only age brings, I believe that we will gain much more through tactful reasoning than through unruly actions.

PEDRO ABUÍN. Those who share this opinion, go ahead, speak first.

THE OLD MAN OF CURES. Amen! The world would be impossible to govern without understanding between the meek and the mighty.

THE VOICES OF THE HERDSMEN. Shoo Marela! Shoo Bermella!

MANUEL FONSECA. Let's wait and see what Quinto de Cures achieves.

RAMIRO DE BEALO. He's got nothing to lose.

THE SHEPHERD. He'll do no better than those who went before him.

PEDRO ABUÍN. He'll get an earful of insults and abuse!

SEBASTIÁN DE XOGAS. Listen! If we really want to cause trouble, we've plenty of time. I think we should leave any possible disputes until after the Corpus Christi celebrations at Viana. Let's go and enjoy ourselves at the fair and waste no further time. There'll be a time and a place on our return to take revenge against Montenegro's decision.

PEDRO ABUÍN. Montenegro! We'll be back!

SEBASTIÁN DE XOGAS. Your days are numbered,
  Montenegro!

THE SHEPHERD. Our only hope lies in setting fire to
  his fields!

The herdsmen ride off, while THE SHEPHERD, *high on a crag
silhouetted against the sky, waves them off with a shout. In the
distance, a flock of doves, flying through the crystal dawn sky,
disperse as they soar over the tower of Lantañon.*

Scene Two
*Morning light dawns on the Lantañon estate. In an inner courtyard
of lemon trees, the arches of a recess with a stone staircase.*
SABELITA *is standing at the top of the staircase, looking up to
the sky. Her honey-coloured hair is tied back in two plaits. She has
a strong, high forehead, fine, delicate features and is dressed in a
plain, purple habit. In a corner of the inner courtyard, a number of
women carrying fruit and other market goods can be heard shouting.*

THE CRIES OF WOMEN. Is it true they've denied access to
  the estate? It takes ages if you have to go all the way around!
  Mother of God! Mother of God! As if we haven't been
  travelling for long enough already! Blessed Mother! We've
  come so far! Our village is further up the mountains than San
  Quinto de Cures!

*THE WOMEN scatter as a horseman approaches. He is a
striking young man, surrounded by greyhounds and other hunting
dogs.* THE WOMEN *rush from side to side, screaming out
blasphemous insults; their faces, masked beneath their caps, are
contorted in anger; their arms are outstretched to protect their
goods.* DON MIGUEL MONTENEGRO, *the handsome son
of* DON JUAN MANUEL MONTENEGRO, *jumps out of
the saddle and ties his horse to the large iron ring fixed to the
wall. He is generally known as* SILVER FACE, *because of his
pleasant, genial nature.*

THE CRIES OF WOMEN. Don Miguelito, please let us cross

through! Have pity on us, Silver Face! We've come from the ends of the earth! Have a heart!

PICHONA THE MUTTERER. Have a heart of gold, a kind face should have a kind heart, Don Miguelito.

SILVER FACE. Go through and take the Devil with you!

PICHONA THE MUTTERER. Long live Silver Face!

SILVER FACE. So Pichona, when do I get my wicked way?

PICHONA THE MUTTERER. You are a right one!

THE CRIES OF WOMEN. God protect you! God protect you!

The group of women rush into the inner courtyard through the large arch adorned with the Montenegro coat of arms. SABELITA begins singing; her sweet, lisping voice echoes through the morning sky. The dramatic violet tones of her habit, standing out against the old stones of the patio and the lush, green lemon trees, create the impression that she is on fire.

SABELITA. How did you leave my godmother?

SILVER FACE. Praying. When do you intend going back?

SABELITA. When my godfather tells me to.

SILVER FACE. My mother is waiting for you.

SABELITA. Why doesn't she call me back? That's what I really want.

SILVER FACE. What? Now that I'm here?

SABELITA. Don't you start.

SILVER FACE. Help me see what's wrong with this dog. He's limping.

SABELITA. If he came through the thistles, it must be a thorn.

SILVER FACE. Come on, over here Carabel!

The dog approaches with one foot in the air. SILVER FACE

turns him over and takes a good look at his paws. SABELITA is now beside him, kneeling on the stone slabs, smiling thoughtfully.

SABELITA. Watch out he doesn't bite you!

SILVER FACE. If he did that, I'm sure you'd nurse me back to health.

SABELITA. I'm no doctor!

SILVER FACE sticks his hand into the mouth of the dog who howls, lashing out in all directions, but does not bite him. SABELITA stares at him intensely, her large, clear eyes as frank and innocent as those of a child.

SABELITA. You're out of your mind!

SILVER FACE. Come on Carabel, attack!

SABELITA. That animal is brighter than you are.

SILVER FACE. Well, let him keep his thorn then.

SILVER FACE jumps up violently. His hair is the colour of gold, his eyes a piercing green, his nose that of an imperial eagle. SABELITA, kneeling beside the dog on the stone floor, tries desperately to remove the thorn stuck in his paw. SILVER FACE returns to her side.

SABELITA. You're mad!

SILVER FACE. Then, you make me well again.

SABELITA. How?

SILVER FACE. With words.

SABELITA. I'm not a faith healer.

SILVER FACE. I need to talk to you tonight, Isabel.

SABELITA. Well, aren't we talking now?

SILVER FACE. I mean a different kind of talking, by the light of the moon.

SABELITA. You really are crazy!

SILVER FACE. Don't you love me, Isabel?

SABELITA. Not the way you think.

SILVER FACE. Well then, you don't love me.

SABELITA. That must be it.

SILVER FACE. I'll come up to your room tonight.

SABELITA. You really are out of your mind!

SILVER FACE. Will you let me in?

SABELITA. Don't even think of it!

SILVER FACE. If I find the door locked, I'll break it down.

SABELITA. You monster!

SILVER FACE. Don't scream when you see me.

SABELITA. Have you no sense of respect?

SILVER FACE. And what would happen if I did come up to your room tonight?

SABELITA. You really do like to play with fire! But you don't frighten me, Silver Face. . . . If you love me, respect me.

DON JUAN MANUEL MONTENEGRO *appears through the orchard carrying a shotgun, with a lively sandy-haired greyhound at his side, and remains by the outer gate. He is a despotic, womanizing nobleman; hospitable yet violent, he is a king from the Suevo tribe and rules from his home at Lantañon.*

DON JUAN MANUEL. Silver Face, leave whatever you're doing and come over here. I was expecting you back yesterday. You've taken your time coming back from Viana!

SILVER FACE. My horse was limping.

DON JUAN MANUEL. I sent someone to find you so that we could count the cattle and brand the young bulls. Your brothers are there already. The best cattle have to be taken down to the fair at Viana. Your elder brothers will take care of all that, they seem to be well-acquainted with the herdsmen's dirty tricks. . . . But I want you to take charge of the money. I hope you don't gamble it away as your thieving brothers are in the habit of doing.

SILVER FACE. Nobody is free from the sin of temptation.

DON JUAN MANUEL. Well, if you feel tempted, make sure you win. Otherwise don't come back.

SILVER FACE. I'll bear that in mind.

DON JUAN MANUEL *looks at him with sly admiration: he has a strong and indulgent affection for this son.* SILVER FACE *is standing in front of his father, his mouth firm and a lively glint in his clear green eyes.*

DON JUAN MANUEL. How is your mother? Is she well?

SILVER FACE. Yes, father.

DON JUAN MANUEL. What was she doing when you left her?

SILVER FACE. Much the same as usual: praying.

DON JUAN MANUEL. She's abandoned me!

SILVER FACE. Mother feels you've done the same to her in Viana.

DON JUAN MANUEL. The stories she comes out with. And now, what about this story that Pedro Rey came to me with?

SILVER FACE. A wild cow fell into the river so I dived in to save her.

DON JUAN MANUEL. That's not what I heard. It seems you were riding the cow and she sank beneath the weight, swallowing so much water that she died soon after under the bridge.

SILVER FACE. She hasn't died. She's on the point of dying.

DON JUAN MANUEL. Pedro Rey thinks I should pay for the

cow. I've told him to bring me the animal, dead or alive, and then I'll make up my mind.

SILVER FACE. He'll steal your money. When I dived in the river, the cow was drowning. Don't pay him for it.

DON JUAN MANUEL. I'm not talking about paying him for it. I want to propose an exchange. He lets me have the cow and I'll let him take you. What do you think?

SILVER FACE. I'm an obedient son.

DON JUAN MANUEL. Let's be serious for a moment. I want you to be a nobleman. And as a nobleman there are certain codes of behaviour you should always adhere to!

SILVER FACE. I know, father.

DON JUAN MANUEL. Your brothers corrupt you with their bad example. Now, listen to me. I'm not asking you to be a saint. Boys will be boys. But don't forget what's expected of you as the other degenerates do.

DON JUAN MANUEL *finishes speaking with a great sigh, his arms resting on the shoulders of the young man. In a gesture of generosity,* SILVER FACE *breaks away to kiss the hand of the old man.*

SILVER FACE. Father, whatever I do, right or wrong, I do without the advice of others.

DON JUAN MANUEL. Well then, go up to the mountains and do what I told you.

SILVER FACE. Amen. What time did my brothers leave?

DON JUAN MANUEL. At dawn.

SILVER FACE *unties his horse, who has been pawing around the shadow of the harsh stone arch where it was tied. Under the proud gaze of his old father* SILVER FACE *mounts the horse in a single leap and rides off at great speed. Up on the patio, as fair as ripe corn, smiling with the innocence of a child, stands the old nobleman's god-daughter,* SABELITA.

SABELITA. Be sensible, Silver Face!

SILVER FACE. I can't when it concerns you!

DON JUAN MANUEL. Is my son trying to win your affections?

SABELITA. It's just a passing infatuation.

DON JUAN MANUEL. What was he saying?

SABELITA. When?

DON JUAN MANUEL. A moment ago.

SABELITA. I can't remember.

DON JUAN MANUEL. Can you recall your reply?

SABELITA. I wasn't listening to him.

DON JUAN MANUEL. You're not meant for him.

SABELITA. I don't claim to be.

DON JUAN MANUEL. You are worth more.

SABELITA. I'm worth nothing more than a lifetime of sorrow.

DON JUAN MANUEL. And who is the source of this sorrow?

SABELITA. He who is the source of everything.

DON JUAN MANUEL. When you're young there is no sorrow. Sorrow came to me with age . . . don't fall for my son!

SABELITA. I don't listen to him, godfather.

DON JUAN MANUEL. If only I were ten years younger.

SABELITA. I wouldn't want you to be ten years younger.

DON JUAN MANUEL. But if I were, you'd look at me, instead of staring at the ground like a damned nun!

In a corner of the courtyard a mad beggar with a disfigured face howls loudly. It is the poor, ragged, mischievous FUSO

NEGRO, *who travels the roads from Lugar de Condes to Lugar de Freyres with a cap full of pebbles.*

FUSO NEGRO. Touporroutou! A great rabble has come together! Touporroutou! They're on their way, they're on their way to burn the tower! Touporroutou!

FUSO NEGRO *sticks his tongue out and twists away in fear. A black buttock protrudes from his patched rags. Touporroutou! Suddenly he returns and begins dancing, his legs weaving from side to side in intricate patterns. Touporroutou!*

Scene Three

The Lantañon estate, lying between Lugar de Condes and Lugar de Freyres. A few isolated settlements, chestnut groves and wheatfields. Lugar de Condes is situated beside a church, Lugar de Freyres buried deep in the mountain. Lantañon lies between them. An ornate, baroque arch, adorned with the Montenegro coat of arms, marks each of the two entrances to the estate. In the clear morning light, a herd of cattle can be seen making its way through the forecourt, the sun glistening on the animals' horns. SILVER FACE, his back to the sun and facing the mountain, rides past. THE OLD MAN OF CURES greets him cheerfully.

THE OLD MAN OF CURES. Noble young man, is it true that access is restricted at present?

SILVER FACE. It is.

THE OLD MAN OF CURES. Do we have to take our cattle around to the river and then over by boat if we want to go to the fair at Viana?

SILVER FACE. That's what the law says.

THE OLD MAN OF CURES. There's an old saying which states that if the law is unjust then let the judges be merciful.

SILVER FACE. My father got tired of being merciful.

THE OLD MAN OF CURES. If we were at least allowed access for the annual Corpus Christi fair, it wouldn't be so bad! Surely it isn't much to ask? According to the old laws, it was a privilege our ancestors enjoyed.

SILVER FACE. My father granted you that, but you took the case to court.

THE OLD MAN OF CURES. That had nothing to do with the village of Cures. Don Juan Manuel is mistaken if that's what he believes. I am the elder of the village. If I include all my sons and grandsons, there are over thirty houses which I, Quinto Pio, can call my own. And that's a fact, as sure as my name is Quinto of Cures. . . . A lifelong Christian, although these days no one seems to recognize the difference between a true Christian and a convert. And that's a fact! That Englishman from Evangelios is the only Jew left around here. Anyway, as I was saying, the people of Cures had nothing to do with the lawsuit.

SILVER FACE. But you acted as false witnesses.

THE VOICES OF THE HERDSMEN. That's not true! We're not like that! You shouldn't let yourself be swayed!

THE OLD MAN OF CURES. Son of Montenegro, you'll never succeed in cutting off all access! It has been allowed since the times of our forefathers, such traditions are the law. We, the people of Cures, will not go against the law, and so from this day forth we shall travel around the river. And that's a fact! But that horseman now approaching won't be denied access. The very King, in the presence of other kings, bows in reverence.

SILVER FACE. Old Man of Cures, if those who go on foot are denied access, let the same rules apply to those on horseback.

THE OLD MAN OF CURES. That used to be the case!

SILVER FACE. It's my father's decision.

THE OLD MAN OF CURES. Amen! Let the father be an example to the son. Let his words be carved in tablets of stone.

THE OLD MAN OF CURES *lifts his staff as he begins to turn the cows around. The cows however, confused by the shouts and prodding of the old man's children and grandchildren, begin knocking into each other. The dark horseman, who can now be seen riding through the sunlight, is* THE ABBOT OF SAN CLEMENTE DE LANTAÑON.

SILVER FACE. Most Holy Abbot, turn your horse around!

THE ABBOT. Why? What's happened?

SILVER FACE. My dear Abbot, you can no longer cross through the estate.

THE ABBOT. Young Absalom, do not delay me with your foolish jokes. I'm on my way to save a soul in Lugar de Freyres!

SILVER FACE. I wish it were a joke!

THE ABBOT. You've been drinking! You want to cause trouble!

SILVER FACE. Really!

THE ABBOT. Get out of the way and let me through!

SILVER FACE. I cannot!

THE ABBOT. Think for a moment before you insult my office, you savage!

SILVER FACE. There is no affront involved in this. I'm merely showing Quinto of Cures justice at work. If those who come on foot are denied access, then the same should apply to those on horseback!

THE ABBOT. Leave such pathetic explanations for another time. Death doesn't wait.

SILVER FACE. Well then, we'll have to break one of her legs.

THE ABBOT. Get out of my way, you disgusting piece of work! How many times do I have to tell you? I'm going to administer the last rites. Move away in the name of the Lord!

SILVER FACE. I cannot!

THE ABBOT. Young man, Satan has taken hold of you!

SILVER FACE. Then I'll make the sign of the cross with my tail.

THE ABBOT. Think carefully about what you are doing!

SILVER FACE. I will.

THE ABBOT. I'm not a boy of your age. Such pranks are ill-suited to a minister of the Lord.

SILVER FACE. My father won the lawsuit. Respect the court's decision, my dear Abbot.

THE ABBOT. Nonsense! Such laws do not apply to me.

SILVER FACE. They apply to you and to the King himself.

THE ABBOT. Nonsense! In Lantañon you have something which belongs to me. Don't forget it for a moment!

SILVER FACE. I won't!

THE ABBOT. I'll come for her!

SILVER FACE. I don't doubt it!

THE ABBOT. Wave her goodbye.

SILVER FACE. I will.

THE ABBOT. We'll see what your father's got to say about this despicable behaviour.

SILVER FACE. The bridge should be opened to no one or everyone. My father can provide no other example.

THE ABBOT. Infidel! Consider the fact that a sinner is awaiting absolution! He is in the clutches of death! You are condemning a soul to eternal damnation and for that you run the risk of excommunication!

SILVER FACE. I'll bear it in mind!

THE ABBOT. And you condemn yourself so recklessly?

SILVER FACE. If there's no other way!

DISTANT VOICES. This bridge belongs to the King! Access is free! No law can close this bridge!

SILVER FACE. In that case, come and fight for it!

THE ABBOT *swings his horse around and rides off. Up on the rocks, silhouetted figures of shepherds shout and gesticulate whilst scattered herds graze on the banks of the river. The shepherds' voices and the barking of the dogs echo through the deep ravine.*

Scene Four

THE ABBOT OF LANTAÑON, *accompanied by an escort of herdsmen and cattledrivers, enters through the green churchyard and dismounts in front of the rectory door. BLAS DE MÍGUEZ, the sexton, helps by taking the horse's bridle. A crowd of voices breaks through the green, rustic silence. THE ABBOT, silent and aloof, enters through the vestry door, his black, sweeping, angular figure disappearing through the dark doorways and past religious statues. He soon returns and stands in the entrance, furtively trying to hide his glances at the herdsmen by appearing to contemplate the weather. The numerous tradesmen and herdsmen argue loudly amongst themselves, raising their staffs with violent, angry gestures. Suddenly a tall, skeletal woman comes out onto the patio. She is dressed in a long, wide skirt and has a distaff pinned to her waist. She turns the spindle, spitting on her finger to help the thread along. She is DOÑA JEROMITA, the Abbot's sister.*

DOÑA JEROMITA. In the name of Jesus! What a commotion! What do you think this is? Some rowdy inn or other! Don't all shout at once, you silly fools! Brother, let's restore some order around here!

THE ABBOT. I don't bloody well feel like it!

DOÑA JEROMITA. Blessed Mary!

THE ABBOT. My clerical office has been insulted by an under-age prick!

DOÑA JEROMITA. Jesus! Have mercy on us!

THE ABBOT *enters once more through the vestry door. BLAS DE MÍGUEZ follows him, jangling the keys to the church. DOÑA JEROMITA, her arms now crossed but with the distaff still pinned to her waist, comes down the patio steps.*

DOÑA JEROMITA. Don't all talk at once! Oh God! Tell

me what happened! Who did my brother have this terrible argument with?

SEBASTIÁN DE XOGAS. One of Montenegro's sons.

DOÑA JEROMITA. But they're family!

PEDRO ABUÍN. In Lantañon, they don't know what family is. All they care about is arrogance and authority.

DOÑA JEROMITA. Are you still disputing access to the bridge? When will this lawsuit finally end!

MANUEL TOVÍO. Our children will be forced to inherit it.

DOÑA JEROMITA. How did the Abbot get involved?

MANUEL TOVÍO. He was on his way to administer the last rites but Silver Face refused to let him through.

DOÑA JEROMITA. That's pure sacrilege! And what about all of you? What do you want?

PEDRO ABUÍN. A man to lead us.

DOÑA JEROMITA. My brother?

PEDRO ABUÍN. Exactly! That's why I'm making this fuss!

SEBASTIÁN DE XOGAS. That's why we're all making a fuss. You're not the only one who's angry. You're just like the rest of us, so don't keep putting yourself forward. We're shouting because we want the Abbot to lead us.

The stark, black figure of THE ABBOT *reappears at the vestry door, carrying the missal. The group of herdsmen and cattledrivers are now silent, waiting for him to speak. The tall, skeletal woman with the distaff pinned to her waist and the spindle dangling to one side, clutches the rim of her skirt with outstretched arms and fingers.*

THE ABBOT. What are you waiting for?

SEBASTIÁN DE XOGAS. We want your decision.

THE ABBOT. And I want to know whether Montenegro's going to stand by his son's appalling misjudgement.

DOÑA JEROMITA. Brother, after such a terrible upset, it's best you let some blood. Now, by Our Blessed Virgin, tell me how this awful thing happened!

THE ABBOT. Why are you asking if you already know?

DOÑA JEROMITA. Jesus! Have mercy on us! Was it with Silver Face?

THE ABBOT. The Devil himself.

DOÑA JEROMITA. He must have been drunk!

THE ABBOT. Damned Montenegros!

DOÑA JEROMITA. Oh brother, don't insult them like this! They're still family, after all! Don't forget that our niece is still in the house at Lantañon! She grew up there!

THE ABBOT. Well, I'll rescue her from their clutches. If the father condones the son's actions, I'll break with them forever.

DOÑA JEROMITA. I'd swear on my life that the father had nothing to do with it! It wouldn't surprise me to hear it come from the other good-for-nothing brothers, but I wouldn't expect this from Silver Face. You know how in love he is.

THE ABBOT. A son of the Devil!

DOÑA JEROMITA. I'm sure he'd just had one too many.

THE ABBOT. I might have had the Eucharist with me!

DOÑA JEROMITA. Jesus! Have mercy on us!

THE ABBOT. He'll suffer damnation! Eternal damnation!

PEDRO ABUÍN. Most esteemed Abbot, as it is a question of justice, place yourself at the head of our parishioners!

THE ABBOT. I've already told you, I'm prepared to wait.

SEBASTIÁN DE XOGAS. It sounds as if you're advising us to be patient.

THE ABBOT. I will wait and wait and wait.

SEBASTIÁN DE XOGAS. And we should do the same until the great fairs at Viana are over. Then we'll see.

PEDRO ABUÍN. It's clear then. We'll have to force our cattle through Lantañon, come what may!

SEBASTIÁN DE XOGAS. Pedro Abuín, there can never be wisdom where sound judgement is lacking. What is the Abbot's advice?

THE ABBOT. I'm not giving any advice. Each is free to protest in whatever way he prefers, through aggressive or through non-aggressive means.

RAMIRO DE BEALO. Don Juan Manuel will change his mind. But we have to wait for the right moment.

DOÑA JEROMITA. Well, go and see him then.

PEDRO ABUÍN. Others have gone and received only harsh words.

THE ABBOT. Well I shall go, and he won't employ such words with me.

SEBASTIÁN DE XOGAS. Whatever his position, he must respect the Church.

THE ABBOT. I shall remove my robes of office.

DOÑA JEROMITA. Stop all this stupid bragging!

THE ABBOT. Jeromita, bring out a jug of wine, so that these men can refresh themselves. I'm off to pray.

THE ABBOT *hurriedly crosses himself and begins praying as he walks beneath the shadow of the wall. The herdsmen scatter along the back wall of the churchyard waiting for the jug of wine. The* ABBOT's *wine has a great reputation in these parts.*

Scene Five
The courtyard of lemon trees on the Lantañon estate. Equipped with a makeshift folding chair, DOÑA JEROMITA *approaches on a donkey; the animal trots along happily,* DOÑA JEROMITA's

*skirt and cloak decorated with brooches covering its flanks. BLAS
DE MÍGUEZ, the sexton, accompanies her, thrashing the donkey's
behind with a rod of green hazelnut. They pass beneath the grand,
feudal arch decorated with the Montenegro coat of arms. The tall,
skeletal woman dismounts at a stone bench, attempting to cover her
spindly legs as she does so. THE SEXTON watches over her with
outstretched arms. He avoids touching her at all costs, respecting her
high-standing position as Abbess.*

DOÑA JEROMITA. Jesus! Have mercy on us!

THE SEXTON. They could well set the dogs on us!

DOÑA JEROMITA. Don't frighten me!

THE SEXTON. I don't see what else we can expect, Doña
   Jeromita.

DOÑA JEROMITA. We'll see about that.

THE SEXTON. We might as well face the fact that we're two
   sheep pitting ourselves against a wolf. Two innocent sheep!

DOÑA JEROMITA. Don't dishearten me with your silly
   stories.

THE SEXTON. The Abbot should have come to sort this out.

DOÑA JEROMITA. My brother and Don Juan Manuel are
   both short-tempered men.

THE SEXTON. That's exactly what I mean! You have to pit
   beast against beast.

DOÑA JEROMITA. Such a heated exchange could have led to
   the scaffold.

THE SEXTON. If you insist on looking at it that way . . .

DOÑA JEROMITA. I think old Montenegro will listen to me.

THE SEXTON. Well, in my opinion, it would have been
   better not to have come at all. We should have waited for a
   coastal wind.

DOÑA JEROMITA. In the meantime, I can't allow my niece
   to remain under this roof.

THE SEXTON. Don Juan Manuel won't give up his precious dove willingly. He loves her like a daughter!

DOÑA JEROMITA. I have the law on my side.

THE SEXTON. Don Juan Manuel doesn't respect the law.

DOÑA JEROMITA. Jesus! Have mercy on us!

SABELITA *appears through the shade of the lemon trees, singing a hymn. She is dressed in a dramatic purple habit, masked by the green shadows and has the sad expression of dahlias in vases. On seeing the tall, skeletal woman she rushes towards her.*

SABELITA. Is anything wrong, aunt?

DOÑA JEROMITA. Haven't you heard?

SABELITA. No!

DOÑA JEROMITA. I sent you a message.

SABELITA. Well, it hasn't arrived.

DOÑA JEROMITA. I've come to take you away. Pack your things.

SABELITA. What's happened?

DOÑA JEROMITA. As your uncle was on his way to administer the last rites, Silver Face blocked his way like a terrible avenging angel.

SABELITA. Blessed Lord!

DOÑA JEROMITA. So I've come to take you out of here.

SABELITA. Does my godfather know about this?

DOÑA JEROMITA. Yes, he knows about it, and what's worse, he condones it.

SABELITA. And what does my uncle think about it?

DOÑA JEROMITA. We've had to resort to bloodletting to calm him.

SABELITA. Oh God! Are you taking me away for good?

DOÑA JEROMITA. That's the general idea, unless your godfather apologizes for that heretic's irresponsible behaviour.

SABELITA. Silver Face! . . . A madman with a fiery tongue! . . .

DOÑA JEROMITA. A damned soul!

SABELITA. He isn't as bad as he looks.

DOÑA JEROMITA. A soul destined for Hell!

SABELITA. Listen aunt, don't talk to my godfather.

DOÑA JEROMITA. What are you afraid of?

SABELITA. Go back to the rectory.

DOÑA JEROMITA. Then you must come with me.

SABELITA. Wait a while, aunt. Don't take me away!

DOÑA JEROMITA. Are you crying already? You show more loyalty to this family of traitors than you do to your own.

SABELITA. They brought me up!

DOÑA JEROMITA. That's it! Rise up against your family! All right stay here!

SABELITA. I'm not going against you!

DOÑA JEROMITA. Jesus! Have mercy on us! Dry your eyes! I don't want to see any tears!

SABELITA. Perhaps . . . I don't know . . . but if I spoke to Silver Face . . . he's not bad, you know.

DOÑA JEROMITA. He's evil itself!

SABELITA. But how shall I go about it?

DOÑA JEROMITA. Jesus! Have mercy on us! Tell me child, what's going on between you?

SABELITA. Nothing!

DOÑA JEROMITA. Is he your lover?

SABELITA. No!

DOÑA JEROMITA. Swear to it?

SABELITA. Why ask if you don't believe what I say?

DOÑA JEROMITA. So what's all this about talking to this heathen boy? What does it mean?

SABELITA. It was just an idea.

DOÑA JEROMITA. Well, it must have come from somewhere.

SABELITA. It could get uncle an apology.

DOÑA JEROMITA. Is that what you're hoping?

SABELITA. I don't know.

DOÑA JEROMITA. Is your influence over Satan's disciple that great?

SABELITA. If only it were! It was just an idea.

DOÑA JEROMITA. With no ulterior motive?

SABELITA. With no ulterior motive.

DOÑA JEROMITA. Wave him goodbye, child! Wave goodbye forever to this personification of evil – and whatever you may feel in your heart, bury it deep beneath seven layers of earth! Now get all your things together so that we can go.

SABELITA. Please wait, aunt!

DOÑA JEROMITA. Why all this delay?

SABELITA. We can arrange everything.

DOÑA JEROMITA. That's why I'm here. Where is your godfather?

SABELITA. Oh aunt, don't see him, don't talk to him!

DOÑA JEROMITA. What are you afraid of?

SABELITA. His arrogant temper.

DOÑA JEROMITA. Don't frighten me!

SABELITA. My godfather is a king!

DOÑA JEROMITA. Well then, I shall be a queen. I'll face that white-haired wolf and discover once and for all if he condones his son's reckless behaviour.

SABELITA. Oh aunt, if you want to take me away, do it before he sees me. Don't let him know!

DOÑA JEROMITA. Jesus! Have mercy on us! You soon changed your mind! What are you afraid of?

SABELITA. He could oppose it!

DOÑA JEROMITA. I have the law on my side! I'll see your godfather, and what he says will decide my course of action.

SABELITA. He's coming!

DOÑA JEROMITA. So much the better.

SABELITA. Don't ask him any questions, aunt.

DOÑA JEROMITA. Come and stand at my side.

DON JUAN MANUEL, *emerging from the door of his tower, remains in the shadows of the stonework.* BLAS DE MÍGUEZ, *the sexton, is jumping and howling at his side. The esteemed gentleman, surrounded by bloodhounds, greyhounds, and an assortment of other hunting dogs, has grabbed him by the ear with a gesture of feudal derision.*

DON JUAN MANUEL. This simpering sexton has brought me a message.

THE SEXTON. A message brought in the service of Our Blessed Lord!

DOÑA JEROMITA. You meddling fool, Blas!

THE SEXTON. The dogs are ripping my clothes!

DOÑA JEROMITA. It should teach you to keep your nose out of things that don't concern you.

THE SEXTON. I wanted to avoid a civil war! The dogs are ripping my clothes to shreds!

SABELITA. Let him go godfather, he's really frightened!

THE SEXTON. Just look at my clothes!

DON JUAN MANUEL. Shut up, you silly idiot! They didn't even touch your skin!

DOÑA JEROMITA. Jesus! Have mercy on us!

THE SEXTON. My clothes hurt me more than my flesh!

DON JUAN MANUEL. You are a true philosopher.

THE SEXTON. A poor, defenceless man!

DON JUAN MANUEL. Go into the kitchen and seek refuge in a jug of wine.

THE SEXTON. My poor clothes!

The limping SEXTON *enters the stone hallway; while in the resonant shadows of the arch, old* MONTENEGRO *laughs in his customary rough, feudal manner.*

DOÑA JEROMITA. What a despicable temper!

DON JUAN MANUEL. And how is my clerical friend?

DOÑA JEROMITA. Furious. He's had to resort to bloodletting, as I suppose you well know.

DON JUAN MANUEL. But he's always seemed so calm, always a picture of decorum and restraint at the table.

DOÑA JEROMITA. Jesus! Have mercy on us! It is something different altogether that's caused this change of temper – the insults he suffered at the hands of a member of your household.

DON JUAN MANUEL. I know what you're talking about.

DOÑA JEROMITA. And what are you prepared to do about it?

DON JUAN MANUEL. I cannot break the rod of justice that the Devil has placed in my hands!

DOÑA JEROMITA. Jesus! Have mercy on us!

DON JUAN MANUEL. I cannot set such an example in my house.

DOÑA JEROMITA. And yet you are prepared to set worse examples.

DON JUAN MANUEL. Perhaps! But this I cannot do.

DOÑA JEROMITA. Jesus! Have mercy on us! Do you mean to say that you condone your son's heretical behaviour?

DON JUAN MANUEL. I must.

DOÑA JEROMITA. Are you fully aware of what he did?

DON JUAN MANUEL. Yes, and I regret it.

DOÑA JEROMITA. Then why are you condoning his behaviour and severing our friendship?

DON JUAN MANUEL. I am not severing our friendship! But I must keep to my decision.

DOÑA JEROMITA. Sooner or later you will crumble.

DON JUAN MANUEL. Don't be so sure. I know what you want and why you're here.

DOÑA JEROMITA. And what do you have to say about it?

DON JUAN MANUEL. Nothing!

DOÑA JEROMITA. You must have something to say!

DON JUAN MANUEL. Nothing!

DOÑA JEROMITA. Aren't you surprised that I'm coming to claim what's mine?

DON JUAN MANUEL. No, I'm not surprised.

DOÑA JEROMITA. Will you stop me taking her?

DON JUAN MANUEL. No!

DOÑA JEROMITA. When there is such animosity between our families I really have no choice but to remove my niece. Don't you agree?

DON JUAN MANUEL. Damn you!

DOÑA JEROMITA. Jesus! Have mercy on us!

SABELITA. Goodbye Lantañon!

DOÑA JEROMITA. Dry those eyes immediately!

DON JUAN MANUEL. Don't cry, child. You'll be back, time passes.

DOÑA JEROMITA. Bringing death.

DON JUAN MANUEL. Yes.

DOÑA JEROMITA. And punishment.

DON JUAN MANUEL. Perhaps! Come here, Sabelita.

DOÑA JEROMITA. Kiss your godfather's hand and let's get going.

DON JUAN MANUEL. Don't cry, child! Try to understand that I must keep to my earlier decision.

SABELITA. I know. Goodbye forever, godfather!

DON JUAN MANUEL. Not forever. You will be back.

SABELITA. Who knows?

DON JUAN MANUEL. If God doesn't will it, the Devil will!

A drunken, dancing BLAS DE MÍGUEZ *emerges from the tower door carrying a jug of wine. The tall, skeletal woman clutches at the rim of her skirt while the old nobleman begins laughing again; he runs his fingers tenderly through the hair of* SABELITA, *who is now kneeling to kiss his hand. In the green shadows of the lemon trees, her purple habit has the dramatic effect of a scream.*

End of Act One

Act Two

Scene One
Viana del Prior: once the heart of the feudal estate, as indicated by its distinguished stonework. Its courtyards and narrow streets are filled with impressive, awe-inspiring echoes. Its history lies in its resonant stones, which tell stories of innocent peasant girls and bright companies of rebellious young men pitted against noblemen and members of the clergy. Grand old houses, prestigious families, and the coats of arms adorning the arches all announce the Gothic myths of this Galician armoury. Viana del Prior! Home of the famous Corpus Christi fair where crowds converge from all parts of Spain and Portugal. A green field filled with oak trees. Prayers. Crowds. Cattle. Banners of all colours. Portuguese swordbelts, saddles from Zamora, brown twill fabric. Petticoats of yellow, green and scarlet. Blue breeches and well-trimmed tunics. Stalls filled with mirrors, knives and ribbons dazzle in the sun as they travel down the Roman flagstone slope on two wagons. They disappear through the arch which joins the church of a convent to a grand palatial house. Fraudulent pedlars set up their stalls under large sunshades, proclaiming the low prices and the high quality of their goods, deceiving astonished peasants with their gypsy charm. Blind men and their guides sing ballads.

A VENDOR'S CRY. Get your copy of *Cipranillo* here! A book for everybody and every house!

ANOTHER CRY. Leeches from Limia! Leeches!

A THIRD CRY. Linen and blankets from Zamora!

A TRAVELLER FROM MARAGATERIA. Go on! Get away, Lucero! Go on! Shoo!

PICHONA THE MUTTERER. Take your pick for a quarter peseta! Rosaries! Cards! Knives! Brooches! Anything for a quarter!

In front of the inn, a sad, sallow-faced peasant dressed in the clothes of a hermit, recites out aloud the story of his once extravagant, now penitent life – sin, blood and the power of miracles.

THE PENITENT. See here the example of a proven sinner

who was warned through signs and omens to break free of his life of gambling and womanizing!

PICHONA THE MUTTERER. Rose-water for the eyes! Tobacco pouches from the prison at Ceuta. On the wheel of fortune there's something for everyone! My friends, don't you recognize Pichona the Mutterer! Come on, take your pick for a quarter peseta! Anything for a quarter!

THE BLIND MAN OF GONDAR. Mouths tire of singing! Feet tire of dancing! Men tire of playing with the same women! But eyes never tire of looking and watching!

The resounding sound of horses and spurs: a group of six horsemen, fine young riders, enter through the main courtyard and dismount at the door to the inn. They are SILVER FACE and his brothers – DON PEDRITO, DON ROSENDO, DON MAURO, DON GONZALO and DON FARRUQUIÑO. This brother, the youngest of the six, wears a three-cornered cap and sash, recognizable emblems of the seminary at Viana del Prior. They hammer at the door with their whips to attract the landlord's attention. A WHORE appears.

THE WHORE. What can I get you?

SILVER FACE. A jug of wine and make it quick.

THE WHORE. Rivero or house wine?

DON PEDRITO. I don't care if it comes from Hell or the Moors.

THE WHORE. They're the same thing.

DON MAURO. A jug of each, woman!

THE WHORE. Don Mauro made an unwise decision.

DON ROSENDO. Who needs house wine when there's Rivero!

THE TRAVELLER FROM MARAGATERIA. There's fine wines in Castille!

DON PEDRITO. Castillian wines are spoilt by the taste of hides.

THE TRAVELLER FROM MARAGATERIA. I don't agree.

DON FARRUQUIÑO. Each wine has its own qualities. White, for example, is suitable for a pork sausage omelette. Espadeiro de Salnés is a most refreshing wine, excellent when one is up in the mountains, at a pilgrimage or playing bowls. Rivero de Avia complements fish pie and pork from Lugo. Each wine has a particular correspondent in life, like everything else. The world is harmony and Pythagorean order. And no one has a right to refute this claim unless they are an ordained theologian!

SILVER FACE. It's not difficult to tell that you spend your time amongst the clergy!

FUSO NEGRO, *his tattered tunic exposing a buttock and his cap filled with pebbles, swears and preaches at the entrance to the church.*

FUSO NEGRO. The end is nigh! Truly nigh! Why change habits and take on new burdens? I will be ordained a bishop! There are too few theologians and the few that exist are corrupted by the female sex.

THE BLIND MAN OF GONDAR. Mouths tire of eating! Bodies tire of sleeping! Only eyes never tire of looking and watching.

DON MAURO MONTENEGRO, *a red-haired, bad-tempered giant, emerges from the inn counting his money. He is wearing spurs, carries a cattle goad and is surrounded by greyhounds.*

DON FARRUQUIÑO. Is there a game indoors?

DON MAURO. They're playing chance.

SILVER FACE. Who's dealing?

DON MAURO. The Abbot of Lantañon.

SILVER FACE. I'll go in and surprise him.

DON FARRUQUIÑO. You may have succeeded in turning him back but I doubt if you'll get him to deal the cards you want.

SILVER FACE. I'm going to surprise him.

DON FARRUQUIÑO. He can perform miracles when he's dealing cards.

THE TRAVELLER FROM MARAGATERIA. He plays fairly but he's got luck on his side.

DON FARRUQUIÑO. He throws down the cards that matter with the skill of a scholar.

DON PEDRITO. If he only knew theology as well as he mis-shuffles cards . . .

THE TRAVELLER FROM MARAGATERIA. I didn't see anything and I was watching as he shuffled them.

SILVER FACE. I'm going to surprise him!

DON PEDRITO. We'll all put something in. It's father's money.

PICHONA THE MUTTERER. Silver Face, buy something off me. This necklace, I'm sure there's plenty of women you could give it to.

SILVER FACE. Keep it for yourself, but I won't pay you for it.

The Montenegro brothers enter the inn, taking their glasses of wine with them. SILVER FACE *remains still for a moment at the door, listening to* THE PENITENT *and* THE TRAVELLER FROM MARAGATERIA.

THE PENITENT. I left my parents' house to see the world disguised as the Devil. I got together with some rough types. I travelled around the fairs with crooked card tricks. With a woman of ill-repute at my side, I suffered scandal after scandal. I was called down many paths! I was warned by many signs!

THE TRAVELLER FROM MARAGATERIA. Come on, cut the stories! Thanks to that habit, you can laze around doing nothing and live off deceit – just like the Royal Government!

THE PENITENT. I do penance for my salvation.

SILVER FACE. What's your crime?

THE PENITENT. Murder. A crime worse than Cain's! I held an axe over my father's head!

SILVER FACE. You killed your father?

THE PENITENT. He collapsed with fear when he saw me. I killed my own father with the air surrounding the axe! My anger was enough to kill him! My parents spoilt me as an only child and that was the real cause of my ruin. I became a reckless, uncontrollable youth.

SILVER FACE. What is your name?

THE PENITENT. Call me damned! A man of evil intention! Evil-minded! A black Hell! A son of Satan!

SILVER FACE. Impostor.

He deposits a silver coin in the beggar's hand as a gracious apology while delivering the insult. He then sweeps elegantly into the inn, the horse's saddle draped casually over his shoulder.

FUSO NEGRO. Rape and envy at your own front door. You killed your father and escaped the executioner. Touporroutou! That must be one of the Devil's miracles. Do you know him? Well! Have you ever met him? He's trying to sell his philosophy to the world. The clergy will have a rough time and pious prostitutes will rush naked into a bonfire.

THE TRAVELLER FROM MARAGATERIA. They may succeed in keeping the Devil away!

FUSO NEGRO. Do you know who I am? Are you aware of the qualifications I have? Do you dare argue with me? If you argue with me, you'll finish up losing! Everything is in a mess! The world is completely misguided. Between a Friday and a Tuesday it explodes into a thousand pieces.

A VENDOR'S CRY. Get your copy of *Cipranillo* here. A book for everybody and every house!

ANOTHER CRY. Leeches from Limia! Leeches!

PICHONA THE MUTTERER. Rose-water for the eyes!
Tobacco pouches from the prison at Ceuta! At the wheel of
fortune there's something for everyone! Take your pick for a
quarter peseta! Anything for a quarter!

Scene Two
*An orchard with sheltered vines at the back of the inn. Carriers,
muleteers, travellers, herdsmen and red-haired clerics are playing
cards in a corner. It is the classic game of the Spanish fairs, referred
to by those who know it as cock and chance.*

THE ABBOT. Ace!

A SPANIARD RECENTLY RETURNED FROM AMERICA.
I'm pulling out! I've been given a dud hand.

A HERDSMAN. I didn't see anything!

DON FARRUQUIÑO. Who was cutting the cards?

PEDRO ABUÍN. I was. What's the problem?

DON FARRUQUIÑO. Blessed are your hands!

PEDRO ABUÍN. Why? Are you winning?

DON FARRUQUIÑO. You must be joking!

  THE ABBOT, *slowly but carefully collects the money, shuffles
  the cards and hands them over to be cut.* DON MAURO
  stretches his giant arm over the cards while THE ABBOT
  watches him.

THE ABBOT. The Priest of Lesón has already agreed.

THE PRIEST. Don Mauro can take my place.

THE SPANIARD RECENTLY RETURNED FROM
AMERICA. What a game! As soon as I leave we get a change
of dealer! Bastard!

THE OLD MAN OF CURES. You know what the old proverb

says: Don't get in fights with queens and kites. It takes a long spoon to sup with the Devil.

DON MAURO *remains arrogantly silent, his eyes fixed on the cards. He places his money on a king. The tall, shrivelled* ABBOT, *with his crooked nose and his mouth shaped like the stone entrance to a cave, watches over the proceedings in a slow, deliberate manner.*

DON MAURO. I'll take to the streets if this king lets me down.

DON FARRUQUIÑO. It will!

DON MAURO. Well, my money's on him.

SILVER FACE. Let's see the cards, my dear Abbot?

THE ABBOT. Blasphemous heretic!

SILVER FACE. How far are you prepared to go?

THE ABBOT. I refuse to reply to such impertinent questions.

THE ABBOT *mutters to himself, his eyes half-closed. The cards lie face down on the table, his hands crossed over them.* SILVER FACE *laughs – a fair-haired, noble figure leaning on his cattle goad, his saddle bouncing gently on his shoulder.*

SILVER FACE. Most Holy Abbot, you know how much I love you!

THE ABBOT. Oh yes! I have proof of that!

SILVER FACE. Well, the truth is that I'm here to gamble away my father's money. Thirty pieces of gold.

THE ABBOT. You're out of your mind.

SILVER FACE. I want you to have a little keepsake, something to remind you of me.

THE ABBOT. Blasphemous heretic!

SILVER FACE. Do you think you can win these thirty Portuguese coins from me? I'm putting them all on the table.

The handsome young man throws a resonant bag of gold on the table in a bold, cheerful manner. THE ABBOT *picks it up as if gauging its contents.*

THE ABBOT. Is it all here?

SILVER FACE. Count it if you like.

THE ABBOT. I cannot allow you to play. You're still a child.

SILVER FACE. Age has nothing to do with it.

THE ABBOT. You blasphemous heathen!

SILVER FACE. You begin.

THE ABBOT. I'll play the game, if that's what you want.

SILVER FACE. I'll put my money on the double. With spades as the trump suit.

DON MAURO. I'll bet on the king.

THE ABBOT. Game! I've a king at the door.

THE SPANIARD RECENTLY RETURNED FROM AMERICA. That squirt was listening to us.

SILVER FACE. Spades. I don't win and I don't lose. I'll play again.

DON MAURO. Remember the words of the oracle of Cures: don't get in fights with queens and kites.

SILVER FACE. We'll see about that.

THE ABBOT. You still have time to pull out.

DON FARRUQUIÑO. Look at this! The king of hearts.

SILVER FACE. This bloody deck has nothing but kings!

THE ABBOT. You were well warned. Don't start saying I stole your money unlawfully.

DON MAURO. I'll say it. You stacked the deck in order to win the game.

THE ABBOT. You bad-tempered insolent rogue!

DON MAURO. Thief!

The red-haired giant picks up the bag of money. The circle of players becomes excited and restless. There is an uneasy feeling in the air, accentuated by the raw mixture of agitated voices and wild gestures. THE ABBOT *takes out a small gun.* SILVER FACE *moves in between them and snatches the bag of money from his brother.*

SILVER FACE. The Abbot has won.

DON MAURO. By cheating.

THE ABBOT. Goliath, I'll burn you alive!

DON MAURO. Cheat!

THE ABBOT. Judas!

DON MAURO *cracks his whip. The sound of a shot; sparks fly from the gun; the smell of gunpowder; barking; insults and threats.* DON MAURO *fights to extricate himself from the scolding clerics and herdsmen who have seized hold of him.* THE ABBOT, *his cassock torn, still holding the smoking gun, walks backwards towards the door of the orchard and runs off. Suddenly the crowd disappears.* SILVER FACE *has the red scratch of a bullet on his forehead and one side of his face has been blackened by the gunpowder. He washes himself with wine. His brothers, gather around him and watch, shouting loudly.*

Scene Three
The green churchyard of San Clemente de Lantañon, with the rectory to one side. The stark, black figure of THE ABBOT *is bidding farewell to three pious old men on the ornate, monastic stone patio. The three men, all with long cloaks, walking sticks and cloth caps, walk in a strikingly similar manner. They kneel together to pray in the green churchyard.*

THE ABBOT. God go with you!

SEBASTIÁN DE XOGAS. And also with you!

THE OLD MAN OF CURES. And may the King of Heaven free us all from arrogant and evil-tempered men!

THE DEACON OF LESÓN. We'd need extra laws before that can happen!

THE ABBOT. And more competent judges.

THE OLD MAN OF CURES. Some competence! How many villains have they failed to send to the gallows! Let's leave all this moaning about judges and laws to those who have nothing better to do.

THE ABBOT. What if we're asked to give evidence?

THE DEACON OF LESÓN. We won't be . . .

THE ABBOT. But if it comes to that . . .

SEBASTIÁN DE XOGAS. Well then . . . we didn't see anything!

THE DEACON OF LESÓN. For my part, I can safely say that I didn't see a thing!

THE OLD MAN OF CURES. It's not as if anything happened which we could really see!

THE DEACON OF LESÓN. Well, that's it then: we can't know anything if we didn't see anything.

THE OLD MAN OF CURES. If we all stick to the truth, there can be no case.

THE ABBOT. I don't think lawyers and bailiffs will come knocking on my door.

SEBASTIÁN DE XOGAS. The legal profession is a law unto itself.

THE DEACON OF LESON. And always at the King's beck and call!

SEBASTIÁN DE XOGAS. Money governs everything, it's just like a king!

THE OLD MAN OF CURES. Most Holy Abbot, may God remain with you!

SEBASTIÁN DE XOGAS. Here's hoping the case doesn't come to court!

THE DEACON OF LESÓN. Montenegros! Savage despots!

They move away into the distance with the ABBOT's *sermon carved in their minds like the Latin lettering on the stonework in the churchyard. They have already disappeared as the crow-like* SEXTON *begins cackling from the bell-tower.*

THE SEXTON. Time will tell. There's no doubt about the weather though!

THE ABBOT. What about those clouds over there . . .

THE SEXTON. They're disappearing. There's a long period of good weather ahead.

THE ABBOT. Blas, go and get some leeches so that I can let some blood.

Just inside the door, the ABBOT's *sister and niece are working the spindle; they are sitting on small benches facing one another, witnessing the events on the patio.*

DOÑA JEROMITA. That devil brings bad luck!

SABELITA. Like thunder!

THE ABBOT. Come down, Blas!

THE SEXTON. Head first! Most lovely and radiant Sabelita, tomorrow there's a mass at San Martiño. Do you want to go over later this afternoon to lay out the altar cloth and replace the candles?

DOÑA JEROMITA. What? No candles left?

THE SEXTON. They disappear like air.

DOÑA JEROMITA. I'll give you air, you stupid fool! Lighting candles left, right and centre and never remembering to put them out!

SABELITA. Where are the candles kept?

DOÑA JEROMITA. In the old chest which used to belong to the Pedrayes sisters.

THE ABBOT *paces up and down, a stark, black-cassocked figure spouting Latin from his missal. He crosses his niece with an armful of brown wax candles, brushing against her shawl.*

THE ABBOT. Where are you going?

SABELITA. To Freyres.

THE ABBOT. Make sure you're back before dark.

DOÑA JEROMITA. Yes, hurry home.

THE ABBOT. I'll rip off this collar if I don't succeed in bringing that damned family to heel!

DOÑA JEROMITA. Don't get excited, brother.

THE ABBOT. I had the missal with me in order to administer absolution. I could have been carrying the Eucharist!

DOÑA JEROMITA. How horrendous!

THE ABBOT. And how sacrilegious!

DOÑA JEROMITA. Those Montenegros have no hearts! Hell-bound souls with no hope of salvation!

BLAS DE MÍGUEZ *emerges from the vestry door jangling a bunch of keys.* BLAS DE MÍGUEZ, *the sexton of San Clemente, a man known for telling ridiculous stories and endless lies, with a face like rancid bacon, an expansive, toothless mouth, sheared eyebrows and dog-like eyes, is an out-and-out villain.* THE ABBOT, *meeting him on the patio steps, takes away his keys.*

THE SEXTON. Montenegros! A pack of ferocious wolves!

THE ABBOT. I am more ferocious than any of them!

THE SEXTON. You'd need to be!

THE ABBOT. Sooner or later they'll bow their heads in shame. And if they don't, well then . . . they'll find themselves Hell-bound!

THE SEXTON. They are already.

THE ABBOT. Hell-bound with twice as many chains.

DOÑA JEROMITA. Chains of flames and serpents!

A horseman approaches the church, silhouetted against the western sun. DOÑA JEROMITA, rises from the bench with outstretched arms and unleashes a torrent of insults.

DOÑA JEROMITA. It's that degenerate!

THE ABBOT. He's just waiting for me to go off the rails!

THE SEXTON. I've been dreaming of grilled mackerel for three nights now!

DOÑA JEROMITA. And our niece still out there.

THE SEXTON. I'm off to warn her.

The scheming, cowardly SEXTON jumps over the wall onto the road. He continually turns his head to catch what is happening in the churchyard. The stark, cassocked figure of THE ABBOT, his cap now cocked to one side, rushes into the nearest door and peers out. He then positions himself at the small window of a disused attic room and points the gun at SILVER FACE.

THE ABBOT. Arrogant Absalom, get on your way. I'm ready to fire this and send you straight to Hell!

SILVER FACE. Most Holy Abbot, I come in peace!

THE ABBOT. Insolent heathen! There can be no peace for an uneasy conscience.

SILVER FACE. I've brought you the money!

THE ABBOT. You must have some perverse, ulterior motive.

SILVER FACE. A good deed to earn a place for myself in Heaven. Most Holy Abbot, come down and take your money.

THE ABBOT. I don't want it! Keep it so that you can condemn yourself forever!

SILVER FACE. My dear Abbot, please, no more slander. Let's forget about the lawsuit!

THE ABBOT. Such a meek proposition does not come from the heart. Your intentions are despicable!

SILVER FACE. Most Holy Abbot, take what's yours and let's celebrate with a jug of wine!

DOÑA JEROMITA. Get away from our door, Satan! Move away, you evil man! Playing humble to steal our precious niece! Get out of here! Go on! Don't waste your time by tempting virtue, Satan!

SILVER FACE. No one can stop me from coming in and taking the jewel you deny me!

THE ABBOT. Proud Tarquin, on your way and pray that I don't kill you!

SILVER FACE. My dear Abbot, God strike you down! Take your money! Here goes! One! Two! Three!

The handsome young man stands in his stirrups and throws the bag of coins towards the window. At the window only THE ABBOT's *horned cap can be seen. The bag flies through the night air like a black bird.* THE ABBOT, *shouting morosely, brings his arms out of the shadows to catch it.*

THE ABBOT. Come back, you insolent heathen! Take your bag! Two can play at that game, you know! Aren't you coming back? I'll throw it out onto the road! I'll leave it on the road! It can stay there! Come back and collect it, you savage! Ten thousand reales! Damn yourself with it!

DOÑA JEROMITA. The end is nigh!

THE ABBOT, *gasping after his threatening outburst, throws the bag of coins onto the road along which* SILVER FACE *is riding away.* DOÑA JEROMITA *falls onto her knees, her arms stretched out as if she were being crucified.* THE ABBOT's *four-cornered cap peers menacingly out of the small window.*

Scene Four
An orchard lit by an evening star. The romantic stones of San Martiño de Freyres lie between four cypress trees. Awe-inspiring mountain peaks can be seen in the distance, at their feet a symphony of violet. The wind murmurs through the nocturnal cornfields. The purple shades of dusk begin to spread over the paths, ochre-red with metallic flecks of blue and white. San Martiño de Freyres, enveloped by a sense of religious duty, begins its evening worship with prayers, miracles and candles for the dead. A woman's hands light the presbytery lamp. An owl flies away in fear. The silhouetted figure of SABELITA *can be seen beneath the lamp.* SILVER FACE *stops his horse at the door.*

SILVER FACE. Isabel!

SABELITA. Don't speak to me!

SILVER FACE. Lift up your eyes for me.

SABELITA. I don't want to look at you.

SILVER FACE. Do you hate me that much?

SABELITA. You frighten me!

SILVER FACE. Do you know where I've just come from?

SABELITA. Some atrocious deed or other.

SILVER FACE. I have just attempted to come to some sort of peaceful arrangement with your uncle.

SABELITA. You're far too arrogant to do anything of the sort.

SILVER FACE. I'm also terribly in love.

SABELITA. It's a bit late to start thinking of love now! What did my uncle have to say about your offer of peace?

SILVER FACE. He whipped a gun out of his cassock faster than I thought possible.

SABELITA. It's a shame he didn't kill you!

SILVER FACE. Why? Are you keen to wear black?

SABELITA. I'd be wearing red if that happened!

SILVER FACE. Liar! Weddings bring peace.

SABELITA. I'll make the sign of the cross to protect myself!

SILVER FACE. If it wasn't for the holy sanctuary of this church, I'd grab you by the waist here and now and steal you away on my horse!

SABELITA. You pirate!

SILVER FACE. Isabel, goodbye!

SABELITA. Goodbye little Silver Face!

FUSO NEGRO *enters through the vestry door, his cap filled with pebbles.* SILVER FACE *can be heard galloping away in the distance.*

FUSO NEGRO. Touporroutou! If you're saving up for a house, you won't even have enough with seven thousand caps! Nowhere near enough! If only it were enough! I need to get my house built and I haven't much time. There's a woman coming over from America. Touporroutou! I've got her pregnant, you see! I've never seen her and yet I spend all night working with her. We sin in the dark. You have to sin! He who fails to sin is damned!

SABELITA. Show some respect for the Church, Fuso Negro.

FUSO NEGRO. I do. Wait until I have the house ready and then we can get together. Touporroutou! The other one's pregnant! She's carrying thirty-seven boys and thirty-seven girls, all in her belly. Tonight I'll ride the wind's horse, I'll work with you and use a knife to put an end to her.

SABELITA. Fuso Negro, stop frightening me! What are you doing here?

FUSO NEGRO. I'm looking at you.

SABELITA. Go away!

FUSO NEGRO. Will you give me enough money for a glass of wine?

SABELITA. Go away!

FUSO NEGRO. Well, if you won't give me the money for a glass of wine, will you let me have a quick look at your legs?

SABELITA. Fuso Negro, stop frightening me!

FUSO NEGRO. Touporroutou! Oh, come on darling! Let me have enough for a glass!

SABELITA. I don't have any money with me.

FUSO NEGRO. Let's make a good idea from a bad idea! What if all the wine in the world could be placed in a giant fountain! What a great idea! And imagine if cows could drop harvests instead of dung from beneath their tails! Another excellent idea! Truly worthy of merit! Everything is in such a state. The world is going crazy. And I know what to do, and so do a few others: but nobody will tell. The first one to open his mouth gets four shots in the back of the head, courtesy of the Government. Satan could govern the world, I'm sure he'd satisfy everyone in some way or other. Touporroutou! He's quick on his feet, he wouldn't find it a problem getting around to meet people.

SABELITA. Show some respect for the Church! Go away, you really do frighten me, Fuso Negro!

FUSO NEGRO. If Satan ruled the world, women could go around naked. Eating, drinking and non-stop fornication from one week to the next. If the world were that badly governed, it would be truly wonderful. Go on lovely, give me a flash of your legs!

SABELITA. Go away!

FUSO NEGRO. I don't want to.

SABELITA. Go or I'll start screaming!

FUSO NEGRO. Let me see your legs, damn you!

SABELITA. Don't frighten me, Fuso Negro!

FUSO NEGRO. Touporroutou! You look so pale and white! Give me a peep, cunt-face! Blessed Mary! What a virgin!

Beneath the romanesque portico, surrounded by stone statues of saints, a phallic triumph accompanied by echoing laughter, fiery eyes and a wild shock of hair. SABELITA *begins screaming, calling out to a distant traveller on the dusky path.*

SABELITA. Help!

FUSO NEGRO. Cunt-face, I'll bite out your tongue!

SABELITA. Help!

A violent black horseman, cursing loudly, leaps unexpectedly over the courtyard wall. The frightening, dishevelled madman falls beneath the hooves of the horse, like the Moors before Saint James. SABELITA, *pale and shaking with fear, is now lifted into the saddle; her head drops onto* DON JUAN MANUEL's *shoulder.*

SABELITA. Godfather, where are you taking me?

DON JUAN MANUEL. Away with me forever!

SABELITA. Forever!

Along the same road AN OLD WOMAN *dressed in sackcloth steps aside. She backs away until she is almost beneath the horse's hooves and makes the sign of the cross.*

Scene Five

A small inn on a steep slope overlooking the sea. Distant beacons which flash on and off with the rhythm of the stars. LUDOVINA's *inn. A half-open door allows the shaft of light from the hallway of the inn to spill out onto the road. Above the counter oozing with the stench of wine and brandy, hangs a brass oil lamp: a spiral of yellow flames and black smoke emerges from its cracked glass and illuminates the room. Behind it, the sordid shelves are filled with tallow candles, baskets of figs and an assortment of bottles, spices and metal tankards.* LUDOVINA *is dozing behind the counter with a cat on her lap. The sound of a horse approaching along the road can be heard in the distance.* PICHONA THE MUTTERER *pokes her head and a bare shoulder through the gaudy curtain of a very small door with three makeshift, wooden steps. The cat jumps from* LUDOVINA's *lap.* PICHONA *conceals herself and closes the door. The horseman approaches.* LUDOVINA *opens her sleepy eyes as* SILVER FACE *enters through the door of the inn. The striking young man, handsome but angry, bends over a chair but still touches the roof with his head.*

LUDOVINA. Mother of God!

SILVER FACE. A glass of brandy.

LUDOVINA. The Devil take me if I didn't recognize you straight away!

SILVER FACE. The Devil take you then!

LUDOVINA. What happened to your other partners in crime?

SILVER FACE. I don't know.

LUDOVINA. They ordered a pie.

SILVER FACE. I hope they choke on it!

LUDOVINA. If you're intending to stay, it's best you tie up the horse outside.

SILVER FACE. He's drenched in sweat.

LUDOVINA. I have to lock up. There's a group upstairs playing cards and they've insisted on it. Don't you feel like trying your luck?

SILVER FACE. Another brandy.

LUDOVINA. You know what they say, lucky in love, unlucky at cards.

SILVER FACE. I'm dogged by bad luck!

LUDOVINA. For Christ's sake! Go out and see to that horse of yours! If it starts panicking it'll bring the inn down on top of us.

SILVER FACE. That wouldn't surprise me. Who's laughing behind that door?

LUDOVINA. Somebody with a big mouth.

SILVER FACE. Is it a woman?

LUDOVINA. I wouldn't know. I haven't seen her naked.

SILVER FACE. Why is she hiding?

LUDOVINA. She must suspect something.

SILVER FACE. Is she a virgin?

LUDOVINA. My dear Silver Face, in this house virgins and good wine are a thing of the past!

SILVER FACE. Fill up the glass.

LUDOVINA. That's three you've had. Isn't your head spinning?

SILVER FACE. The world's spinning! Fill up the glass.

LUDOVINA. I'm not filling it again.

SILVER FACE. That noisy curtain's beginning to irritate me.

LUDOVINA. Don't look at it then.

SILVER FACE. Who's in there?

LUDOVINA. A scorpion.

SILVER FACE. I'm going to drag it out by its ears.

LUDOVINA. Mother of God, strike down and paralyse this irreverent anti-Christ!

SILVER FACE *strides back to the horse. The horseshoes glisten for a moment in the shadows of the hallway. They crash down onto the makeshift, wooden steps and resound savagely through the night.* PICHONA, *dressed in a jerkin and a flared skirt, emerges from one side of the curtain. Over her bare, milk-white shoulders, the twisted corner of a fichu.*

PICHONA THE MUTTERER. What can I do for you?

SILVER FACE. Let me look at your face.

PICHONA THE MUTTERER. There's not much to see.

LUDOVINA. It's worse than being hit in the face by a cloud of stone!

SILVER FACE. Come and have a drink, Pichona.

PICHONA THE MUTTERER. No thanks.

SILVER FACE. Drink or I'll baptize you in it.

PICHONA THE MUTTERER. All right! All right! Don't get angry, my dear Silver Face! Pass the glass over! A toast to your health and to the love you keep so secret.

SILVER FACE. It's not love.

PICHONA THE MUTTERER. It must be jealousy then!

SILVER FACE. The same again, Ludovina.

PICHONA THE MUTTERER. Not for me.

SILVER FACE. For me and for you.

PICHONA THE MUTTERER. I don't want any more to drink.

SILVER FACE. Drink!

PICHONA THE MUTTERER. My head's spinning.

SILVER FACE. Drink!

PICHONA THE MUTTERER. What do you say about him forcing me to drink like this, Ludovina?

LUDOVINA. I say drink and be happy!

PICHONA THE MUTTERER. You're not much help against this Moorish king.

SILVER FACE. Before the night is out you'll be dancing naked.

PICHONA THE MUTTERER. You're a Montenegro through and through!

SILVER FACE. Drink!

PICHONA THE MUTTERER. Anything for a quiet life.

SILVER FACE. Are you happy, Pichona?

PICHONA THE MUTTERER. Walking the streets! I suppose it all depends on what you mean by happy.

SILVER FACE. How would you define happiness?

PICHONA THE MUTTERER. Not looking back, Silver Face, and making sure you've always got a peseta in your pocket.

SILVER FACE. Shall we get together and travel the world?

PICHONA THE MUTTERER. You may think I'm lying but you aren't the first to have made such a suggestion. There have been others and they weren't having a joke at my expense!

SILVER FACE. Make a decision so that we can pool our money.

PICHONA THE MUTTERER. Do you mean to put in a large amount?

SILVER FACE. Whatever you decide to lend me.

PICHONA THE MUTTERER. And what do you intend to bring with you?

SILVER FACE. The pleasure of my company.

PICHONA THE MUTTERER. Very funny!

SILVER FACE. I'll give you what I have.

PICHONA THE MUTTERER. And I'll take it like the greatest prize on earth.

SILVER FACE. I'll parade you through the fairs on my horse.

PICHONA THE MUTTERER. I'm not the type of woman who ought to be riding at your side.

LUDOVINA, *still behind the counter, nods; on her lap the cat, its eyes half-closed, snores through its whiskers.* PICHONA's *face lights up as she laughs, adjusting the fichu across her shoulders.* SILVER FACE *sinks a hand into her breasts.* LUDOVINA *walks out through another door, rubbing her eyes.*

SILVER FACE. Why did God make you a woman?

PICHONA THE MUTTERER. Don't start!

SILVER FACE. They're firm.

PICHONA THE MUTTERER. Get your hands off me.

SILVER FACE. Why did God make you a woman?

PICHONA THE MUTTERER. I'm sure you know the answer.

SILVER FACE. Well I don't!

PICHONA THE MUTTERER. I'm the sort of woman you can come to for a year and a day if you want – or for as long as it lasts. And if I have the time and the money, we can spend a peseta or two together. But I don't want you shouting it about for all to hear.

SILVER FACE. Why did you hide when I came in?

PICHONA THE MUTTERER. So as not to be blinded.

SILVER FACE. Give me a kiss.

PICHONA THE MUTTERER. Not here. Let's go back to my place in Cures. If you come I'll lay out my best sheets edged with lace.

SILVER FACE. I won't let you leave until you've danced a fandango.

PICHONA THE MUTTERER. It would be a sin to do it here.

SILVER FACE. Ludovina, another couple of drinks so that she can dance.

PICHONA THE MUTTERER. Please Silver Face, don't make me drink any more. After being out in today's heat, my head's all over the place.

SILVER FACE. Drink so that you can dance.

PICHONA THE MUTTERER. I'll dance if it makes you happy.

SILVER FACE. Nothing makes me happy.

PICHONA THE MUTTERER. My poor darling!

SILVER FACE. Go to Hell!

SILVER FACE, *still bending over the chair, suddenly goes outside onto the road and disappears into the night.* PICHONA *and* LUDOVINA, *who has now returned, look at each another and smile with the mischievous expression of two people who think alike.*

PICHONA THE MUTTERER. I'm off, while there's still enough moonlight to guide me home to Cures.

LUDOVINA. Is there anyone waiting for you?

PICHONA THE MUTTERER. The cat.

LUDOVINA. You didn't tell me whether you had a good time with that traveller, you know, the one who just got back from America?

PICHONA THE MUTTERER. What a bore!

LUDOVINA. The world is full of them!

PICHONA THE MUTTERER. One of those silly sanctimonious fools who are scared out of their wits at the thought of death! He turned the colour of wax when I showed him the three and the seven of hearts set against each other.

LUDOVINA. Did you read the cards for him?

PICHONA THE MUTTERER. He wanted me to.

PICHONA *begins to leave, her final words spoken with the shawl already wrapped around her head. Her dark body fills the doorway. As she steps out she is suddenly frightened. Along the road, in a violent blast, a horseman seems to fly by, a black flash of lightning which moves the fortune teller to make the sign of the cross.*

LUDOVINA. Pichoneta, that horse has gone mad!

PICHONA THE MUTTERER. It certainly looks like it! As if the road were on fire!

LUDOVINA. Who was the rider?

PICHONA THE MUTTERER. A man with a woman. She seemed to have fainted.

LUDOVINA. Mother of God!

PICHONA THE MUTTERER. God protect me from sin!

LUDOVINA. Did you recognize either of them?

PICHONA THE MUTTERER. I couldn't say for sure. But it looked like Don Juan Manuel.

LUDOVINA. Dirty old bugger!

PICHONA THE MUTTERER. And what if father and son were to meet along the way?

Scene Six
The rectory. The bare, whitewashed hall adorned with ancient arches and black beams is lit by a single oil lamp. THE ABBOT is pacing up and down – gun, cassock and cap. The flames from the oil lamp flicker uneasily across the walls; the trembling light amidst the shadows makes the wind seem almost visible along the pale limestone. The ecclesiastical cap hanging on a nail dances from side to side, while on the chest of tithes, a small dog, grumbling and yawning, wags his tail. The silent, nocturnal churchyard reaches out to the doorway. In the moonlight, THE ABBOT's tall, skeletal sister, her arms outstretched, stands afraid. The flame of the oil lamp flickers in the wind. The black dance of the ecclesiastical cap's tassle can be traced along the wall.

THE ABBOT. Will that Satan come back?

DOÑA JEROMITA. Look out for his tail!

THE ABBOT. Damn him!

DOÑA JEROMITA. And the bag of money lying there on the road! Jesus! Have mercy on us!

THE ABBOT. Let's hope that arrogant sod has to beg for alms!

DOÑA JEROMITA. Well, when it comes to arrogance, my brother, you aren't far short of the mark! This will drive me to an early grave! The first person who happens to pass by will pick the bag up! Just look at the way that blasted moon shines down on it!

THE ABBOT. Stop all this moaning and get inside. I want to lock up.

DOÑA JEROMITA. That moon has no conscience! I wish it would hide its interfering self behind some black cloud or other!

THE ABBOT. Shut up! I'm sick of all this witch-like hocus-pocus!

DOÑA JEROMITA. And not a living soul passes by! Jesus! Have mercy on us!

THE ABBOT. Is this what you're moaning about?

DOÑA JEROMITA. This shock will be the end of me! All that money! Brother, think for a moment, you're condemning a soul!

THE ABBOT. Shut up, serpent!

DOÑA JEROMITA. Isn't the money justly yours? Didn't you win it playing cards?

THE ABBOT. The cards were stacked!

DOÑA JEROMITA. You are letting yourself be ruled by petty scruples. You condemn yourself through pride. It's the sin of pride that's eating away at you!

THE ABBOT. Perhaps . . .

DOÑA JEROMITA. When it comes to an argument, you're never prepared to let anyone get the better of you. Brother, think of your age, your responsibilities, don't throw money away like that reckless youth!

THE ABBOT. I have to get the better of him. Go inside and don't mention the subject again!

DOÑA JEROMITA. Kill me if you want! But I'll defy your orders. I'll pick up the bag and keep it.

THE ABBOT. I'll shoot your bloody head off!

DOÑA JEROMITA. A small question of pride and you're prepared to assassinate your own sister! I'm horrified!

THE ABBOT. Come in and shut up!

DOÑA JEROMITA. This will be the death of me!

THE ABBOT. And me! But I won't let that Satan get the better of me. Get in, I want to lock up.

DONA JEROMITA *falls onto her knees and begins begging with outstretched arms before the clear moon.* THE ABBOT, *stark and black, is standing at the door – cap, gun and cassock. The dark shadow of an* OLD WOMAN *approaches along the path.*

THE OLD WOMAN. Sabeliña! Sabel! Come out a moment, dearie. Is Sabelita not in?

DOÑA JEROMITA. What are you up to? I don't want any gossip in my ear. I know your evil ways.

THE OLD WOMAN. Mother of God! Spare me such accusations!

THE ABBOT. Why are you looking for her?

THE OLD WOMAN. I'm not.

DOÑA JEROMITA. You were calling her.

THE OLD WOMAN. I was calling out to reassure myself.

DOÑA JEROMITA. To reassure yourself of what?

THE OLD WOMAN. Of whether it was actually her. I thought I saw her along the road so I thought I'd rush over . . . I'm sure you can let me have a little something. Even if it's only a cup of flour for tonight's soup!

DOÑA JEROMITA. Where did you see the child? Jesus! Have mercy on us!

THE OLD WOMAN. The end is nigh!

DOÑA JEROMITA. Don't frighten me! Answer!

THE OLD WOMAN. At my age you can never rely on what you see.

THE SEXTON *appears through a clearing in the rocks and jumps over the wall of the churchyard. He looks frightened and breathless as he makes his way through the moonlight.*

THE SEXTON. Sin is running rampant! A black dream! Fish frying in the flames of his pan! A black dream!

THE ABBOT. Where is my niece?

THE SEXTON. Sin is running rampant! Satan himself, blacker than Hell, carried her away on his horse!

DOÑA JEROMITA. Jesus! Have mercy on us!

THE OLD WOMAN. Sabeliña in the arms of that Turkish brigand like a harlot Mary Magdalene!

DOÑA JEROMITA. That irreverent child had this planned! The whore deceived me!

THE ABBOT. Have we ever known a darker hour?

THE SEXTON. All Hell has broken loose!

THE OLD WOMAN. The Devil loves to corrupt young virgins!

THE ABBOT. That black sheep will return to her fold tonight: even if I have to drag her here myself. Blas, follow me!

DOÑA JEROMITA. And tomorrow, my dear brother, bury her in a convent!

THE SEXTON. Requies in pace!

THE ABBOT. In which direction were the criminals heading?

THE SEXTON. Towards the estate, I think.

THE ABBOT. Let's go!

DOÑA JEROMITA. Brother, try not to get lost!

THE OLD WOMAN. Perhaps you'll be able to find someone who'll be willing to marry her! Most Holy Abbot, are you sure you haven't any scraps you can spare?

THE ABBOT. I hope your tongue falls out!

DOÑA JEROMITA. Blessed Virgin! Brother! . . . Look out there! . . . The money! This will kill me! Thirty gold coins ripped from my entrails!

DOÑA JEROMITA *opens her arms to heaven and screams aloud, piercing the silent, starry night. In the moonlight, along the silver road,* FUSO NEGRO *can be seen. Touporroutou! He stumbles across the bag of money and runs off with it.* THE ABBOT *fires his gun at him. The distant barking of dogs.*

Scene Seven
Nocturnal singing and the sound of horses. The distant laughter of the fair – tambourines, acrobatics and strumming guitars – are keeping PICHONA THE MUTTERER *awake in bed. The roaming woman with large, bright eyes listens to the sounds of the fair, her red hair spread across the pillow. A small, greasy oil lamp hangs from a corner above the oven. A hen is huddled beneath it. In the darkness, a cat lazily opens its green eyes. The sound of a horse. The girl sighs, the hen begins to stir, and the cat arches its back and disappears. The cat's piercing green eyes are seen along the shadow of the wall. A knock at the door.*

SILVER FACE. Open up, Pichona.

PICHONA THE MUTTERER. I'm in bed and I haven't any clothes on.

SILVER FACE. Less for me to do.

PICHONA THE MUTTERER. You Moorish king! Tell me who you are!

SILVER FACE. As if you didn't know.

PICHONA THE MUTTERER. No, honestly, I don't recognize you.

SILVER FACE. Open up!

PICHONA THE MUTTERER. Hold on a minute while I put on a slip. Don't knock down the door, my darling!

SILVER FACE replies with a heartless laugh. The knocking has stopped. PICHONA hurries to open the door without having properly tied up her loose dress. Standing on the deserted road, beneath the light of the moon and against a distant backdrop of stars and fairground tambourines, the handsome young man holds onto the horse's reins.

PICHONA THE MUTTERER. Standing there in the moonlight, it really does look as if your face is made of silver.

SILVER FACE. Were you waiting for me?

PICHONA THE MUTTERER. In a way. Come in and take me if you want, but don't mistreat me, my darling.

SILVER FACE. Get out of the way!

SILVER FACE pushes the girl out of the way and walks in through the door, pulling the horse's reins. The cat spits, the hen cackles, the candle flickers. The horse is suddenly frightened; its great eyes glint with fear.

PICHONA THE MUTTERER. Where are you planning to leave the horse?

SILVER FACE. Under the bed.

PICHONA THE MUTTERER. The brandy's gone to your brain.

SILVER FACE. I'll tie him to the door like a town crier!

PICHONA THE MUTTERER. What's he going to shout about? The fact that there's someone in my bed? We're young and we've a right to enjoy ourselves. Come in and shut the door.

The handsome young man bends slightly in order to enter the door. PICHONA places the bar on the door while the horse neighs outside. SILVER FACE goes straight over to the rickety old bed and sits down; the semi-naked girl, full and white, turns to smile at him.

SILVER FACE. Pichona, pull off my spurs and shut up. For Christ's sake, shut up!

PICHONA THE MUTTERER. You can tear the bedspread with your spurs if you want to, and then you can start on me! Go on, hit me! Enjoy yourself!

SILVER FACE. I'm not going to enjoy myself like that!

PICHONA THE MUTTERER. Why? Don't you like me?

SILVER FACE. I ought to laugh because you're amusing, but I don't . . .

PICHONA THE MUTTERER. You're upset over something, that's why you were drinking so heavily at Ludovina's. Am I right? Don't you want to answer?

SILVER FACE. I don't know what you're talking about!

PICHONA THE MUTTERER. Forget your dark obsession and take me in your arms. This trouble will soon pass and then you'll be the first to laugh. That's the way it is! No problem lasts forever. Your lips are as cold as death!

SILVER FACE. You're tiring me.

PICHONA THE MUTTERER. Well then, do something about what's bothering you. Luck changes. Shall I read your fortune?

SILVER FACE. Were you taught the art by a witch?

PICHONA THE MUTTERER. There was no witch involved. I was taught by a friend in Monforte.

SILVER FACE. She must have been quite a teacher!

PICHONA, *her shift slipping across her shoulders, looks through the chest and then begins walking around the foot of the rickety old bed, holding the oil lamp and the deck of cards. She hands the deck to the handsome young man to cut and then places it on the flowered bedspread.*

PICHONA THE MUTTERER. Give me the secret, Book of Vilham, or else I'll have to resort to a reading of the palm.

Show us the paths that lie ahead. Cut the cards so that I can read the good and the bad.

SILVER FACE. Don't overdo the prologue.

PICHONA THE MUTTERER. Raise your left hand and turn a card over. I will read them in the Portuguese manner. Diamonds followed by spades. Jealousy and anger. Notice the three of hearts below the seven of spades. Hearts here mean bells and spades indicate a death wish. Does it make any sense?

SILVER FACE. What a load of claptrap!

PICHONA THE MUTTERER. This two, this four and this six, offset pairs, signify the lights of a funeral wake. The queen of diamonds is a person in love. It could be you. I see no one else in sight. The jack of spades, face down, is a crying woman. Well, that's what it looks like to me, anyway! And the five of hearts is permission crossed with sin, as shown by the king of clubs which was on top of the pack. Here are the three aces, they're powerful. And then three queens set against each other. Queens signify virility. Does that tell you anything?

SILVER FACE. Nothing!

PICHONA THE MUTTERER. I'm going to shuffle them again to see if the message is any clearer.

PICHONA *begins collecting the cards which lie across the bedspread. When she picks up the queen of spades, she holds the card still for a moment as if reminded of something.*

PICHONA THE MUTTERER. Have you ever thought of killing anyone?

SILVER FACE. If the thought had crossed my mind, I'd have done it by now.

PICHONA THE MUTTERER. You're a right Robin Hood!

SILVER FACE. I'm worse!

PICHONA THE MUTTERER. But you don't kill or steal! The cards link you with a dead man. It's in the two of hearts, although that's never a reliable card. But the fact that it was followed by the queen worries me. The queen of diamonds forever in love is you. Now you can't get any clearer than that!

SILVER FACE. Enough!

PICHONA THE MUTTERER. Enough! Take me in your arms, my darling. Take me in your arms, my Spanish Moorish king! It's the first time you've come looking for me! What is it you want? Your lips are cold! Take me in your arms, my treasure!

End of Act Two

Act Three

Scene One
*A large, dark room in the grand house at Lantañon. A painting
of Christ dressed in a loin cloth suffers against the darkness of
the wall. The yellow, nail-like flame of the oil lamp appears to
hypnotize the room. Through the hollow of the arch the table can be
seen, laden with food. Dogs and cats wander aimlessly around. The
feudal lord, sitting in an armchair, raises his glass. SABELITA,
standing at the far end of the room beside the door, covers her face.
Her hands are exquisitely pale!*

DON JUAN MANUEL. Take your hands away from your eyes
and look at me.

SABELITA. I can't!

DON JUAN MANUEL. Do what I say, Isabel!

SABELITA. Godfather, take me back to San Clemente.

DON JUAN MANUEL. We'll go after supper. Sit down.

SABELITA. Let me serve you.

DON JUAN MANUEL. Stop crying and do what I say.

SABELITA. It is my fate to cry.

DON JUAN MANUEL. Take my glass and drink.

SABELITA. Don't embarrass me, godfather!

DON JUAN MANUEL. Damn your embarrassment!

*DON JUAN MANUEL smashes the glass and rises from the
chair, knocking the table as he goes. The sudden judder of the
furniture spills the wine and blows out the oil lamp. In the
dark room, as if by magic, the moon throws a silver beam of
light through a stained glass window. As the figures disappear
once more into the darkness, the spell of the voices and the
shadows grows.*

SABELITA. Godfather, please allow me to return to San
Clemente.

DON JUAN MANUEL. The door is open. Go and don't bother coming back!

SABELITA. That wretched Fuso Negro!

DON JUAN MANUEL. Why are you still here?

SABELITA. I'm afraid!

DON JUAN MANUEL. Go!

SABELITA. Calm yourself, my restless soul! Away with you fear! Don't tie me to this house, you magnet from Hell!

DON JUAN MANUEL. Damn it! Go! Don't hang about!

SABELITA. King of Heaven, set me free or I shall be lost!

DON JUAN MANUEL. Aren't you going?

SABELITA. I can't.

DON JUAN MANUEL. You belong to me.

SABELITA. My soul is damned!

DON JUAN MANUEL. Let me have it!

SABELITA. What do you want with my soul?

DON JUAN MANUEL. I want to keep it. Let me have it!

SABELITA. I'll hand it to Satan.

DON JUAN MANUEL. It's mine!

SABELITA. Godfather, save me!

DON JUAN MANUEL. I am Satan and you are lost!

SABELITA. Godfather!

DON JUAN MANUEL. Call me a monster from Hell. Cursed a thousand times for not even respecting the flower of your innocence.

The stark, black ABBOT rushes in through the moonlit door.

Behind him, miming a gesture of lascivious fear, the repellent
SEXTON OF SAN CLEMENTE.

THE ABBOT. Pharoah king, I've come for my sheep!

DON JUAN MANUEL. There she is!

THE ABBOT. I think badly of you, barbaric Montenegro.
Your behaviour appals and angers me! But I never thought
you so low as to receive your sons' whores as dinner guests!

DON JUAN MANUEL. You unscrupulous cleric, my
god-daughter is not a bastard's whore!

THE ABBOT. What do you have to say, you shameless harlot?

SABELITA. I'm not guilty of anything.

THE ABBOT. Who brought you here? You were seen being
carried away on a horse. If that isn't a clear indication of
your whoring ways, I don't know what is!

DON JUAN MANUEL. I brought her here!

THE ABBOT. Vade retro!

DON JUAN MANUEL. What are you afraid of?

THE ABBOT. You took her?

DON JUAN MANUEL. Yes.

THE ABBOT. Why?

DON JUAN MANUEL. To comfort me in my solitude.

THE ABBOT. Montenegro, I'm warning you, hand back my
precious sheep.

DON JUAN MANUEL. It was her decision.

THE ABBOT. Montenegro, I come in peace.

DON JUAN MANUEL. I'm not proposing war.

THE ABBOT. We were once friends who treated each other as

family – and yet you denied me the right to cross through the estate as I was on my way to administer the last rites.

DON JUAN MANUEL. That wasn't me. That was my son.

THE ABBOT. But you stood by his decision.

DON JUAN MANUEL. It was my obligation.

THE ABBOT. That sinner died without my benediction. We can only suppose that he is suffering in Hell.

DON JUAN MANUEL. The Devil will no doubt be grateful to my son for that.

THE ABBOT. You irreverent blasphemer!

DON JUAN MANUEL. I call it sacrilege! You want her as some sort of recompense! We understand each other!

THE ABBOT. Barbaric Montenegro! You'll get the war you have so carelessly provoked! I shall trample on your estate and rescue my wayward sheep.

DON JUAN MANUEL. Take her, I hand her back in peace. Isabel, you are free to stay or go as you please. Make your decision.

SABELITA. I choose to die!

THE ABBOT. Shut up, you irreverent child! Don't publicize your lewd behaviour! Follow me!

SABELITA. My feet are pinned here. I can't move. I'm soiled by evil!

THE ABBOT. Come with me!

SABELITA. Shackles tie me down. My feet won't move!

THE ABBOT. I'll drag you out of here by your hair.

SABELITA. Godfather, don't keep me in chains! Break this black magnet that pins me down! Let me go, let me go free!

DON JUAN MANUEL. You are free.

SABELITA. Away, fear! I pray, my soul be brave! Be strong! Godfather, free me from this wretched captivity! And if you cannot, if it is my fate to be lost, arrange for me to remain here.

DON JUAN MANUEL. Let the sin fall on my conscience. Stay!

THE ABBOT. Montenegro, you have the power of the Devil! And in that power may you find solace! You don't frighten me, Montenegro! You will be summoned! We will meet again!

DON JUAN MANUEL. Go to Hell!

THE ABBOT. Just to punish your arrogance, I'm prepared to light a candle to the Master of Hell! You should tremble in fear!

THE ABBOT *exits through the moonlit door like a black blast.* DON JUAN MANUEL *raises his glass and offers it to the huddled shadow of his new whore.*

Scene Two
The crossroads at San Martiño de Freyres. A sky filled with stars. The murmur of the wind through the cornfields. The moaning sound of the mill, its fearful sound prolonged by a cluster of trees. The moon weaves silvery mists across the pond. At the place where the four paths meet the long, cassocked figure of THE ABBOT *appears. Beneath the starry sky, his black arm and peaked cap – weapons of curses and anathema – appear especially pronounced.* BLAS DE MÍGUEZ *is huddled like a dog over the elongated shadow of the cleric.*

THE ABBOT. Damn that arrogant family!

THE SEXTON. Don Juan Manuel is quite a man!

THE ABBOT. You degenerate, Montenegro, I'll punch you in the face, like this!

THE SEXTON. What perfect justice!

The holy man slaps his own cheek while THE SEXTON *crosses himself repeatedly, groaning and beating his chest. The faint sound of barking dogs in a distant village.*

THE ABBOT. Satan, I'll sell my soul if you protect me at this difficult time. Not even sacrilege frightens me!

THE SEXTON. Most Holy Abbot, don't ask Hell for assistance!

THE ABBOT. Today, I'll gamble my soul!

THE SEXTON. If you gamble it, you'll lose it.

THE ABBOT. And you will be damned alongside me!

THE SEXTON. What do you need me for?

THE ABBOT. My fate will be your fate.

THE SEXTON. As long as it doesn't have any influence over Saint Peter.

THE ABBOT. You'll do as I say.

THE SEXTON. As long as I save my soul!

THE ABBOT. When you arrive home, you'll begin to die.

THE SEXTON. Holy Mother!

THE ABBOT. While in the clutches of death, you'll bid farewell to your wife and children and ask for confession!

THE SEXTON. I start to die and yet I won't die.

THE ABBOT. What do you propose to suffer from?

THE SEXTON. A pain in my side.

THE ABBOT. From the moment you set foot in the churchyard you'll be in pain, cursing the gods.

THE SEXTON. I'm afraid of what you're suggesting.

THE ABBOT. It is important that you do what I say without question.

THE SEXTON. I begin dying . . . I receive confession and communion, which never comes amiss . . . I've got it. But I won't go further than that . . . I could refuse to die.

THE ABBOT. You'll do as I say!

THE SEXTON. If my wife gets suspicious . . .

THE ABBOT. Go!

THE SEXTON. I'll have to whack her across the bum!

THE ABBOT. If need be, you will die.

THE SEXTON. Keeping one eye open. That's all I'll agree to!

THE ABBOT. Start walking!

THE SEXTON. I'll go no further than that.

THE ABBOT. You'll do whatever I say!

THE SEXTON. I won't even think of dying!

THE ABBOT. You will begin dying and if necessary you will die. Those are my orders and you will obey them.

THE SEXTON. Bloody orders! I refuse to comply!

THE ABBOT. You're placing your trust in Satan.

THE SEXTON. So that he can then scorch me! I detest him!

THE ABBOT. Go!

THE SEXTON. Fool! We could be opening our path to Hell!

THE ABBOT. I feel like sinking this fist between your horns! Open your eyes, you idiot! Can't your black conscience see Hell beneath you?

THE SEXTON. This will ensure our excommunication! We are profaning the sacraments!

THE ABBOT. Fall down in horror! Tremble with fear!

THE SEXTON. Dies irae! Dies illa!

*The sacrilegious cleric begins to slap his cheeks, howling like a
dog as he does so. The frightened, cowering* SEXTON, *his face
turned away, runs off in his wooden clogs, as if dancing on the
moonlit country path. As he enters the churchyard – all haycock
and moonlit sky – the shouting begins.*

THE SEXTON. I'm dying! This is the end! This sudden
seizure will kill me! It will leave me excommunicated! Life,
don't leave my body! Let me see the light of day!

THE ABBOT. Satan, help me and I'll pledge you my soul!
Help me, King of Hell, for no evil is beyond you! Satan, by
my holy vows I call you! Satan, for you I will recite aloud
the entire black missal! I renounce Christ and give myself to
you! King of Hell, unleash your north winds! Arouse your
serpent! Shake up your furies! Satan, answer my call!

FUSO NEGRO. Reporting for duty, Sir!

*The madman begins a frenzied dance on the white path. The
bag of money, placed within the torn schismatic cap, dances
with him. He dances past the sacrilegious* ABBOT OF SAN
CLEMENTE.

Scene Three
*Quintán de San Martiño. Haycocks and moonlit roofs. Distant
barking. Hanging vines cast purple shadows in front of the doors.
A solitary house at the edge of the churchyard. A black and red
fireplace where a naked old woman is delousing herself. Through
the chimney which peeps through the tiles, the rising smoke of pine
needles and the smell of grilled sardines. The old woman continues
delousing herself while a child whines. Her* LAZY DAUGHTER
is sitting beneath an oil lamp, patching up a large clerical cloak.

THE SEXTON'S WIFE. Good God, I'm seeing things again!
The wind's carrying your father's voice!

THE LAZY DAUGHTER. Rubbish!

THE SEXTON'S WIFE. Listen carefully. Can't you hear it?
It's the voice of a very distraught person. Do you hear it?

THE LAZY DAUGHTER. It's the wind on the roof.

THE SEXTON'S WIFE. Don't you think it sounds familiar?

THE LAZY DAUGHTER. Mother, you've been drinking!

THE SEXTON'S WIFE. Talk of the Devil! It's time for
a drink!

*The naked old woman reaches out for the greasy tankard on the
kitchen shelf, knocking down a trivet in the process. The cat runs
away in fear, leaping over the dirty old bed. Three children peep
out from a corner of the patched blanket. The old woman drinks
from the tankard, slowly savouring the contents.*

THE CHORUS OF CHILDREN. Give us a swig, mum! Give
us a swig!

THE SEXTON'S WIFE. Get me a pitchfork! Quick!

THE CHORUS OF CHILDREN. A swig!

THE SEXTON'S WIFE. Celonio! Gabino! Mingote! You
venomous troublemakers! Do you want Saint Benitiño of
Palermo to pay you a visit? Do you want a drink, Ginera?

THE LAZY DAUGHTER. The boys will smell it on my
breath.

THE SEXTON'S WIFE. Keep your mouth well-shut, you
irresponsible slut! Get close to boys and you'll soon see what
you end up with. What a hopeless case! If you get pregnant,
you're out of this house. It's a damn good drop of anis! Take
a swig, girl!

THE LAZY DAUGHTER *resolutely grabs the tankard which
the old woman offers her. Having taken a drink, she wipes her
lips with the attractive scarf draped around her shoulders.*

THE LAZY DAUGHTER. It's good stuff!

THE CHORUS OF CHILDREN. Give us a swig, mum! Give
us a swig!

THE SEXTON'S WIFE. Give those bloody children a
swig.

Peeping out from the patched blanket on the dirty old bed, THE

CHORUS OF CHILDREN *continue to beg.* CELONIO, GABINO *and* MINGOTE *fight over the tankard, with outstretched arms and pointed talons.* THE LAZY DAUGHTER *hands over the tankard which smashes to the ground as it is juggled between the many hands.*

THE SEXTON'S WIFE. Bloody brats! Let's hope some ill wind comes and takes you all away! You'll end up on the gallows! You good-for-nothing lot! You little buggers!

THE LAZY DAUGHTER. Put on your shirt, mother.

The old woman listens to the screams as she shakes the tongs across the frightened heads of the now spoiled altar-piece and then returns mournfully to the fireplace. She searches in a large bundle of clothing for her handbag and counts out eight copper coins.

THE SEXTON'S WIFE. It was the best money could buy! Like the stuff the Queen of Spain drinks! Ginera, tie up your petticoats and go and get me a glassful.

THE LAZY DAUGHTER. What sort do you want?

THE SEXTON'S WIFE. Plain anis, you stupid bitch! Go on, get out of here! All you can think of is boys! Anis, you silly girl! Anis! Take a candle.

THE LAZY DAUGHTER. There's a full moon!

A DISTANT VOICE. I'm dying! The end is nigh!

THE SEXTON'S WIFE. Jesus Christ! There it is again! Bloody wind! It sounds just like your father having a good moan!

A trembling GINERA *opens the door. Below the mosaic moonlight of the vines, the kneeling shadow of* THE SEXTON *can be seen, with outstretched arms in the shape of a cross.*

THE SEXTON. Where am I? The pain clouds my vision and I don't recognize this place!

THE SEXTON'S WIFE. What stupid story is this?

THE SEXTON. Grant me confession! I'm asking for God's forgiveness!

THE SEXTON'S WIFE. It's not the time for that!

THE SEXTON. My vital humours are in revolt. Beloved daughter cover yourself with a shawl and head to San Clemente!

THE LAZY DAUGHTER. Don't be stupid, father!

THE SEXTON. A sudden seizure will take me from this world!

THE SEXTON'S WIFE. We should be so lucky!

THE SEXTON. Sudden seizures at times like these are lethal.

THE SEXTON'S WIFE. Well then, hurry up and die!

THE SEXTON. You'll go before me, whore!

THE SEXTON'S WIFE. Drunkard!

THE LAZY DAUGHTER. Lie down, father!

THE SEXTON. I give you my blessing, beloved daughter.

THE SEXTON'S WIFE. How generous of you!

THE LAZY DAUGHTER. It's almost as if he were delirious.

THE SEXTON'S WIFE. He's delirious with drink!

THE SEXTON. You wicked woman, just respect the sacrament of marriage at my chosen moment of departure from this world!

THE LAZY DAUGHTER. My father was never as wise as this!

THE SEXTON. Beloved daughter, I give you and these three growing sons my blessing. Call yourselves orphans from this moment on!

THE SEXTON'S WIFE. Celonio, Gabino, Mingote! On your knees, you good-for-nothing threesome!

THE CHORUS OF CHILDREN. Our father, Blas! Our father, Blas!

THE SEXTON. Mother of God, come to the assistance of this devoted servant about to appear before the Supreme

Tribunal! This pain gnaws at me like a dog with rabies!
Mother of Sinners! It gnaws at my bones, Supreme Mother!
Here on earth we call it a sudden seizure, Mater Immaculata!

THE SEXTON'S WIFE. Shut up, you thieving liar! Shut up
and don't bother calling that stupid tart again! Do you want a
rubdown?

THE SEXTON. I want the final sacrament!

THE SEXTON'S WIFE. You fool, don't leave this world. It
still needs you!

THE SEXTON. The Lord is calling me. I'm on my way. Tell
our daughter to hurry.

THE SEXTON'S WIFE. You seem to be quite happy about
all this.

THE SEXTON. Such is the duty of every good Christian.

THE SEXTON'S WIFE. Oh, Blas, you were never as wise as
this! It's quite clear that you're heading towards death! Oh,
Blas, don't leave this life! Blas de Míguez, are you aware of
what awaits you?

THE SEXTON. Leave all this until I've been visited by a priest.

BLAS DE MÍGUEZ *winks an eye, twists his mouth and sticks
out his tongue, creating an altogether tragicomic, carnivalesque
picture. The balding old woman makes the sign of the cross and
puts on a shift with trembling hands.*

THE SEXTON'S WIFE. Oh death, it was all right when you
kept your distance! Ginera, get going!

THE CHORUS OF CHILDREN. Oh, our poor father! Oh,
our poor father!

THE LAZY DAUGHTER. Beloved father, don't leave this
world while you are still needed!

THE SEXTON. Don't upset my peace of mind!

THE SEXTON'S WIFE. Blas, don't go! All-engulfing death,
why are you taking him?

THE SEXTON. You're talking too much!

THE SEXTON'S WIFE. Was the life I gave you so bad?
Answer me, you useless piece of shit!

THE SEXTON. Do not insult me at this difficult time, whore!

THE SEXTON'S WIFE. Answer me!

THE SEXTON. I recognize your merits and so I bless you!

THE SEXTON'S WIFE. He's delirious again! Hurry up and
get going, Ginera!

THE CHORUS OF CHILDREN. Oh, our poor father! Oh,
our poor father!

THE SEXTON. Shut your mouths, you fortunate angels!
Death, move away!

THE LAZY DAUGHTER. This is true delirium!

THE LAZY DAUGHTER *escapes from the house, wrapped in
a large cloak, and carrying a small oil lamp. She can be heard
wailing along the road.*

THE LAZY DAUGHTER. Goodbye, father! Never again will I
receive your teachings!

THE SEXTON. Nitwit, I'll thrash you!

THE SEXTON'S WIFE. Don't start swearing when you're like
this, you stupid man! Whatever happened to that forbearance
you were talking about?

THE SEXTON. I'm about to die, it's not surprising that I
should say such crazy things.

THE CHORUS OF CHILDREN. Oh, our poor father! Oh,
our poor father!

THE SEXTON'S WIFE. Shut up, you thieving liars!

BLAS DE MÍGUEZ *lets out a loud shrill and throws off a
clog. He jumps off the dirty old bed and begins hopping, grabbing
the children by their mop-like hair. They begin to howl in fear,
tearing at the old woman's shirt.*

THE SEXTON'S WIFE. Calm yourself, Blas! The enemy's

trying to force his way inside you! Stand firm and pray to the Blessed Trinity! Sinner, save your soul!

THE SEXTON. Shut up, you fool!

THE SEXTON'S WIFE. Don't swear! Think of your soul!

THE SEXTON. I may be dying but I'm still able to give you a good thrashing! I'll come through this!

THE SEXTON'S WIFE. Don't rebel against the wishes of the Lord!

THE CHORUS OF CHILDREN. Oh, our poor father! Oh, our poor father!

THE SEXTON. I'm going to cut your bloody throats, you irreverent bastards! Warm up some wine with cinnamon for me, you pious grief-stricken woman.

THE SEXTON'S WIFE. Your true self is coming back! The curse that was there inside you has taken the form of a cat running across the floor.

THE SEXTON. A feeble lie! Don't try and invent things! Shut up, you pitiful heretic! World of perdition, it has been said already that you are a well of poison, all bitter absinth wine! When my time comes, I'll not be sorry to leave. Goodbye, my children, a true chorus of angels!

THE CHORUS OF CHILDREN. Oh, father! Father! Father!

THE SEXTON'S WIFE. Shut up, you thieving bastards and get on your knees! Can't you see that he's trying to knock some sense of decency into you!

THE SEXTON. Orphaned children! Delicate shrubs!

THE SEXTON'S WIFE. For God's sake, pull yourself together! You need the strength of a man for this part of the send-off!

THE SEXTON. Tender shoots, in this valley of tears we find our only protection in the bosom of our Holy Catholic Church. Never forget that! Life is nothing but a brief passage!

FUSO NEGRO. Toupourroutou!

A cautious FUSO NEGRO *appears at the door. His shadow lies in wait, spying from the path with an aggressive, wolf-like expression. He laughs loudly, shaking the divisive bag of Portuguese gold with a hand that lies hidden between his shirt and his skin.*

THE SEXTON. Get out of there, Fuso Negro.

FUSO NEGRO. I'm going.

THE SEXTON. I don't want you at my door.

FUSO NEGRO. Will you let me have Ginera? I'll pay her weight in gold.

THE SEXTON. Get out of here, you irreverent villain! Don't joke about death!

FUSO NEGRO. Do you have any fresh pilchards?

THE SEXTON'S WIFE. Look at the light of our Blessed Lord! Look, over there in the distance in the courtyard, come over and take a look! Listen to the bell!

THE SEXTON. I refuse to die!

BLAS DE MÍGUEZ *jumps off the dirty old bed with his hair standing on end. As he is wearing only one wooden clog, he wobbles as he goes. His wife stands in front of him with the mop-haired children clinging to the rim of her shirt.*

THE SEXTON'S WIFE. Lie down, Blas.

THE SEXTON. I refuse to die. What was the agreement? I would only close one eye! We have to be clear about this! I don't want any lights! Put all the lights out! I'm asking the wind to blow them all out! I refuse to die! The lights! I won't go, even though the candles are calling me. Let me go! Get out of my way, woman!

Scene Four
PICHONA's *bed. Silence, broken only by sighs and giggles. The rustle of the straw mattress.* SILVER FACE *and* PICHONA *are*

fornicating beneath a wonderful Portuguese bedspread. Toc! Toc! Toc! A stone rolls along the roof. The lovers are silent.

PICHONA THE MUTTERER. Don't go! Kiss me! Don't think about your problems!

SILVER FACE. Shut up!

PICHONA THE MUTTERER. What are you listening out for?

SILVER FACE. Shut up!

PICHONA THE MUTTERER. The wind disrupting the tiles, perhaps?

SILVER FACE. It's not the wind.

PICHONA THE MUTTERER. What do you think it is?

SILVER FACE. Some goblin or other wearing wooden clogs.

PICHONA THE MUTTERER. Darling, don't frighten me, you know how I believe anything I hear! Kiss me! Don't move your mouth away! Kiss me!

The wooden clogs of the 'goblin' crack against the rooftiles. Laughter filters through the black smoke, making its way down through the serpent-like chimney, scattering ashes. The trivets dance from side to side.

THE VOICE FROM THE CHIMNEY. Toupourroutou!

PICHONA THE MUTTERER. Is that what you were talking about, my love.

SILVER FACE. Sounds like it.

THE VOICE FROM THE CHIMNEY. Who's that bastard in your bed, Pichona?

SILVER FACE. Get down, sonny, we know each other.

PICHONA THE MUTTERER. If you start encouraging him, we'll have trouble. Now my darling, take me in your arms!

THE VOICE FROM THE CHIMNEY. Throw that poxy bloke out of your bed, Pichona!

PICHONA THE MUTTERER. Go away!

THE VOICE FROM THE CHIMNEY. I've got a bag of gold coins for you. Can you hear them?

PICHONA THE MUTTERER. It sounds like a trick to me.

THE VOICE FROM THE CHIMNEY. Now is the time to be happy! Let the pig's tail dance in its jar! Pichona, shall I warm your legs? And between one sin and the next, a fish pie!

SILVER FACE. And wine from Rivero.

THE VOICE FROM THE CHIMNEY. Crafty bastard, you seem to know what you're talking about!

PICHONA THE MUTTERER. If that's you, Fuso Negro, I'll cut your balls off! Don't break my tiles, you bastard!

THE VOICE FROM THE CHIMNEY. Toupourroutou! This bag is for you, you gentlemen's whore! Can you hear it singing?

PICHONA THE MUTTERER. I can hear it singing in your mind.

SILVER FACE. Sonny, you found that bag lying on the road.

THE VOICE FROM THE CHIMNEY. You can see the cat's eye beneath its tail!

SILVER FACE. We're two of a kind.

PICHONA THE MUTTERER. Go away, Satan!

THE VOICE FROM THE CHIMNEY. Toupourroutou! This treasure gives me more power than the Pope!

SILVER FACE. At least as much.

THE VOICE FROM THE CHIMNEY. I can sleep in the convent with the blessed nuns and bed them seven at a time.

SILVER FACE. Of course you can!

THE VOICE FROM THE CHIMNEY. You certainly know your theology!

SILVER FACE. Weren't you about to get married, sonny?

THE VOICE FROM THE CHIMNEY. Toupourroutou!
I've four peaks on my cap! Black goat, if we come to some
agreement, I'll put a padlock on you!

SILVER FACE. Who seduced your woman, sonny?

THE VOICE FROM THE CHIMNEY. A Turkish cock that
got between us.

SILVER FACE. Couldn't you frighten him off?

THE VOICE FROM THE CHIMNEY. He came dressed as a
black flame.

SILVER FACE. But what of your erudite knowledge, sonny?

THE VOICE FROM THE CHIMNEY. The Devil doesn't
recognize erudite knowledge! Toupourroutou! What a clear
moon! Come up, Pichona, so that we can have a dance!

PICHONA THE MUTTERER. I need some ointment for my
armpits.

THE VOICE FROM THE CHIMNEY. Stick a horn in
your ear. Pichoneta, come up so that we can dance in the
moonlight. Toupourroutou! Come up, skimpy shirt!

PICHONA THE MUTTERER. You great, fat, castrated pig,
change the subject!

THE VOICE FROM THE CHIMNEY. Toupourroutou! I'm
naked so that we can dance a fandango!

PICHONA THE MUTTERER. This is like a bloody carnival!

THE VOICE FROM THE CHIMNEY. Toupourroutou!

PICHONA THE MUTTERER. You're going to bring down
my chimney with all this shouting!

THE VOICE FROM THE CHIMNEY. Listen to the gold
coins calling out to you!

PICHONA THE MUTTERER. Sonny, you've come too late.

THE VOICE FROM THE CHIMNEY. Throw that bastard
out of your bed!

PICHONA THE MUTTERER. He's a king!

THE VOICE FROM THE CHIMNEY. Cut off his head!

PICHONA THE MUTTERER. I'm tied to him.

THE VOICE FROM THE CHIMNEY. If you pee in the bed, the bond is broken.

PICHONA THE MUTTERER. What a wonderful idea!

SILVER FACE. Sonny, that money isn't yours!

THE VOICE FROM THE CHIMNEY. Who says so?

SILVER FACE. You discovered that money thanks to the moon!

THE VOICE FROM THE CHIMNEY. What a feeble lie!

SILVER FACE. You picked it up along a deserted road.

THE VOICE FROM THE CHIMNEY. You're making that up because you want the money!

SILVER FACE. It was already night when you passed through the churchyard at San Clemente.

THE VOICE FROM THE CHIMNEY. Who are you since you know so much?

PICHONA THE MUTTERER. Give the money back to its rightful owner, sonny!

SILVER FACE. The owner doesn't want it.

THE VOICE FROM THE CHIMNEY. Bloody hell! Who have you got in your bed, Pichona!

SILVER FACE. If you want to see my face and know my name, come down.

THE VOICE FROM THE CHIMNEY. I'm still scratching one of my scorched buttocks. In the flash of gunpowder I recognized the cap, hidden and waiting; the gun aimed and ready to fire.

SILVER FACE. Come down, sonny!

THE VOICE IN THE CHIMNEY. Oh no, I don't! Death passed by me as I was standing by the churchyard. In the explosion I saw four peaks and a face covered in blood.

SILVER FACE. And was that my face?

THE VOICE FROM THE CHIMNEY. Toupourroutou! Most Holy Abbot, don't play with that black goat anymore. Look at those habits!

SILVER FACE. Sonny, you're making a big mistake!

FUSO NEGRO. Toupourroutou! I can see the peaks on the cap! The sunflower on your patio, a Turkish cock is ready to peck at it. Toupourroutou! Listen to the screams echoing through the night. The virgin niece has been carried away by the thieving nobleman!

SILVER FACE. What a ridiculous story this is, you evil-minded bastard!

FUSO NEGRO. Naked, with her hair loose, screaming and covering her breasts in a cave at Lantañon. The Turkish cock is crowing on the white crystal ball!

SILVER FACE. What is this black light you place before me? My father is the thief who steals from me!

THE VOICE IN THE CHIMNEY. Bloody hell, who are you?

SILVER FACE. Satan protect me!

SILVER FACE *lets out a deafening roar. He looks frenzied and furious; his eyes are on fire. He takes the axe from the chopping block, lifts his arm and buries the axe in the door. He then rushes out into the starry night.*

PICHONA THE MUTTERER. What dark idea is going through your mind? Wait! Hold on! Don't leave my arms to rise against your own father! Stay and I'll serve you for the rest of my days! I'll be your slave! I don't want to go back to a life of mourning! I am the woman of ill repute for whom Benitiño the penitent killed his father! Possessed of the same anger, he escaped from my arms! Stay my love! I'll wait here and pray for you!

A VOICE FROM THE FAIR.
>Wizards and goblins travel through the night
>To the mill of a friend:
>They were carried there by the wind and
>Returned through the air.

Scene Five

The courtyard of the estate, filled with the fragrant smell of lemon trees. Moonlit arches and a still, black cypress tree at the foot of the steps. DON JUAN MANUEL's *remorseful shadow passes by. His knock-kneed fool follows him, exaggerating his limp.*

DON GALÁN. Jujú! An old man in love means a broken heart!

DON JUAN MANUEL. Shut up, you fool!

DON GALÁN. The pronouncement of a wise man!

DON JUAN MANUEL. The pronouncement of a scoundrel!

DON GALÁN. It's useful for old bodies to remain on good terms with Saint Peter.

DON JUAN MANUEL. Don Galán, I'm tempted to become a hermit.

DON GALÁN. I'll come with you and carry your saddle-bags.

DON JUAN MANUEL. Saints don't have servants.

DON GALÁN. We'll be equals.

DON JUAN MANUEL. You can't be a saint.

DON GALÁN. Blas is like Bonifas before the table of God!

DON JUAN MANUEL. Don Galán, to be a saint one has to pass through Hell. As you have never known how to be a sinner, you can't possibly know how to be a saint. I do!

DON GALÁN. Naturally!

DON JUAN MANUEL. But is it worth repenting and becoming saintly at this precise time, when the World, the Devil and the Flesh can offer me such few opportunities to sin? If only I'd thought about it thirty years ago! Now it looks like the doubts of a hypocrite. It's hardly worth it! Tonight I'll be eating grapes! Don Galán, you don't understand a word I'm saying.

DON GALÁN. I understand enough!

DON JUAN MANUEL. In all my life, I've never lifted such a black pack of cards as the one in front of me at this moment!

DON GALÁN. As black as coal!

DON JUAN MANUEL. Hideous!

The muffled sound of pacing and prayers. THREE OLD WOMEN, *like three owls with lanterns and long cloaks, bend and stalk as they pass beneath the arch. The liturgical tolling of a bell in San Clemente de Lantañon. Distant lights.*

THE VOICE OF AN OLD WOMAN. Ave María! The moon shines down on the lord of the estate! The moon deserves its prize! From here he looks like an apostle dressed in silver.

DON JUAN MANUEL. Where are you going?

THE VOICE OF AN OLD WOMAN. We are accompanying the Blessed Eucharist on its way to a dying man.

DON JUAN MANUEL. This Abbot will provoke me into committing sacrilege! Don Galán, untie the dogs and get my gun!

DON GALÁN. Master, don't fly away on Satan's wings!

The sound of an approaching horse. Upset and angry, SILVER FACE *gallops into the courtyard. His fair hair glistens exquisitely beneath the moonlight, the axe in his hand gleaming like a black flash of lightning.*

SILVER FACE. Father, I'm going to kill you!

DON JUAN MANUEL. Then don't hold back, you wretch! Raise your arm and open the doors of Hell to me!

SILVER FACE. Where is Isabel?

DON JUAN MANUEL. Under lock and key.

SILVER FACE. Isabel is mine!

DON JUAN MANUEL. When did you win her love?

SILVER FACE. Father, don't make me angrier!

DON JUAN MANUEL. There are plenty of women at your age. If one doesn't want you, there are hundreds of others to choose from. There are women born every hour of the day but you only have one father.

SILVER FACE. And the love of one woman!

DON JUAN MANUEL. Women either die or grow old. Disobedient son, blinded by deceit and dreams, observe these approaching lights! Do you see this procession of gossips wrapped in cloaks and carrying lanterns? The Blessed Sacrament is coming to visit me with the procession that my sins deserve. Don't be crueller than the executioner, wait until the person under sentence of death has confessed and received Holy Communion. I am going to provide you with a fine example.

A slow procession of lanterns and cloaks enters through the imposing arch adorned only by the Montenegro coat of arms. The sacrilegious ABBOT OF SAN CLEMENTE comes hidden beneath an ecclesiastical cloak of gold cloth and a four-cornered cap. In his black, claw-like hands, he carries the silver chalice which holds the Holy Sacrament.

DON JUAN MANUEL. Stop!

THE ABBOT. Montenegro, the Church asks your permission to pass through with the Body of Christ!

DON JUAN MANUEL. Who's dying?

THE ABBOT. Blas de Míguez!

DON JUAN MANUEL. Let the Devil take him! I know what you're up to, you fake priest!

THE ABBOT. Pharoah! Bow your arrogant head before the king of kings!

VOICES OF THE OLD WOMEN. Montenegro! Your soul is

as black as pitch! Your heart is black with sins! Black as the cauldrons of Hell!

DON JUAN MANUEL, *holding two dogs back by their collars like lions, makes his way down the stone steps. He walks between the lights in gloomy silence. Beneath the cloak,* THE ABBOT OF SAN CLEMENTE *lifts the silver chalice.* DON JUAN MANUEL, *a sullen, mocking, enigmatic figure, kneels on the ground, forcing his dogs to do the same.*

DON JUAN MANUEL. Sacrilegious Abbot! What are you looking for?

THE ABBOT. A sinner at the point of death.

DON JUAN MANUEL. Well, here you have him! A master at the art of decadent living with the axe suspended over my head. This bastard that I call my son is planning my death. And to absolve my sins you, my dear Abbot, have fallen straight from heaven. I confess my sins here publicly. I am the worst type of man. No one can have been more fond of gambling, wine and women. Satan has always been my patron. I cannot rid myself of all these vices. I'll burn in them. I never recognized anyone else's laws. In my adolescence, I killed a card-player in some dispute about a game. I forced one of my sisters to become a nun. I insulted my wife with a hundred women. This is the man I've been! I don't expect to change! The days of miracles and repentant saints are over! Give me absolution, Abbot!

THE ABBOT. Get out of my way, blasphemer!

DON JUAN MANUEL. This is sacrilege!

A CONFUSION OF VOICES. Montenegro! As black as Hell and excommunicated forever!

The crack of a catapult. A stone ricochets off the tower wall. An owl flies away from the chimney. DON JUAN MANUEL *stands with firm resolution and grabs the chalice from* THE ABBOT.

DON JUAN MANUEL. Move back!

THE VOICES OF THE OLD WOMEN. Christ! Christ!

Blessed, tortured Christ! Night close in! Conceal this horrific act!

DON JUAN MANUEL. Silver Face, let your horse loose on this procession of gossips!

SILVER FACE. Where is the bolt that will destroy us all?

SILVER FACE *recovers the reins lying on the mane of the frightened horse and gallops through the arch. Hooded cloaks and the lights of the pious procession start to move away. Superstitious voices. Elusive shadows. Holy fear.* DON JUAN MANUEL, *still holding the silver chalice, sits on the steps.*

DON JUAN MANUEL. I'm afraid I may be the Devil!

End of play

Further Reading

G G Brown, *A Literary History of Spain: The Twentieth Century*, London, Ernest Benn Ltd, 1974.

Gwynne Edwards, *Dramatists in Perspective: Spanish Theatre in the Twentieth Century*, Cardiff, University of Wales Press, 1985.

Ricardo Gullón (ed.), *Valle-Inclán Centennial Studies*, Austin, Texas University Press, 1968.

Robert Lima, *Valle-Inclán*, New York, Columbia University Press, 1972.
——, *Valle-Inclán: The Theatre of his Life*, Columbia, University of Missouri Press, 1988.

John Lyon, *The Theatre of Valle-Inclán*, Cambridge, Cambridge University Press, 1983.

C B Morris, *Surrealism and Spain 1920–1936*, Cambridge, Cambridge University Press, 1972.

José Rubía Barca, *A Biobibliography and Iconography of Valle-Inclán (1866–1936)*, Berkeley, University of California Press, 1960.

Verity Smith, *Valle-Inclán*, New York, Twayne, 1973.

Anthony N Zahareas (ed.), *Ramón del Valle-Inclán: An Appraisal of His Life and Works*, New York, Las Americas Publishing Company, 1968.

Major Productions

Divine Words

Produced by the Margarita Xirgu and Enrique Borras Theatre Company at Madrid's Teatro Español, opened on 16 November 1933, designed by Castelao and directed by Cipriano Rivas Cherif.

Produced at the Gothenburg City Theatre, Sweden, opened on 3 February 1950, directed by Ingmar Bergman.

Produced by the Lope de Vega Theatre Company, opened at Madrid's Teatro Bellas Artes in 1961, designed by Emilio Burgos and directed by José Tamayo.

Produced by the National Theatre of Costa Rica, opened at the National Theatre in San José in 1961, designed by Emilio Burgos and directed by José Tamayo.

Opened at the Odéon Théâtre de France in Paris on 21 March 1963, translated by Robert Marrast, designed by André Acquart and directed by Roger Blin.

Opened at the Teatro Coliseo in Buenos Aires on 6 September 1964, designed by Krystina Zachwatowicz and directed by Jorge Lavelli.

Opened at the Stuttgart Theatre in 1971, designed by Dirk von Bodisco (costumes) and Klaus Gelhaars (set) and directed by Hans Neuenfels.

Opened at the Kammerspiele Theatre in Munich in 1974, designed by Rolf Glittenberg and directed by Johannes Schaaf.

Produced by Teatro Circo di Roma, opened at the Teatro di Roma on 28 May 1974, translated by María Luisa Aguirre D'Amico and directed by Franco Enríquez.

Produced by the Nuria Espert Theatre Company, opened at the Teatro Auditorium in Palma de Mallorca in October 1975, designed by Víctor García and Enrique Alarcón and directed by Víctor García.

Opened at La Maison de la Culture de Bourges, France, on 10 October 1989, designed by André Acquart and directed by Jean-Marie Broucaret.

Bohemian Lights

Produced by the Théâtre National Populaire, opened at The Théâtre du Palais Chaillot, Paris, in March 1963, translated by Jeannine Worms, designed by Jacques Le Marquet and directed by Georges Wilson.

Produced by the Lope de Vega Theatre Company, opened at Madrid's Teatro Bellas Artes in 1971, designed by Emilio Burgos and directed by José Tamayo.

Opened at the Kiel Theatre, Germany in 1974 designed by Hans Vietor and directed by Dieter Reible.

Produced by La Cooperativa Teatro Tre, opened at the Teatro Ex-Cantieri Navali della Giudecca in Venice in July 1976, translated by María Luisa Aguirre D'Amico, designed by Elena Mannini (costumes) and Erico Job (set) and directed by Mina Mezzadri.

Produced by the Mexican National Theatre Company, opened at the Teatro del Bosque in 1978, designed by Emilio Burgos and directed by José Tamayo.

Produced by the Centro Dramático Nacional, opened at Madrid's Teatro Maria Guerrero in 1984, designed by Fabià Puigserver and directed by Lluís Pasqual.

Silver Face

Produced by the Cámara y Ensayo National Theatre Company, opened at Madrid's Teatro Infanta Beatriz in 1967, designed by Emilio Burgos and directed by José María Loperena.

Opened at the Theater Stadt Schauspielhaus in Frankfurt on 29 March 1974, as part of the trilogy, *The Savage Plays*, designed by Augusto Fernándes and Klaus Gelhaar and directed by Augusto Fernándes.

Produced by the Centro Dramático Nacional, opened as part of the trilogy, *The Savage Plays*, in 1991, designed by Pedro Moreno (costumes) and José Carlos Plaza (set) and directed by José Carlos Plaza.

Produced by Paris's Théâtre National de la Colline, opened at the Avignon Festival as part of the trilogy, *The Savage Plays*, in July 1991, translated and adapted by Armando Llamas, designed by Graciela Galán and directed by Jorge Lavelli.